I0530359

THE UNBOUND HEART

Copyright © 2024 John Driggs

All rights reserved. No new contribution to this publication may be reproduced, stored in a retrieval system, or transmitted, in any form or by any means, electronic, mechanical, photocopying, recording, or otherwise, without the prior consent of the author. Copyright fuels creativity, promotes free speech, and creates a vibrant culture. Thank you for supporting the author by buying an authorized edition of this book and for complying with copyright laws.

SPACE OF POSSIBILITY
Heber City, Utah 84032
Author: John Driggs | Title: The Unbound Heart
Subtitle: Spirituality Without Dogma or Superstition
ISBN 979-8-9892273-1-0 (Print) | 979-8-9892273-2-7 (E-book)

Neither the publisher nor the author are engaged in rendering professional advice or services to the individual reader. The ideas, procedures, and suggestions contained in this book are not intended as a substitute for consulting with your physician, licensed therapist, or other professional. All matters regarding your health require medical supervision by a licensed professional. Neither the author nor the publisher shall be liable or responsible for any loss, damage, or illness, mentally, physically, financially or otherwise, allegedly arising from any information or suggestion in this book.

Cover Design by Corbin Olson

Dedicated to Karl Popper,
Joseph Goldstein, Sam Harris,
Loch Kelly, & Deborah Adele

CONTENTS

AUTHOR'S NOTE I

THE POWER OF BELIEF II

1. REASON 2

The Poetic Art of Understanding.................................... 2

The Poetic Art of Understanding.................................... 3

The Critical Art of Understanding 7

2. FREEDOM 17

Self-Responsibility 20

Tyranny 24

3. WISDOM 30

Words, Persons, & Things... 31

The Truth of Emptiness.. 37

Who Are You? 41

What is Vipassana? 44

What is Mindfulness? 47

Not-Two 52

4. LOVE 55

Metta | Loving-Kindness.. 57

Karuna | Compassion.. 61

Mudita | Sympathetic Joy 69

Upekkha | Equanimity 73

5. TRANSFORMATION 84

The Truth of Suffering.. 86

The Cause of Suffering 93

6. WORLDVIEW 103

The Possibility of Wellbeing 104

Cause & Effect or Inter-Relation 106

Perception 108

Thought.. 112

7. COMMUNICATION **117**

Four Measures of Speech.. 118

Is Your Speech Honest?... 119

Is Your Speech Beneficial?... 124

Is Your Speech Kind?.. 126

Is Your Speech Skillful? 130

8. WISE ACTION.. **133**

Skillful Precepts 134

Committing to Non-Harm 138

Refrain From Taking What Is Not Given 147

Wise Livelihood... 151

9. MIND... **155**

Virya | Effort 158

Mindfulness | Establishing Our Foundations.................... 166

Concentration 192

10. DEATH **200**

A Brief History of My Relationship With Death 201

Recent Experiences of Grief.. 203

Letting Go 208

"Life consists in learning to live on one's own, sponta-neous, freewheeling: to do this one must recognize what is one's own---to be familiar and at home with oneself."
- Thomas Merton

"The only true wisdom is knowing you know nothing."
- Socrates

"When we try to pick out anything by itself, we find it hitched to everything else in the universe."
- John Muir

AUTHOR'S NOTE

Dear Reader,

You might consider this a book about spirituality but, really, it is about life—your life and how to live it authentically, to the fullest. The words in these pages will encourage you to look not outside of yourself but to your own heart and mind to understand yourself, the world, and your place in it. It will encourage you to take responsibility for your own life, to blaze your own trail, to sculpt your own being.

Another way to think about this book is as a kind of Traveler's Guide—a collection of maps, compasses, and other tools from the world's wisdom traditions—to support you as you learn to walk your own path in peace. I want you to be able to live in your own skin. I want you to make peace with Nature, to come into harmony with the Dharma, the truth of the moment's experience, so that you may navigate your life, your relationships, your work and your art with a bit more ease, a bit more freedom, a bit more love and understanding.

May you feel safe and secure on your journey. May you have profound experiences of truth, beauty, and goodness. May you establish deep and meaningful relationships—with yourself, with others, and with the natural world around you. May you know Love directly. May you embody a lasting peace. You are undeniably beautiful, a truly remarkable fact of existence.

John P. Driggs
June 26, 2024

THE POWER OF BELIEF
- BY WAY OF INTRODUCTION -

"The purpose of education is to show a person how to define herself authentically and spontaneously in relation to her world—not to impose a prefabricated definition of the world, still less an arbitrary definition of the individual herself. It is to help the student discover herself: to recognize herself, and to identify who it is that chooses." – Thomas Merton

It's spring in Salt Lake City. I've been writing at my desk all day and my back is painfully aware. I glance out the window and see that the morning's storm has washed out the pollution and left a soft blue sky. I figure it's time to give my back a break and take a walk before day turns to night, so I hit the streets with no destination in mind.

Before long, I find myself wandering up a steep hill in an unfamiliar neighborhood. At the top, I'm met by a beautiful view of the Salt Lake Valley tucked up against the snow-capped mountains to the east. I breathe in the fresh spring air with a subtle smile as I watch the setting sun drape the valley in a warm glow. I sit down on a patch of grass to take in the moment. As I scan the valley, my eyes lock onto the pearl-white Mormon temple that sits at the heart of the city. It inspires in me the power of beliefs.

Beliefs not only build temples, mosques, and synagogues. They build smartphones, spaceships, and self-driving cars. They determine what clothes we wear, what company we keep, and what food we eat. They establish businesses and nations. They run courts of law, fuel economies, and spark revolutions. They push mountaineers to the highest peaks and launch astronauts into space. They shape our identities, mold our fears, and carve out our dreams. Beliefs frame our experience. They propel our entire lives.

I've been fascinated with beliefs since I was a kid. Growing up in a devout Mormon home and community, I watched the Mormon belief system propel my friends and family to do all kinds of things. Their beliefs put them on their knees every day to pray, put scriptures in their hands, sent them to church every Sunday, encouraged them to perform wonderful charity work, and to abstain from coffee and alcohol, among many other things.

Why? Because they believed the Church to be true. When I was a kid, I guess none of this really mattered much. If my parents, whom I love beyond words, and the rest of my community said that's the way things are, what choice did I really have?

One day, though, during a Sunday school lesson, I ran into a problem—the doorway to all new spaces of possibility. I confronted some moral and philosophical issues with the Doctrine, which sent me on a search for truth and understanding. And once the floodgates opened, the rapids never let up. Each question compelled me to seek out an answer. But every time I'd catch a glimmer, I'd just end up with more questions. Essentially, my initial problems grew deeper and deeper. I learned more and more about what I do not know. But as I became better acquainted with my ignorance in this way, I was able to ask better questions and, in turn, create better answers.

The evolution of these problems has consumed me now for decades. It has led me to explore the life and physical sciences, to pour over the world's religions, past and present. It has given me a relentless appetite for Eastern and Western philosophy. It has sent me around the world to explore people and customs, to break bread with Hindus, Muslims, Christians, Buddhists, and non-believers. It has led me to explore the nature of my own mind, to sit for week- and month-long meditations, to trek the Himalayas in silence for a month, to experiment with many psychedelics and entheogens, including participating in several traditional ayahuasca ceremonies with the Shipibo tribe in Peru, both in the Amazon Jungle and in the Sacred Valley, as well as inhaling vaporized Sapo Toad venom (5-MeO-DMT), otherwise known as the 'God Molecule'.

And after all this—books, travel, meditation, experience—I am now confident about one thing: that I know nothing, that whatever knowledge I have will always be engulfed by my infinite ignorance, that I'm just a kid playing in this Cosmic sandbox without a clue about much of anything.

While this Socratic ignorance has kept me open, while it has kept my wings uncaged from predetermined belief systems, while it has allowed

III

me to soar through the infinite and unbounded space of thought and mind, there is still much I have learned from the world's wisdom traditions. There are many philosophies that have helped orient me in this endless mystery of existence, many frameworks that have helped me better understand myself, the world, and my place in it, many ideas that have allowed me to sink roots deep into the earth, bringing a stability and strength to my life.

I've also come across some non-conceptual, or experiential, practices and meditations from various wisdom traditions that have helped soften my heart and open my mind. They have made me more composed and resilient, less reactive to people and situations. They have ultimately given me more freedom—freedom from distraction, freedom from mindless attention, freedom from suffering. I've also discovered meditations that have moved me past concepts and connected me directly to the unformed space of awareness, meditations that have pointed me to a boundless love and unshakeable peace.

I'd love to share them with you. But again, nothing in this book should be taken on authority. I have no desire to convert you to a specific belief system or to tell you to live a certain way or anything like that. I simply want to offer my support as you blaze your own trail. I want you to live authentically from your own heart.

This, I believe, will require you to open to the beliefs you have constructed over your bare, ever-changing flow of experience, and to examine with a caring attention how these beliefs propel you through the world, how they shape your life and your being. It will require you to learn to live with uncertainty, and to be at ease with it. Rather than live with concrete answers, it will require you to live from your questions, to live with the humility of not knowing.

What conceptual frameworks do you have constructed over your bare, ever-changing flow of experience? What do you believe to be true? What really propels you? What shapes you? How do you view and relate to yourself, the world, and your place in it? How will you paint your life? How will you sculpt your being?

Again, there's no right way to build a belief system, no right way to live your life, no right way to be. It's largely a poetic and artistic pursuit. But just as an artist must keep an open and honest conversation with her art, so too must you remain open and honest about your creation—about your beliefs, about your life, about your experience. Only then can you hope to understand and, therefore, truly love your yourself. Only then can you find lasting peace.

IV

So, as we move through this book, I'll encourage you to get out your paints and brushes, your bricks and mortar, to create the most important thing you can—the authentic you.

1. REASON

"I may be wrong, and you may be right,
and by an effort, we may get nearer to truth."
-Karl Popper

"The only true wisdom is knowing
you know nothing."
-Socrates

When I reflect on my life to see what has motivated me most, what has really driven me, it is without a doubt truth. I am a realist in every sense of the word. It's expressed in my writing, in my speech, and in my very being. I simply can't fathom a life, a point, a purpose, a relationship, or anything else for that matter, without a commitment to reality. If we're not oriented to reality, if we're not trying truly, humbly, and honestly to understand ourselves, others, and our world, then what are we doing?

As you know from the introduction, this commitment began early for me. Steeped in the Mormon culture of the Salt Lake Valley, everyone around me was telling me what was true. My friends and family made claims about God, claims about the creation of the heavens and earth, claims about the afterlife, claims about good and evil, claims about how I should live my life. And because these beliefs were so important to them, I couldn't simply say to my family and community, "No thanks, the Church is not for me." I had to defend myself and my choices. I had to bring my reasons.

This marked the beginning of a lifelong passion for me—epistemology, or the study of knowledge. I've read, studied, and thought about epistemology more than any other topic. What do I know to be true? How do I know it to be true? What is knowledge? How is it created? How does it grow or evolve? What power does it have in our lives and in the world? Can knowledge ever be demonstrated, proven, or justified as True, with a capital T?

These kinds of questions have continued to orient me not only in my intellectual life but in my moral and spiritual lives too. Everything unfolds from understanding. What we believe to be true shapes everything. It shapes how we think, it shapes how we talk and act, it even shapes how we experience the world. And underneath all our beliefs, the foundation to everything we know, is our epistemology—the how we come to hold our beliefs.

In this chapter, then, rather than tell you what to believe or what path to follow, the solution I have to offer, the common ground I believe we must all attempt to share, is not blind adherence to some set of truth claims. It is to investigate humbly and honestly how we know, to open ourselves to our epistemological foundation, which holds everything we believe to be true. And we will do this by tracing Western epistemology to its roots, so that the depths of these roots can bring a strength and stability to our lives.

It is my hope that this chapter brings you discerning wisdom. I hope it makes you better situated to align yourself, your heart and mind, with truth. I hope it helps you find lasting peace.

The Poetic Art of Understanding

It's midnight. I'm alone in southern Thailand, floating on my back in the calm ocean water. The brushstroke of glimmering white light that cuts through the heavens is breathtaking. Reverence and wonder push outward on my being as I float amongst the stars. I feel some thoughts burgeoning. The wonder entices them to run freely. "Not yet," I think to myself. "Right now, just bathe here, in the fullness of existence. Feel yourself without shapes or borders, without words or concepts. Let go entirely and just be. Soak in the simple and unanswerable marvel of being."

After fifteen minutes or so of total surrender, of non-doing, I work my way back to the shore. "Yum," I think to myself, "how healing." I sit down on my towel and acknowledge the little blooms, the thoughts that eagerly awaited my attention. I feel a sense of communion as I imagine the first kid to look up at the stars and wonder. What a sacred moment that must have been.

Wonder is the beginning. It is the space from which all things unfold. It gives birth to questions. Wonder is the womb of understanding. It molds from the empty formless space of awareness all that can be known.

Our relationship with the stars, the awe and reverence we hold for them, is not only a great starting point for the history of thought. It is also largely what it means to be human. Children across space and time have looked up to the stars and been swept away by their beauty and deep mystery. And some of these brave little cosmologists, desperate to know more about their home, the cosmos, eventually began to speculate answers.

In Thailand, there's an ancient story about how a particular star cluster known today in the West by its Greek name the Pleiades came to occupy the night sky. As the story goes, a monk made camp one night near a poor couple's little hut. The couple was worried because it was their culture's tradition to feed monks, who often swore off all possession, and the couple had only some brown rice, a hen, and seven chicks. It was also a common belief that such an act of generosity, especially to a monk, would lead to rewards in a future life. So, despite their worry, the poor couple decided to give the monk the best food they had — their hen. The hen overheard this, so she took her chicks aside and said, "I love you, but I must go now. It's time for you all to take care of yourselves." Early the next morning, the couple killed the hen and began to roast her. The chicks were so overcome by grief that they ran and jumped into the fire, hoping to remain with their mother. And as legend has it, the seven chicks were reborn as stars in the sky, now called Dao Look Kai.

The Kiowa tribe, an indigenous people of the Great Plains of North America, tell a different story about this same constellation. It goes something like this. A group of seven women snuck away one night to dance under the stars. But suddenly, the Bear People showed up and started to chase the women. So, the women ran and climbed onto a large rock for safety. But the Bear People too started to climb. Panicked, the women asked the rock for protection. And because no one had honored it before, the rock agreed to help. So, it shot out of the dirt and knocked the Bear People to the ground. The women were safe for now, but they quickly realized that they were now stranded on the rock. "What are we going to do now?" they said with worry on their faces. Desperate, they sang prayers to the stars for help. Happy to hear their praise, the stars took the seven women into the sky. In midwinter, you can still see them sitting above the Devil's Tower in Wyoming, smiling down on the rock spirit with gratitude.

What wonderful stories—attempts at explaining the world! Just imagine, faced with their ignorance, hearts eager and full of wonder, they had to start somewhere. What can you do but throw some color onto the canvas and go from there? We simply don't know what we don't know. So, we can only guess.

To really feel into this problem situation, the problem situation of understanding, let's step into a thought experiment. Go ahead and rewind the tape of your life until you first come out of your mama's womb. What did you know at this point? Did you know who you were? Did you know yourself? Probably not. In fact, you probably didn't have any concepts. Sure, natural selection armed your body with innate impulses, genetic algorithms, to cry and breastfeed, say. But it seems unlikely you experienced your 'self' as distinct, separate from the world. Your experience would have been full, seamless, without division.

So, how did you come to hold concepts, including the concept of yourself? Only with time and experience, as the environment got in the way of your innate impulses, like hunger, could you start to tease the world apart from you, from your desires and impulses. Only then, it seems, could you learn that there are things out in the world for you to manipulate, navigate, avoid, use, dissuade, or persuade to act out your innate impulses.

To better understand what I mean, consider handing a chimp a treat. The chimp will grab the treat without thinking about it. There is not much need for thinking. But if you block the treat with obstacles, the chimp must be creative. It must use imagination, the little problem solver in the head, to satisfy its desire or innate impulse. "Hmm...here are some boxes. Maybe I can stack them up and climb on them to get the treat!" So, the chimp, in solving its problem, paints concepts or imagery around those parts of the world that stand in relation to its impulses. So, we continue to learn about our "selves" through this conditioning. As our innate impulses drive us, we get feedback from the environment about where we believe our "edges" to be.

Now, consider again our chimp who is forced to pause and reflect. While the chimp's action is suspended, what do you think it feels? What does it experience during that pause? Frustration? Resistance? And where does the chimp believe this resistance exists? Is it in the object or does the chimp think it comes from within itself—that it's a psychological phenomenon? What is this invisible power the chimp needs to overcome? What is this resistance?

Now consider how the chimp might feel about the boxes when the chimp realizes the boxes will help it get the treat. Does the chimp believe the boxes are on its side, like many of our ancestors who tried to make the rain or sun (gods) happy so they too would be on their side? Or again, does the chimp think this is an inner state, an inner feeling that is not apart from the chimp?

These invisible forces are, of course, elements of the chimp's mind.

But I doubt the chimp understands this (or the earliest humans as they began to wake up to the objects of consciousness). Rather, it's likely that these feelings are naively projected onto the objects, like a kid who kicks his toy because it pinched his finger. "Why would the toy do such a thing!?"

A survey of the world's ancient religions seems to support this view—that these invisible 'forces', or numina, were believed to be separate from who or what we are. In Ancient Rome, for example, Janus is not a fully personified god who presides over doorways and gates but is simply 'the spirit of door-ness,' a spiritual power present in all doors that can help or harm one who passes through them.

Magic, mythology, and religion, it seems, find their roots here. As these numina accumulated, we would have needed a way to organize, navigate, and make sense of all the unseen forces in the world. So, mythology and religion became the vessels for magic and the supernatural, which allowed us to paint these unseen powers with more definite shapes and qualities, giving them an increasingly concrete form. In time, some of these supernatural entities became beings of their own, eventually transforming into complete anthropomorphic gods, like the gods of Egypt, India, Greece, and all the rest.

Supernatural knowledge became knowledge of a higher order, knowledge of the gods revealed only to the inspired or, as the Greeks said, to the 'divine' man—the prophet, poet, and priest. It is here, around the time of the Agricultural Revolution that our ancestors' beliefs shifted from animism to polytheism.

As agriculture developed and cities expanded, our ancestors developed entire pantheons of gods to explain all kinds of phenomenon—gods of war, water, fertility, wisdom, music, death, love, and so on. Before long, there was a god or goddess for everything. Our polytheist ancestors began to see the world as their own, as something given to them by the gods. And if they made the gods happy, the gods would reward them with plenty of food, water, and good fortune. But if they upset the gods, well, then the capricious gods would punish them with droughts, earthquakes, plagues, and other catastrophes.

Over time, though, as more kingdoms arose, each with its own pantheon of gods, the arena started to get overcrowded. And when you have so many gods in charge of so many things, odds are you are going to offend at least some of them. So, people started to pick favorites, worshipping only one god, even though they believed other gods existed. This is a form of worship known as henotheism, which seems to have first appeared in India during the Vedic period (c. 1500 — c. 600 BC).

You can also see traces of henotheism in the Bible. In the book of Jeramiah, for example, Yahweh gets upset at his people for worshipping Ishtar: "Don't you see what they are doing in the...streets of Jerusalem? The children gather sticks, the fathers build the fire, and the mothers knead dough, to make cakes for the Queen of Heaven [Ishtar], and they pour libations to other gods, to vex Me." (Jeremiah 7:17–18).

Jeremiah and Ezekiel, two prophets from the Abrahamic religions, were early missionaries of the idea that all gods except one are false. They even went so far as to argue that the one true God punishes idolatry. Like Jeremiah and Ezekiel, many polytheists became so fond of their preferred god that, over the generations, people began to believe the god of their ancestors was the only true god. Thus, the seeds of monotheism were sown, which have evolved down to the present day.

As you can see, though there is a kernel of truth to our ancient myths, our early speculations of the world were...well, naïve. But what do you expect? We had to start somewhere. We owe all our knowledge to these brave little cosmologists. It's their wonderfully imaginative stories that mark our first brave steps into the darkness of our ignorance. But imagination alone, of course, won't get us any nearer to truth. We also need a way to reign in our poetic maginations. Let's see how a small group of Greeks in the Ionian colonies finally figured out how to get purchase on our wonderfully creative stories.

The Critical Art of Understanding

It's Tuesday, a typically confused Spring morning here at the edge of the Uinta National Forest in Utah, where Winter refuses to go down without a fight. I wake up to my 6:00 AM alarm clock—my baby's voice: "Morning snuggles, daddy?" I open the covers and cuddle up to that sweet angel. After each of my babies cycle through, I get out of bed, make my tea, do my chores, and then the family gathers for Morning Devotional, where we devote ourselves to Love. We read from one of the world's wisdom traditions, discuss our monthly virtue, work on memorizing a poem, and then soak in silence together for a few minutes to find our way back to stillness, that boundless open space that sits at the core of our beings, uniting us to all things.

After we close our morning devotional with meditation, I remind the kids, "It's Tuesday! Go ahead and get dressed so we can go to the library."

Living on the edge of National Forest, with no neighbors, and because I homeschool the kids, it's fun for them to get out and interact with the other homeschooled kids at the library. Plus, there's nothing quite like being surrounded by so many books. I can feel the authors with me. Their spirits live on through their words. The thought, the passion, the tedious care they put into extracting their ideas from their minds to put onto paper—it's inspiring!

Once at the library, surrounded by so much knowledge and creativity, I start thinking about the kids' philosophy lesson I'll be having with them in the afternoon. Today, we're going to start learning about the ancient pre-Socratics, who I absolutely adore—a bunch of renegade thinkers who invented the Ionian tradition, a creative and critical method for understanding. I notice a wave of gratitude move through me. I think about how much this group of rebels has influenced me and realize that none of this influence would have been possible if their ideas weren't written down, translated, and preserved by so many brave people—people who faced religious and political persecution for holding such dangerous and heretical knowledge.

So, what was so dangerous about the Ionian tradition? Well, to get a glimpse of the problem, let's head back in time some nine thousand years, to when the book of Deuteronomy was written.

> *What thing soever I command you, observe to do it: thou shalt not add thereto, nor diminish from it. If there arises among you a prophet, or dreamer of dreams, who asks you to serve other gods, then that prophet, or dreamer of dreams, shall be put to death. If thy brother, the son of thy mother, or thy son, or thy daughter, or the wife of thy bosom, or thy friend, which is as thine own soul, shall entice thee by saying, 'Let us go and serve other gods,' thou shall not consent unto him, nor hearken unto him; neither shall thine eye pity him, neither shalt thou spare him, neither shalt though conceal him: But thou shalt surely kill him; thine hand shall be first upon him to put him to death.* (Deuteronomy 12:32–13:9)

This scripture was not unusual. In fact, it was par for the course. Nearly every civilization throughout history created a dogmatic school whose main task was to pass on the doctrine of its founder intact to each generation. And in the rare event a person criticized the doctrine or proposed a new idea, the heretic would've been silenced, expelled, or even killed.

New ideas would occasionally arise, of course. But to survive, it couldn't be presented as a new idea but would rather have to be presented as a return to the founder's original doctrine, which the person would have to argue had been perverted or distorted in some way. And if it was convincing enough, the school would split, and a conflict would naturally arise. (Just consider the dozens of branches of Islam and Christianity, including the religion of my upbringing, Mormonism. Joseph Smith, the founder of Mormonism, did just this—he argued that Christ and God visited him, told him that their doctrines had been distorted, and gave him the pure teachings.)

Some six hundred years before Christ, though, a few Greeks in the Ionian colonies, after experiencing several culture clashes with nearby civilizations, finally thought, "Hold up. With so many competing claims and explanations of the world, don't you think we could be wrong about ours?"

You can see the role these clashes had on Greek philosophy quite clearly in the writings of the poet, philosopher, and all-around badass Xenophanes (c. 570 — c. 475 BC):

> *The Ethiopians say that their gods are flat-nosed and*
> *black*
> *While the Thracians say that theirs have blue eyes and*
> *red hair.*
> *Yet if cattle or horses or lions had hands and could draw*
> *And sculpture like men, then the horses would draw*
> *their gods*
> *Like horses, and cattle like cattle, and each would then*
> *shape*
> *Gods in the likeness, each kind, of its own.[1]*

With so many competing beliefs about the world, the Ionians concluded that we humans are fallible—that our explanations of the world are made of bold guesses. But rather than throw their hands in the air and abandon their search for truth, they invented the single most important tradition necessary for the growth of human knowledge—a tradition of reason; a tradition of an open and honest critical discussion where the aim is to move nearer to truth. This is also spelled out quite clearly by Xenophanes:

> *The gods did not reveal, from the beginning,*
> *All things to us; but in the course of time,*

Through seeking we may learn, and know things better...
These things we learn are like truth.
But as for certain truth, no man has known it,
Nor will he know it; neither of the gods,
Nor yet of all the things of which I speak.
And even if by chance he were to utter
The final truth, he would himself not know it:
For all is but a woven web of guesses.[2]

Xenophanes, in a few short verses, not only highlighted the conjectural nature of human knowledge but he also designed an elegant theory of objective knowledge. He knew that though our knowledge of it could never be certain or final, a real world nevertheless exists, the world behind appearances, and that through seeking we may come to understand it better. Objectivity arises because of this very fact that we make mistakes, that we can and do error—objectivity is the standard from which we fall short. In other words, our failure to solve a problem gives us a window into an objective reality.

Though Xenophanes spelled it out explicitly, it was actually his older contemporary Thales of Miletus (c. 624–546 BC) who invented this revolutionary new school—a school that engages in a creative and critical discussion, where the aim is to move nearer to truth. Thales was one of the first to conjecture natural explanations of forces in the world. To explain earthquakes, for example, he conjectured that 'the earth is supported by water on which it rides like a ship.'[3] And when the water stirs violently, it causes the earth to shake. This isn't bad considering he threw it down some six hundred years before Jesus. But what was even more impressive about Thales is that he seemed to have encouraged his student Anaximander (c. 610 — c. 546 BC) not to dogmatically accept his explanations of the world but to criticize and improve upon them!

Anaximander took on Thales' challenge and accomplished something truly remarkable. He took issue with Thales' claim that the earth is supported by water. 'If the earth is supported by water,' he wondered, 'what supports the water? And if the water is supported by something in turn, what supports it?' Each time you add a level of support, you're still faced with the same problem.

To fix this infinite regress, Anaximander argued that the earth is held up by nothing but remains suspended in space because it is equal distance to all things.[4] This novel idea, if followed through to its logical conclusion, should have led Anaximander to propose that the earth is shaped like a sphere. But it's likely that his experience of walking on what appeared to be a flat surface deceived him. So instead, he argued that the earth is shaped like a drum, and that we walk on one of its flat surfaces.[5]

This, to me, is one of the most inspiring moments in the evolution of human thought. And it gets even better. Anaximander recognized that there was an obvious objection to his own claim that the earth was equal distance to all things—one just needs to look at the sun and moon. To resolve this problem, Anaximander imagined two large rims rotating around the earth, a rim one hundred twenty-seven times the size of the earth and the other eighteen times its size, the sun and moon respectively. Both these rims, he tells us, are filled with fire and each has a breathing hole through which the fire is visible. The fixed stars are also rims of fire with breathing holes. And each of these rims rotates on a common axis, which together form a sphere around the earth.[6]

Unbelievable! By criticizing and finding gaps not only in Thales' ideas but also in his own, Anaximander was able to throw down the first spherical theory of the cosmos!

Next, Xenophanes, inspired by this remarkable new school, applied it to a problem he had encountered during his travels throughout Greece as a bard, a professional reciter of Homer's and Hesiod's poems. As you saw above, Xenophanes encountered many conflicting claims about the gods' appearances, which led him to wonder, 'If the gods aren't shaped like us, how should we imagine them?' His solution was a single, all-encompassing, unmoving force:

One God, alone among gods and alone among men is the greatest.
Neither in mind nor in body does he resemble mortals.
Always in one place he remains, without ever moving,
Nor is it fit for him to wander here or there.
Effortless over the cosmos he reigns by mere thought and intention.
All of him is sight; all is knowledge; and all is hearing.[7]

Xenophanes's solution—a pantheistic and monistic force—is remarkable, no doubt. But perhaps his greater achievement was to admit that it was no more than a guess, one that is highly fallible and open to improvement. This left the door open for Heraclitus (c. 535 - c. 475 BC), the next Greek on our list, to run with Xenophanes's idea.

Heraclitus was inspired by Xenophanes's idea of a monistic god or force. But unlike Xenophanes's god, who remained in one place, Heraclitus argued that God was continually in flux. He arrived at this claim after noticing a deep paradox in nature. The world appears to be filled with things. Yet all these things change in time, even if we don't perceive the change directly. Winds blow, rivers flow, and children grow. Even something as stable as a bronze cauldron eventually rots away. So how, Heraclitus wondered, can something change yet remain the same?

This problem of change led Heraclitus to propose that, in truth, there are no things but, rather, only a single continuous process. The world is on fire, he claimed. Those who look but do not think believe only the fuel burns, while the bowl in which it burns remains unchanged. Yet the bowl burns. It is eaten up by the fire that holds it. Fire—or change—is all there is. Everything is like a flame—though it appears to have a shape, it is actually just a part of the Everlasting Fire. And the apparent stability of things is merely an illusion, an illusion which Heraclitus believed is due to a transition in opposites:

> Life and death, being awake and being asleep, youth and old age, all these are the same...for the one turned round is the other and the other turned round is the first.... The path that leads up and the path that leads down are the same path.... For God all things are beautiful and good and just, but men assume some things unjust, and others to be just.... It is not in the nature or character of man to possess true knowledge, though it is in the divine nature.[8]

Heraclitus's originality and deep skepticism of common sense are truly astonishing. But there appears to be a logical inconsistency in his solution. If opposites are identical and all things are one, isn't change impossible by definition?

Parmenides (c. 514 - mid 400s BC), Heraclitus' younger contemporary, certainly thought so. He therefore proposed a radically different solution to the problem of change: he denied it completely, and instead argued that the world is one unchanging spherical block. Parmenides arrived at this conclusion by way of something like a logical proof, which went something like this:

> Only what exists, exists.
> What does not exist, therefore, does not exist.

And because change requires the non-existent,
that is, what once was or what will be,
change is impossible.
Thus, the world is full.
It is timeless, uniform, and unchanging.
The world (or mind) just is.[9]

What the hell do you do with that! Especially considering this was the first time someone deduced a conclusion from a tautology or analytic statement like that—what exists, exists. His conclusion seems almost foolproof. Yet it's completely absurd. One just needs to look around to see that everything is changing all the time. So, how could Parmenides have possibly reconciled his unchanging block universe with our perception of change?

This, I believe, is what led Parmenides to distinguish between Truth (alêtheia) and Opinion (doxa). Though Xenophanes and Heraclitus had already vaguely distinguished true reality (ultimate truth) from the world of appearances (relative truth), Parmenides was the first to formulate a criterion to cut through the world of appearances and get at absolute Truth. His criterion is simple. Truth, he argues, can be obtained only by deducing conclusions from premises that are certain, like the tautology 'only what exists, exists.'

Parmenides, no doubt, deserves a top spot in the philosophical hall of fame. Not only was he among the first to employ a hypothetico-deductive argument to make a metaphysical claim about the world. But to follow his critical reasoning to a conclusion that so vehemently opposes our common sense, as he did, is some next-level reasoning.

As remarkable a thinker as he was, though, Parmenides' criterion of truth is surely wrong. There's no denying the power of deduction, especially to the extent it's used to refute a theory, which is largely what Parmenides did. But as Xenophanes had already highlighted, human knowledge is and always will be conjectural. Because, even if we could prove that our logic is sound (which is an impossible task since it requires logic to prove logic, which is circular), our premises are never certain.

All premises are made of concepts. And all concepts are created. They are just noises and scribbles. They are abstract symbols we use to paint over the boundless and inseparable space of existence. Each word is defined by other words, which in turn are defined by more words, and on and on ad infinitum. We agree to these words by convention, which is helpful, but no word or concept can be certain, they can never be what things are in themselves. Words, as we'll see in the next chapter, are just pointers. There's no escape—our words, theories, ideas, and understanding of the world will never be able to penetrate the veil of appearances. They will always be but a web of guesses.

Now, before we move onto the last Greeks we'll explore in this chapter, let me just mention one more thing about Parmenides's theory—that is, it is an empirically falsifiable claim. Falsifiability is a modern requirement for scientific claims. It was introduced in the beginning of the twentieth century by the philosopher Karl Popper to distinguish metaphysical, supernatural, and pseudoscientific claims (like Marxism, Psychoanalysis, Astrology, etc.) from the empirically rigorous claims of science (the theory of relativity, natural selection, plate tectonics, etc.).

If a claim is to reach the status of a 'scientific claim,' it must in principle, Popper argued, be able to conflict with some observation or experiment. That is, it needs to stick its neck out, leaving itself vulnerable to refutation. And the further it sticks its neck out, like Einstein's theory of relativity, the better.[10]

In any case, it was the atomists, the last of the Greeks we'll meet in this chapter, who recognized and took advantage of this fact. Leucippus (c. 5th century BC) and Democritus (c. 460 — c. 370 BC), like Parmenides, believed that our senses can't be trusted. And so, like Parmenides, they believed logic is necessary to transcend our faulty senses. But Democritus realized that it would be impossible to improve upon Parmenides' theory without our senses, even if they can't be trusted fully. He expresses this in his famous dialogue between the two caricatures he created for the Intellect and the Senses:

Intellect:
Colored by convention; sweet by convention; bitter by convention. But in truth, atoms and the void.

Senses:
Poor intellect! You take your credentials from us and want our downfall? But by casting us down, you fall yourself![11]

So, to move past Parmenides' seemingly final-say on philosophy, the atomists used both logic and the senses to refute Parmenides' block universe and replace it with their theory of atoms and the void. And because Parmenides had created an empirically testable theory, the atomists were able to start from an observational refutation—that there is clearly change in the world. Taking this as their starting premise, they then flipped the coin on Parmenides' logic, which went something like this:

There is change.
And because change requires the non-existent,
the non-existent does exist.
Thus, the world consists of the existing,
the hard and full, and of the non-existent:
The world exists of atoms and the void.[12]

Atomism was incredibly successful. It lasted for over two thousand years and culminated in Newton's mechanics. It wasn't abandoned until the middle of the nineteenth century, when Michael Faraday and James Maxwell showed us that electricity, magnetism, and light are all manifestations of the same thing, the electromagnetic field, pushing us back in the direction of a Parmenidean view of the physical cosmos. But I digress.

Here, I just want to highlight the stark contrast in the Ionian school versus the dogmatic school. The goal of the Ionian school was not to preserve the doctrine of the school's founder intact but to improve upon it. They didn't expel or kill someone for criticizing a teacher's idea or for proposing a new one. They encouraged it. They understood that criticism is necessary to progress our imaginative and, thus, highly fallible explanations of the world. And that it is only after we find a hole in an existing explanation, like the infinite regress in Thales' argument or the logical inconsistency in Heraclitus' claim or the empirical absurdity in Parmenides' block universe, that we can hope to propose a better solution.

The birth and development of the Ionian tradition is a marvelous story. It has given us so much of what we have come to appreciate—our electricity, computers, internet, medicine, engines, and infrastructure. It's critical, then, to understand not only how it works but also how fragile it is. As a tradition, aside from a few sparks in China and India, it has been invented only once. It began with Thales and Anaximander and lasted only a few hundred years before taking a series of blows, beginning with the Persian empire's invasion of northern Greece and, again, when the Greeks exchanged their words for swords under the Macedonian and Roman empires. It was eventually pushed to near extinction when the Catholic Church, largely under the spell of Plato, suppressed all free thought and claimed that the Bible was the only true source of knowledge. And though it was picked up briefly during the Golden Age of Islam by the Abbasid caliphate, it didn't make a stable recovery until after the fall of Constantinople in 1453, when scholars migrated to Italy, bringing with them what ancient writings had survived.

Questions & Reflections

Where does wonder, reverence, and awe show up in your life? What opens your eyes wide and makes you feel vast, open, and interested? What brings vitality to your being? What motivates you to learn and understand and grow? What demands a story? What demands understanding?

How does art, poetry, or storytelling personally help you understand yourself and the world? What myths or archetypes help you make sense of life? Do you have any stories that shed light on your own internal world of thought, feeling, and emotion? How does your understanding of reality shape how you live and relate and be? Who or what do your stories say you are?

How do you distinguish between reality and fantasy? Where does criticism show up in your life? Do you keep people close who are willing to give honest reflections, even if they are critical and sometimes hurt? Are you able to listen to opposing views and opinions with composure and interest?

Write down your most deeply cherished beliefs, your strongest convictions. Then, consider, for even a moment, that you might be wrong about them. After all, these beliefs are just words on a page. What lies behind them? Isn't there just *This*, whatever *This* ineffably is? Isn't there just existence? Is there more space, more ease, more discerning wisdom when you can hold these beliefs with an open hand rather than a clenched fist?

2. FREEDOM

"The willingness to accept responsibility for one's own life is the source from
which...self-respect springs."
– Joan Didion

When the kids and I get home from the library on Tuesdays, I start our philosophy lesson with the question, "Why is philosophy important?"

"It's a love of wisdom," they all reply. "Philo is the Greek word for 'love,' which can be translated more specifically as 'tending to.' And sophia is the Greek word for 'wisdom.'"

"Nice! And why should we tend to wisdom?" I ask them.

"Because wisdom brings us peace since it seeks to align ourselves with Nature, with the Dharma, with the truth of the moment's experience!" they all shout.

I like the word "align" here because it signifies that philosophy is, at its root, an activity, a moral system, a way of life. And if we look etymologically at wisdom, we indeed find that the root *wis* carries the active function of discerning or judging; to discern the way forward. Think of the word clock-wise, the way of the clock, or like-wise, in the same way.

Now, I bring this up because philosophy is often met with boredom, and sometimes even scorn. People believe it is too far removed from our everyday lives. And there is a kernel of truth to this. From the late 1800s to the mid 1900s, with the rise of the philosophical schools known as Logical Positivism and Analytic Philosophy, philosophy desiccated, and most philosophers stepped away from moral problems, leaving them to the preachers and politicians. It really wasn't until the Vietnam War and the "Hippy Movement" that philosophers once again began to investigate moral questions. The Philosopher Peter Singer even opened space to explore our ethical duties toward non-human animals in his 1975 book Animal Liberation, which gained wide attention in the public sphere.

Despite its detour from moral problems, though, philosophy is of central importance to our everyday lives. Each of us is constantly trying to align ourselves—our body, heart, mind, desires, impulses, interests, values, aims—with reality, with the dharma, a Sanskrit word that means the truth of the moment's experience, which is always new, original, unique. Every day, we face judgment calls and must skillfully discern the best course of action.

At the political and societal level, we confront decisions about abortion, global alliances, military strategies, the misuse of police force, political funding and campaigning, healthcare, immigration policies, the growing threat of A.I. and synthetic biotechnology, etc. At home and at work, we have to figure out how to best approach a loved one who hurt us, a colleague who has a drug or alcohol problem, or a friend who is cheating on their partner. And at bottom, each of us, in each moment, is always faced with the problem of what to do next, which is always new and unpredictable. Popper put it succinctly when he said, "All life is problem solving."[13]

In this chapter, then, we will trace the roots of moral philosophy back to the ancient Greeks, who were among the first to awaken to their personal moral responsibility, without authority from the gods. But before we jump in, let me just say that moral philosophy is arguably the most confused and misguided arena of philosophy. On the one side, there are still many, mostly on the political Right, who believe that reason and science can't shed light on morality. It belongs to religion, they argue. Only God can determine what is good and evil.

And on the other side, mostly on the political Left, there are many, even philosophers and scientists, who deny any objectivity to our morals. Following David Hume, an eighteenth-century Scottish philosopher, they argue that it's impossible to get an ought from an is—that is, a moral proposition from a factual statement. "Tis not contrary to reason," Hume famously wrote, "to prefer the destruction of the whole world to the scratching of my finger." This view, known as moral relativism, claims that our norms, values, and behaviors have no universally objective basis but instead depend entirely on the culture we grew up in.

Were philosophy confined to old men in tweed jackets, this wouldn't be much of a problem. But ideas are powerful, and they can—and do!—have drastic consequences on our lives and on our society at large. For those who believe morality comes from god, there is the obvious problem of which god to listen to—for there are thousands of gods on offer. There is also the problem of jihad, martyrdom, patriarchy, sexism, racism, homophobia, forced marriages, genital mutilation, honor killings, mass genocide, and all the rest that are brazenly forced onto society.

And in the other camp, with the moral relativists, we are left with the absence of any rational moral framework. Morality amounts to nothing more than a fiction, each of us confined to the fiction of our cultural inheritance. This view not only renders us entirely incapable of moving toward a global order, as we must, but it makes diverse countries like the United States, a nation built of immigrants, equally incapable of healing its divisions. Just think, if the moral relativists abide by their own logic, the Northern States in the U.S. had no bases to tell the Southern states they were wrong to have slaves. Slave trading is a deep part of their cultural inheritance. It's there in the Old Testament, in Leviticus and Deuteronomy. In fact, many of the patriarchs of the Bible were slave owners.

Consider also, in this same vein, that we in the West currently have no place to stand to tell Hamas to stop killing Jews for Allah. We can't tell ISIS it is wrong to stone their daughters to death for having sex outside of marriage or to beat women who learn to read. We can never tell the Saudi Arabian government it is wrong to hang gays in the street by the dozens or for the Taliban to stop performing beheadings at their soccer game halftimes. Why? Because we in the West don't share the same Quranic values as Hamas, the Taliban, or the Islamic Theocracy of Saudi Arabia. So much for spreading safety, peace, political freedom, free speech, gender and racial equality, and other basic human rights to the world's precious children.

Moral relativism is not only misguided, it is lazy, irresponsible, cowardice, and downright cruel. I think many people on the Left who take this position are more worried about appearing racist, bigoted, xenophobic, Islamophobic, et cetera than they are actually concerned about the wellbeing of the people, children, women, gays, scientists, and critics who live and suffer under these harmful frameworks. Of course, not all are worried about their appearances. There are also many of us empaths, whose tender hearts are easy targets for manipulation. And many of us just don't have the information. Plain and simple, our culture is in a state of mass moral confusion.

In any case, until recently, moral relativism didn't have any teeth since most people still looked to their religion on matters of morality. However, as more of us leave religion behind in this Information Age, the danger of collapsing into moral relativism is becoming more imminent and the need for a secular and rational morality more pressing.

So, let's go ahead and explore the problem and hopefully clear up the confusion. For there is a simple one on offer, which to my surprise has been largely overlooked by philosophers, scientists, and intellectuals alike. The solution is this: all knowledge—whether physical, biological, social, political, moral or otherwise—evolves through the same humble method of trial and the elimination of error. So, in the field of morality, Hume's problem disappears.

We can concede that it is impossible to derive an ought from an is. But that's no matter, since all knowledge is conjectured anyway, including our values and aims—our moral propositions, what we ought to do. This, however, does not mean we need to abandon our pursuit of moral progress. When we own up to our fallibility in the moral sphere, when we admit that not only our behaviors, norms, and traditions are conjectured but that so too are the very aims they attempt to achieve, then we can work together openly and honestly to move toward a better world, toward a better life, toward a better experience.

This is what the Ancient Athenians did when they established the first free and open society under the leadership of Pericles. Let's see how they got there.

Self-Responsibility

Before cultures clashed, our social norms, rites, and traditions would have seemed as natural as the seasons—each were believed to be controlled by the gods, or by nature. So, no one would have thought to question the social structures and cultural dogmas that had evolved. The clothes men and women wore, the duties each performed, the rituals they observed—that's just the way the world was.

Some five hundred years before Christ, though, as civilizations near the Mediterranean expanded and clashed, people were finally given reason to question their social structures and traditions. The Persian King Darius I (550–486 BC), for example, in a rather inspired moment of teaching and no doubt to mess with some Greeks living under his rule at the time, asked the Greeks how much money it would take to convince them to eat the flesh of their fathers when they died.

The Greeks, whose custom was to burn their dead, freaked out and said no amount would convince them. So, King Darius summoned the Callatians, whose custom was in fact to eat their dead, and asked them how much money it would take to persuade them to burn their dead. They also freaked out and asked why he would suggest such a thing.[14]

Whatever the effect was on Darius' subjects, there was one Greek who learned a great deal from these culture clashes. Growing up in a city under the control of Darius' son Xerxes, Protagoras (c. 490 — c. 420 BC) witnessed firsthand the clash of beliefs, norms, and traditions from those cultures that had been swallowed by the Persian empire. It led him to conclude that our social norms and behaviors are quite different from natural laws, like the seasons. Social norms, he argued, are created and enforced not by god, or by nature, but by each of us.

This had dramatic consequences because it shifted the burden to distinguish between right and wrong from god, or nature, to each individual. Only you, the individual, he claimed, can judge whether a behavior, norm, law, or institution is right or wrong. The burden is yours and yours alone. You can't shift it to god, nature, history, or even to society because, whatever authority you accept, it is still you who must accept that authority. "The individual," he famously said, "is the measure of all things."[15]

Talk about the ultimate self-responsibility! Heavy, I know. But heavy as it may be, this ability to paint our morals onto the world is, I agree with Protagoras, incredibly motivating and inspiring. It allows us to bring purpose and meaning into our lives. Unlike our critter friends, who are confined to the narrow and automatic range of aims and behaviors carved out by natural selection (or the religious, by god's creed), you and I, as we wake up to our social and cultural conditioning, can examine, criticize, and then change our aims and behaviors. And what's more, we can now even change our genes, which have their own morals, or operating instructions, built into them!

We can ask what problem a particular norm, tradition, or gene is meant to solve (that is, we can examine the underlying aim and motivation), and then we can work toward improving the norm, tradition, or gene to better accomplish the underlying aim. And if through critical discussion we decide to change or readjust the underlying aim itself, we can do that too. We can even toss the aim altogether if we find it objectionable. So, as you can see, the epistemological method here is the same as that used by the Ionians to learn more about our physical world—a cyclical process of criticism and creativity. Through open critical discussion, experimentation, observation, and a heavy dose of creativity, we can continue to carve away at our mistakes. In a way, we can pull ourselves up from our own bootstraps.

The biggest failure of contemporary philosophy, in my opinion, is its failure to consider the objectivity of our morals. Our morals do indeed exist objectively. One way of life, or one set of values, may certainly be incom-

21

patible with another way of life in the same way a scientific theory is logically incompatible with another. Do these incompatibilities, these clashes, not exist objectively? Certainly they do. How else would Protagoras have been able to distinguish social norms from natural laws? The most important role philosophy can play in our lives, I believe, is to discover where our virtues, aims, and behaviors clash, and then discuss them openly, honestly, and critically.

Socrates (c. 470–399 BC) is the symbol of this wisdom. He spent his days questioning people about things like justice, goodness, and beauty, artfully walking them to their own ignorance, to their own contradictions, to clashes in their own beliefs, morals, and assumptions. And in the end, he even gave his life to defend the right to do so.

Looking for a scapegoat to blame for the Athenians' misfortune in the Peloponnesian War, the jury sentenced Socrates to death for corrupting the youth and undermining the state religion. Had he apologized, he probably would've been exiled. But Socrates refused to abandon reason. "To put it bluntly," he tells the jury, "I've been assigned to this city as if to a lazy horse who is in need of a great stinging fly. All day long I will rouse and criticize every last one of you." Not flattered, the jury sentenced Socrates to death.[16]

Socrates wasn't stupid. He understood what his provocation meant. But to him, the unexamined life isn't worth living. Reason, he believed, is what makes us human. It is the divine spark, the spirit of progress, the path to truth, beauty, and goodness. So, he courageously gave his life to defend it.

Nor was Socrates an enemy of democracy, as some believed. Rather, he criticized the State's government as any responsible democrat should—to find holes in the state's laws and institutions to clear the way for a better life. He seemed to have understood that democracy is the only system of government that allows people to reform their institutions with reason rather than bloodshed.

He also understood that democracy itself can't provide reason. Only the individual can. It wasn't the Athenian democracy that turned its back on reason and sentenced Socrates to death. It was the individual people. Governments and institutions are merely fictions that live in the minds of individuals. They have no existence or power apart from us. The responsibility to engage in reason is always up to the individual. The heavy lifting is on you. It is up to you and you alone to build a better life.

Democritus (c. 460 – c. 370 BC), the co-inventor of the atoms and the void, also believed that each of us carries the burden to create a better life for ourselves. He believed that every person is a little world of her own. Only the individual can suffer. Only the individual can feel love, joy, and happiness. It is up to each individual to put social laws and institutions into place. It is up to each of us to judge and improve them. And if necessary, it is up to each of us to defend them.

Pericles (c. 495 – 429 BC), the general of Athens at its peak, took this burden seriously. Before him, Athens was essentially an oligarchy in all but name since the aristocrats still held all the wealth. So, to even out this imbalance, Pericles created the first civil project in history—a state-sponsored economic incentive to inspire all of Greece. 'We will build all kinds of enterprises,' he declared, 'to provide inspiration for every art and to find employment for every hand.' True to his word, the project was a success. It created many jobs for the middle and lower classes and produced art that is still admired to this day. He also introduced state salaries for jurors and soldiers. He even used the state treasury to pay for the occasional public festival.

Pericles believed that the whole of Athens was an education. It doesn't compete with other nations. It sets an example. And so, it did. Under the influence of the great thinkers of Pericles' generation, Pericles and his fellow Athenians not only created a world empire. They implemented the world's first free and open society—a society whose values are sketched out beautifully in a speech he gave at the end of the first year of the Peloponnesian War:

> "The laws afford equal justice to all alike in their private disputes, but we do not ignore the claims of excellence. When a citizen distinguishes himself, then he will be called to serve the state, in preference to others, not as a matter of privilege, but as a reward of merit; poverty is not a bar. The freedom we enjoy extends also to ordinary life; we are not suspicious of one another, and do not nag our neighbor if he chooses to go his own way...But this freedom does not make us lawless. We are taught to respect the magistrate and the laws, and never to forget that we must protect the injured. And we are also taught to observe those unwritten laws whose sanction lies only in the universal feeling of what is right...And although only a few may originate a policy, we are all able to judge it. We do not look upon discussion as a stumbling block in the way of political action, but as an indispensable preliminary to acting wisely...We believe that happiness is the fruit of freedom and freedom that of valor...."[17]

Pericles' words symbolize a new commitment—a commitment not to the gods or to the state or to a specific group, but to each individual. It is a commitment to freedom—the freedom to express one's self, the freedom to distinguish between right and wrong for one's self, the freedom to vote for public matters, the freedom against institutional prejudices and biases, the freedom against unwanted physical force, and the freedom to go your own way if you so choose.

Our political motivations should not and cannot be framed around the state, the dollar, the economy, or any other fiction. They must find themselves rooted in the minds of free individuals—the only place where truth, beauty, and goodness, or anything else for that matter can exist.

Let us turn our gazes inward, as Socrates did, to establish our politics and morality. Know your true Self. Know the nature of your own mind. Let this exploration of yourself, of your own heart and mind, guide you as you work to create laws and institutions, as you build out and conduct your communities. Let the exploration of yourself guide you as you paint the masterpiece that is your life.

Just remember—freedom does not come free. As the great thinkers of Pericles' generation stressed, only you can build these freedoms into our institutions. Only you can criticize and improve them. And if necessary, only you can defend them. Nature, god, and society cannot do this for you. The future depends on you. The burden is on you to build a better future, to build a better life, to build a better world.

Tyranny

This, of course, is no easy task. It takes great courage to navigate the darkness of your ignorance in search of a better life. If you feel the weight of this burden, no worries. You aren't alone. In fact, many Greeks were suffocated by it and tried desperately to shift the responsibility back to god, or nature.

But there were also some in Ancient Greece (and even today) who were aware of this strain and used it as leverage to maintain their power—to return to the so-called 'natural' state, where the rulers rule, the workers work, and the slaves slave. One of the earliest attempts was put forward by the Greek poet Pindar. It is natural law, he argued, for the strong to make slaves of the weak. Democracy, or anything else that protects the weak, is not only arbitrary, but also a disgraceful perversion of god's natural law.[18]

Many "naturalistic" arguments have been proposed since Pindar—many out of fear, some with good intentions, and others...well, not so much. And though most of these arguments admit that we do in fact create our own social norms, they nevertheless claim that our norms ultimately rest on nature.

I see at least two common objections to these arguments. First, I'm not sure nature is the best place to rest your morals. I mean, isn't it more natural to leave your shoes and clothes behind? The farther we trace our lineage back, isn't it more natural to rape than 'make love'? Shouldn't you give up your cellphone, car, and home? What about the arts and sciences? Should we give them up too? Isn't it obvious? If you want moral progress, you can't look back at nature. You must look forward, out into the darkness, beyond the wall of ignorance.

The second point these naturalistic arguments overlook is the fact that it is still you who must decide which aspects of nature to ultimately rest your morals on. And, as I'm sure you know, we each have several competing 'natural' instincts. Just consider another argument put forward in the same vein by another Greek sophist Antiphon:

> "*The nobly born we revere and adore, but not the lowly born. These are barbarous habits. For as to our natural gifts, we are all on an equal footing, on all points, whether we now happen to be Greeks or barbarians...we all breathe the air through our mouths and nostrils.*"[19]

No doubt Antiphon's heart is loads kinder than Pindar's. But his claim is just as unstable. No matter what aspect of nature you rest your morals on, whether it be your narcissistic or empathetic tendencies, it is still you who must decide to rest them there. Once you are aware of a behavior, there's no escape, only you can decide whether to continue the behavior, modify it, or toss it altogether.

In any case, although I think Plato was aware of the weaknesses in these naturalistic arguments, he nevertheless tried to rest his moral and political theory of tyranny—the Philosopher King—on the 'natural' inequality of people.[20] No two people are alike, he claims. And no one is self-sufficient. Each of us has a peculiar nature—some are fit for one type of work and some for another. To further our own interests, then, we gather in one place to share our goods and services.

Okay. So far, so good. He's essentially beat Adam Smith to his theory of the division of labor. But in the end, the only important division for Plato turns out to be the one between the wise philosophers, who should be the city's rulers, and the rest of us fools. Let's see how he gets here.

Plato's aim is simple: arrest all political change! Why? Because for him, the material world consists of only copies of those perfect forms and ideas which exist for eternity in the immaterial realm. And these material copies, he argues, decay from their perfect form. (This was Plato's clever solution to dovetail Heraclitus's Everlasting Fire with Parmenides's Block Universe). So, to stop the decay, Plato made it his aim in the Republic to arrest all political change in order to maintain the ideal state, the natural state, where the rulers rule, the workers work, and the slaves slave.

Those who can peer into the realm of forms—that is, the wise philosophers like Plato—will tell you that the ideal state requires strict class division. And since the state is in the hands of its rulers, all efforts shall be aimed at preserving the ruling class. The ruling class will oversee all military, legislative, and religious affairs. It will be the only class to be educated, and all other intellectual activities will be prohibited. Anyone outside the ruling class who innovates in education, legislation, or religion will be put to death.

Whoa! What happened here? Didn't Plato's teacher Socrates give his life to defend the individual's right to pursue wisdom for herself? And didn't he also defend the egalitarian theory of justice—the unprejudiced and equal treatment of free citizens under the law? So, how did Plato get here, defending a tyrannical form of government. And how did he expect his fellow Athenians to go for it?

Plato knew, of course, he'd have to pull some intellectual gymnastics to sell this to the Athenians. So, he laid a classic bait-and-switch. Because even the word 'justice' carried so much weight in Athens, Plato knew it would be hard for people to turn their backs on 'justice,' especially if Plato put the words in the mouth of Socrates (the main character of Plato's fictional dialogue), and even if he had tainted its meaning. So, he stirred up some confusion and laid the bait.

After Plato's fictional Socrates, in the Republic, speaks about how the rulers will be the city's judges, the fictional Socrates asks his interlocutor Glaucon, "Will it not be the judges' aim to make sure that no man takes what belongs to another?"[21]

"Yes," Glaucon replies.

"Because that would be just?" Socrates asks.

"Yes, because that would be just."

The two therefore establish that to keep and to practice what belongs to one's own is justice. Okay, fair enough. But here comes the switch. "Now see whether you agree with me," says Socrates. "Do you think it would harm the city if a carpenter became a shoemaker and the shoemaker a carpenter?"

"No," says Glaucon, "not very much."

"What about if someone who by nature was a worker became a member of the ruling class?" Socrates asks. "Would this kind of underhand plotting mean the downfall of the city?"

"Most definitely it would," replies Glaucon.

Socrates continues, "We have three classes in our city, and I take it that any such plotting or changing from one class to another is a great crime against the city and ought to be considered utterly wicked, no?"

"Certainly," Glaucon confirms.

"And you would agree that such wickedness towards one's own city is injustice?"

"I would."

"Then, this is injustice," the fictional Socrates concludes, "And, conversely, it is just when each class attends to its own business."[22]

There you have it. This is how one of the most adored philosophers in the West tactfully commandeered the meaning of justice to pursue his political theory of tyranny.

Throughout Plato's political writings, especially as he gets older, it becomes clear that he doesn't care about the individual's freedom. He cares only about the philosophers, the ruling class—that is, him and his close group of friends—which he disguises as the 'ideal state.' In fact, in his Laws, when describing the Constitution of the Republic as the highest form of the state, he tells us that there shall be common property of wives, children, and chattel. Life shall be spent in total community. We must do all that is possible to eliminate private possessions. From childhood on, we should stand under leadership of the state. All traces of anarchy and independence shall be eradicated. And all people and all laws shall be used to protect the state (a.k.a., him and his fellow philosophers).[23]

Plato's morality is simple: something is 'good' if it furthers the interest of the state, and 'bad' if it hinders it. Consider the implications of this moral system. The state can never be wrong in its actions as long as it is strong, as long as it survives. It can lie, cheat, steal, and kill so long as it is 'good' for the fictional state. Might is right.

Plato even goes so far as to argue that, because us unsophisticated folk can't grasp logical arguments, the rulers should tell lies and create religious myths to persuade us to do what is in the best interest of the state. And anyone whose beliefs deviate from those of the state shall be sent to the inquisitors. And if he refuses to retract his heresies, he will be put to death.[24]

Did Plato forget that his dear teacher was sentenced to death just twenty years earlier for this very charge? Socrates gave his life to defend reason. And now Plato, his most brilliant student, was trying to destroy it. Why?

Well, to give Plato the most charitable view—I think it is possible that he saw how much instability and upheaval the fight for democracy was causing and so he was genuinely interested in saving the state rather than seeking glory or riches for himself. For he says in the Republic, "If they [the ruling class] are not satisfied with a life of stability and security, ... and are tempted, by their power, to appropriate for themselves all the wealth of the city, then surely they are bound to find out how wise Hesiod was when he said, "the half is more than the whole.'"[25]

Examining Plato's political writings with critical eyes, however, I think there is a strong argument to suggest that Plato wanted to become Philosopher King. After all, Plato tells us that only few are eligible for the post. And it's hard to deny that he speaks of himself when he says, "He who belongs to the small band [of philosophers]...can see the madness of the many, and the general corruption of public affairs. The philosopher...is like a man in a cage of wild beasts. He will not share the injustice of the many, but his power does not suffice for continuing his fight alone, surrounded as he is by a world of savages."[26]

And then there's my personal favorite: "It is not in accordance with nature that the skilled navigator should beg the unskilled sailors to accept his command .... But the true and natural procedure is that the sick...should hasten to the doctor's door. Likewise, those who need to be ruled should besiege the door of him who can rule; and never should a ruler beg them to accept his rule, if he is any good at all."[27]

Arrogant much? Check me out, Plato says, your natural born king. But don't expect me to come begging to you fools. If you want me, get down on your knees and pray I accept the post as Philosopher King.

Plato couldn't have strayed further from the humble teachings of Socrates. A wise philosopher in Socrates's eyes is someone who admits she knows nothing. The wise philosopher understands that her knowledge, however impressive, will always be engulfed by her ignorance. And she knows that what little knowledge she has is likely wrong. She therefore commits herself to reason, the spirit of progress, to find and correct her errors, so that she may pursue a better life.

In Plato's eyes, however, the wise philosopher is no longer a modest seeker of knowledge but a proud possessor of Truth, with a capital T. He is an omniscient demigod king, who can peer into the immaterial Realm of Forms, a clairvoyant, a seer. The wise philosopher, to Plato, no longer encourages critical thought and open discussion. But instead indoctrinates minds. The wise philosopher makes people utterly incapable of having a free and independent mind. He must convince all to stand under leadership of the Philosopher King, using whatever lies and deceit are needed.

Poor Plato never did become Philosopher King. His ideal state was not realized until much later when, in the Dark Ages, the leaders of the Catholic Church became the privileged holders of divine Truth.

Questions & Reflections

How do you navigate the moral sphere? How do you determine which foot to put in front of the next? How do you make value judgments—how do you discern right from wrong? Do you take responsibility for yourself, for your own actions and decisions, or do you play the victim to god, nature, society, corporations, institutions or some other fiction? How could you take more responsibility for yourself and your own actions? How can you take responsibility for your own life?

What problems do you consistently face? How are you framing the problem? Is there a way you could frame the problem more skillfully? What posture are you taking to these problems? Are some solutions to your problems better than others? How do you resolve conflicting judgments or misaligned values with your partner, family, neighbors, or co-workers?

Where, if at all, do you confront authority, dogma, or tyranny in your life? Who or what is getting in the way of your freedom? Are you yourself curbing your own freedom in any way? When was the last time you stood up to authority because your own heart, your own conscience, alerted you to some kind of injustice? Is there any relationship in your life that requires you to set and enforce boundaries to provide you with more freedom? How might you do that skillfully?

3. WISDOM

"Learning to be oneself means learning to die in order to live. It means discovering in the ground of one's being a 'self' which is ultimate and indestructible, which not only survives the destruction of all other more superficial selves but finds its identity affirmed and clarified by their destruction." – Thomas Merton

Something I absolutely admire about my partner River is how well she knows her way around words. I learn at least one new word a day and, in the time we've been together, I can still count on my fingers how many times I've stumped her. She grew up in a very literal family. At the dinner table as a child, her dad would challenge her and her siblings about how they used a word. If he felt they used it incorrectly, he would have them grab a dictionary and defend themselves. She has also consumed books like they were candy since she was very little and has written poetry for just as long.

This is one of the aspects that made me so attracted to her. I was looking for someone who could keep me sharp, articulate, and well-spoken. I was keenly aware that the specific words and frames we use, not only out loud but in the privacy of our minds, shape our life and experience. So, it was important that the human closest to me would provide a good example and clear reflection. Throw my oldest kid into the mix, whose lexicon is becoming more astonishing each day, and there's no escape now—if I don't articulate myself well, the reflection is crystal clear. I need to either clear up my expression or clarify my actual thought.

There is a trap here, though, for those of us who, like me, have the tendency to fixate on words, a trap that keeps us ostensibly cut off, isolated, and alone. As you will come to see, it distracts us from our true spiritual nature, disconnecting us from ourselves, from our friends and neighbors, from the world, from the spirit, from god, from awareness. It is a trap that makes us vulnerable to prophets and soothsayers, a trap that imprisons us in our own frameworks and beliefs.

It's critical, then, that we understand it, not just intellectually but also as a matter of direct experience. So, in this chapter, we will first explore the problem intellectually, so the thinker in our heads can get a grasp on the situation. And then, we'll see if we can meet this understanding with our direct experience, the place where true transformation happens.

Words, Persons, & Things

The earliest Greek philosophers didn't really ask 'what is?' questions. That is, they didn't get bogged down in defining and analyzing each of their terms. Rather than quibble over the meaning of words, they tried to solve specific problems by creating bold explanatory theories. And if critical discussion revealed that an explanation didn't hold up, then they'd try to create a better one. Now, of course, if they needed to clarify a specific term, they would. But again, it wasn't so much the specific words, but rather the overall message, problem, framework, or explanation that mattered. Beginning with Socrates, however, this explanatory approach to knowledge started to fade into a descriptive one.

After Socrates recognized that the philosophers before him had explained the world using only physical or mechanical causes, without considering the intentions of living beings, he turned his gaze from the heavens to the soul—to problems a bit closer to home, to things like justice, beauty, and goodness. In Socrates' words:

> "It was as if somebody would first say that Socrates acts with reason or intention; and then, in trying to explain the causes of what I am doing now, should assert that I am now sitting here [in prison] because my body is composed of bones and sinews... and that the sinews, by relaxing and contracting, make me bend my limbs now, and that this is the cause of my sitting here with my legs bent.... Yet the real causes of my sitting here in prison are that the Athenians have decided to condemn me, and that I have decided... it is more just if I stay here and undergo the penalty they have imposed on me. For, by the dog... these bones of mine

would have been in Megara or Boetia long ago... had I not thought it better and nobler to endure any penalty my city may inflict on me, rather than to escape and run away." (Phaedo 98c-99a)

Seeing the absence of our intentions at play, Socrates quite naturally turned to political and moral questions. He wanted to know what things are in our inner worlds, in and of themselves. If, for example, someone claimed that people ought to be happy, he would ask what happiness is, and then watch them stumble to describe it. Do we really know the things we speak so confidently about?

We all know what things like happiness, heartbreak, and hope are like, but does anyone know what they really are? Is happiness, say, made of some kind of substance, some kind of essence? Does it have a shape? Does it exist apart from someone who is happy? What about something more concrete, like a car? No two cars are really the same, but we all know what we mean when we say 'car.' But is a car no longer a car if it loses its headlights? Its doors? Steering wheel? Frame? What if we got rid of every actual car, would the concept of car still exist? If so, where would it exist? And what would its existence be like?

This is classically known as the problem of universals. Socrates's solution to the problem was: though we can never know what happiness really is, we can still improve our understanding—our definition or description—of it by criticizing our assumptions. That is, we can improve our understanding of what things are by committing ourselves to reason.

Socrates's student Plato agreed that definitions are key to our understanding. But because Plato was convicted in Heraclitus's Everlasting Fire, he thought it was impossible to define anything. The moment you define it, it will have changed in the next moment. So, to square the problem of change with the problem of universals, Plato argued that universals exist in an eternal and immaterial Realm of Ideals, a place where mathematics, numbers, ideas, and other concepts are frozen in perfect form—a Parmenidean world where everything just is. And material things that share some characteristics of these forms are imperfect, decaying copies of the immaterial form.

Okay, weird but original and cool. So, did Plato believe we could ever come to truly know what these things are? Did he believe we could access this immaterial realm of forms? Well, yes and no. In Plato's earlier works, still under the influence of Socrates, he believed we could come to know things better through his famous theory of anamnēsis, but not know with certainty.[28] According to the young Plato, before birth, our souls were inextricably tied up, at one with, the Ideal Realm. So, it knows all things. But when we are born, we forget. At birth, we fall from heaven, we fall from grace, we fall from a divine state of knowledge and into ignorance. (Here may be the seed of the Christian idea that ignorance is sin, or at least related to sin; cp. Phaedo, 76d.) We become trapped in our decaying material bodies.[29]

As the result of anamnēsis, though, we can once again contact truth. We can recover our memory and knowledge, though only partially, through a recollection process, where a teacher questions a student in an attempt to provoke a memory of the object at hand. Plato's fictional character Socrates demonstrates this in a passage of the Meno by helping an uneducated young slave to 'recall' the proof of a special case of the theorem of Pythagoras. So, for the early Plato, all knowledge is re-cognition, recalling or remembering the essence or true nature of things that our souls once knew.[30] (Note that Plato's influence now reaches not only into mathematical and philosophical circles but into spiritual circles too, like the Theosophists and Anthroposophists—those who seek spiritual clairvoyance.)

Aristotle, however, a top student at Plato's Academy, didn't buy this. To him, Plato's immaterial realm doesn't solve the problem of universals. It duplicates it. Form, Aristotle believed, doesn't exist apart from particular things. To say that Billie Eilish and Nina Simone are both women is not to say that over and above them there's a third thing—womanhood—to which they are each related. Rather, womanhood is simply a characteristic they share. And we recognize this shared characteristic because we learn about womanhood through repetition: after examining many women, we eventually discover those similarities that lead us to the true description, or essence, of womanhood.

So, for Aristotle, we aren't born with innate knowledge of universals, as Plato believed. Rather, we discover the true essence of a thing through induction—the repetition of observation and experience, which he believed can somehow lead us from particular instances to universals, ending with that Ah-hah! moment, where we suddenly grasp the concept. This, at first sight, seems like a much more grounded theory of knowledge than Plato's. But Aristotle's solution to the problem of universals fails for at least three reasons.

First, he completely ignores Heraclitus's argument that it's impossible for anything to exist in a world of constant change, since the moment you define something, it will have changed in the next moment. The second reason Aristotle's solution fails is due to his belief that repetition can somehow create knowledge. Don't get me wrong: repetition, or practice, is central to the human learning process, no doubt. But repetition doesn't create anything new, which the growth of knowledge requires. Rather, repetition familiarizes and fine tunes an existing solution, one that's already been created through trial and error. That is, it helps you form habits, which frees up your conscious attention to focus on new problems. The more practiced we become at a task, the less awareness we require to do it. Just think, for a moment, about when you first learned to drive or tie your shoes. At first, it required a lot of attention. But with practice, more and more you were able to accomplish these tasks subconsciously. How long has it been since you put thought into tying your shoes?

The last but not least of Aristotle's mistakes was his assumption that knowledge is passively imprinted on our minds through observation. This idea was picked up and developed by Francis Bacon during the Scientific Revolution and later defended by John Locke, who said the mind is like a blank slate which is filled by sensory experience. This 'tabula rasa' or 'bucket theory of mind', also known as Empiricism, was the mainstream view until finally, in the twentieth century, the humble philosophical giant Karl Popper cleaned up the confusion. But unfortunately, still to this day, I find people falling into its trap—scientists, politicians, and spiritual seekers alike. So, let's give this a good critical look.

Despite what Aristotle, Bacon, and Locke believed, it's impossible to read or infer knowledge from nature. After all, a blank slate can't do anything. To 1) collect data from the world, and 2) do something with it, requires creative theories or inventions. Again, a blank slate can't do anything with light waves. To do something with that information, those 1s and 0s, first requires a theory about how to capture the waves, like our visual systems do. And then that data needs to be organized according to an aim, a 'why' or a problem to solve. We don't just have visual systems for the hell of it. Our visual system was shaped and molded by the problem of survival and replication, by evolution. It's aim is to help us navigate our terrain.

To demonstrate this point—that you need theories in place to catch and use data—Popper would ask his students on the first day of class simply to observe. Finally, after a long, awkward silence, a brave student would muster up the courage to say, 'Um...Professor, what exactly do you want us to observe?'

'Ah hah!' Popper would reply, 'Precisely the point. To observe, you must first have in mind a definite problem and hypothesis to guide your observation—to tell you what you seek and where to seek it.' Charles Darwin also seemed to find this point obvious when he said, 'How odd it is that anyone should not see that all observation must be for or against some view....'.[31] You may have noticed this on the road when you're looking to buy a new car. Suddenly, you start seeing the car you want everywhere.

There's no escape from it. Every observation is theory laden. None of your sensory perceptions represent how the world actually is, at least in any complete sense. You don't, for example, experience the nerve signals traveling from your sensory receptors to your brain as electrochemical wave patterns, which again are just concepts we use to paint over some narrow region of reality. Nor do you experience these electrochemical signals as traveling through your neurons.

No, instead, you believe they're out in the world somewhere. But yellow, say, doesn't really exist 'out there.' Rather, your brain creates the experience of yellow through a computational process of electrochemical signals. When you perceive yellow, you're really detecting a pattern of incoming electromagnetic waves that repeat themselves about 520 trillion times a second. And after they're captured by a molecule in your eye, the signal is then relayed through several biological systems—again, theories—before yellow finally arises in consciousness. As with all knowledge, your sensory experience of the world is but a web of guesses.

An additional point to consider is the perception of different animals. As you know, animals perceive the world differently than we do. Bats use sonar or echolocation to see and navigate through the world. Vipers see in infrared. Mantis shrimp see in sixteen dimensions, as opposed to our three dimensions. Which animal has the correct view of the world? None. We each see and know the world only from behind the veil, from the world of appearances. And because the world of appearances is creative, because it is only a model of the universe, each of us sees only a fraction of this infinite potential. We each have created (or evolved) our own models of the impenetrable world behind appearances, the ultimate reality. We've created nets, if you will, that are cast over only small portions of the world.

Well, so much for Aristotle's epistemology. But let's not stop here. We have only half of his theory. Though induction fails for the reasons we have explored, I think it is still worth our time to hear him out, since the belief that something can be proven, demonstrated, justified, or verified as positively true still haunts the halls of humanity to this day. Just ask Muslims, Christians, Hindus, the Far Right, the Far Left, the Marxists, the Anthroposophists, or sadly even some scientists.

Okay, so what's the other half?

Well, for Aristotle, induction merely gives the premises or concepts which you can then use to deduce the ultimate secrets of the cosmos. So, the real power for Aristotle lies in deduction. Deduction, Aristotle believed, is the key to demonstrably true knowledge, or episteme.

And hey, can you really blame him? After all, you can't deny its power. We rely heavily on it to bring order and meaning into an otherwise chaotic and meaningless world. When I tell you 'I love the warmth you bring into this world,' it means something. But 'Into warmth I you world this love the bring' is just noise. Likewise, if we cut a pie into thirds and it creates only two slices, then we'd be in big trouble, no? Coding and software development, constructing bridges and buildings, and everything else that requires logical steps—math, algorithms, instructions, recipes—would all fall apart. My grandma's oatmeal cookie recipe would be doomed!

Logic holds our concepts together. It puts them in relation to one another. Words and concepts have no teeth without it. Concepts need to be put into a thought, idea, or explanation—a relational scheme—to mean anything. Logic, or relational properties, are necessary for us to paint stories, to pin characteristics to people, to build relationships, and to choreograph dances. Our words, symbols, and concepts are empty without logical consistency.

So, we probably both agree to some extent with Aristotle that deduction is necessary to understand the world. It's necessary for a world of order and meaning rather than chaos and noise. The problem though, which Aristotle himself recognized, is that, if the key to demonstrably true knowledge is deduction, then our premises or concepts must also be demonstrated. And if our premises are demonstrated, then they too must have been deduced from something, which in turn must have been deduced from something else, and so on *ad infinitum*.

"How," Aristotle wondered, "can I get around this infinite regress?"

First, he figured that, because words get their definition by convention, they must be true by convention—in other words, that truth is relative. But this would mean that knowledge is true only by convention, which he didn't like. So, it was here that he turned to induction in hopes of securing demonstrably true conceptual knowledge.

Aristotle's epistemology, then, relies on both induction and deduction. Once we've acquired the true essence of a thing through induction, through the repetition of experience, once we have that Ah-hah! moment, we will have an infallible definition of it. And once we've built a big enough dictionary in this way, we should be able to use our definitions to deduce the ultimate explanation of reality—one that is eternally infallible.

That's some big talk for a goofy little creature of this small blue planet we call Earth. Aristotle was right on his first go-round—words are created by convention. They are relative, relational. How can they tell us the true essence of anything? They can't. Knowledge is and always will be but a web of guesses, a limited collection of concepts or divisions that we paint over the seamless whole, relating each concept to the others to solve our problems and achieve our aims.

There is no certainty. No finality. No capital T Truth. There is only the World, God, Mind, Awareness, or whatever you want to call This, and then there are our thoughts about *This*.

See if you can start to pay attention to this difference. See if you can move past thoughts and meet experience directly. Meet experience as a phenomenon. As the spiritual teacher Krishnamurti said, "Once a child learns the word 'bird', she may never see a bird again." From then on, the mind takes a shortcut and just sees the concept 'bird.' The ineffable aliveness of experience is obscured by the mental label. We lose what is called "beginner's mind" in Zen. We confuse the finger pointing at the moon for the moon. The Mormon Buddhist Thomas McConkie said, "We adults, we learn words. And with these words, we just carry this mental map around the world like, 'Oh, there's that thing. I've seen that before. Oh, today's Wednesday, just another Wednesday.' And these labels, we wear them like straitjackets in our lives." So, again, see if you can notice those times when the mind is covered by a sticky film of thoughts, concepts, and ideas and those times when it is bright, clear, and open, moving effortlessly with the ever-changing flow of experience.

Words are powerful and they bring meaning and order into our lives. Just don't be fooled by their illusory nature. Don't be fooled by prophecies and signs and stories about who you are or what life ultimately means. Awareness, which is boundless and unformed, can never be reduced to a string of words or imagery—a thought, idea, or story. Everything arises in awareness. So how can this next thought, this next string of words, images, or concepts, be who or what you are. It obviously can't. You are without beginning or end. You, my dear reader, are divine.

The Truth of Emptiness

It's no secret everything changes. You know this, I know this, we all know this. We watch the sun rise and set. We feel the seasons turn. Every experience we have ever had has come and gone. The anger you felt yesterday isn't here anymore. You and everyone you know will someday die. Entire species and civilizations have come and gone. Stars and galaxies are born and fade away. Not even the very fabric of space and time is stable.

But how many of us really understand the implications of this truth? How many of us live as if we understand this—that there are no stable, unchanging things, that everything is always in flux? As Heraclitus said, "You can't step in the same river twice. For it is not the same river and you are not the same person."

Around the same time as Heraclitus, the Buddha came to this same conclusion in his search to understand suffering and its end. What the Buddha realized is that suffering arises when we lose direct sight of this truth of change and identify ourselves with the world of appearances. We mistake ourselves for the flames and forget that the flames are not apart from the Everlasting Fire.

All suffering and discontent, he says, stem from the mistaken view that an independent and stable self sits at the center of experience, clinging to things it believes to be its own—"my" anger, "my" body, "my" pain, "my" joy. If we hold onto that which by its nature changes, which is everything, we will suffer. His solution to alleviate suffering, then, is to simply let go and float seamlessly through the stream of nirvana (nibbana in Pali). He encouraged each of us to recognize directly for ourselves that, as a matter of direct experience, nothing can reliably be identified as "I" or "mine."

Can you find any place the "I" can take a stand? Can you call these things that are constantly changing the self? Is the changing physical body the self? Are the changing sensations in your body the self? Are the changing feelings and perceptions the self? Are the changing thoughts, emotions, mind-states, and mental formations the self? No. Each of these, when you put them under scrutiny, are found to be selfless.

What we take to be our "self" is a temporary and illusory identification with some process of experience. The sense of self arises and solidifies itself like ice floating in water. Though ice is actually made of the same substance as water, we harden a portion of the water into ice when we mistakenly identify ourselves with some appearance in the vast, seamless ocean of mind.

Now, I know that this understanding of emptiness or selflessness can seem bleak and even nihilistic. But once you understand it as a matter of direct experience, it is quite the opposite. It is incredibly uplifting, liberating, and empowering. Our sense of self doesn't disappear but grows incredibly vast and connected. Our heart becomes filled with love and compassion not only for the world and everyone in it but also for our little self—the flame, who lives and relates to others; the person we are in the world.

So, the truth of emptiness is not a denial of things like people, creatures, democracy, justice, and all the rest. It is simply a denial of their substantial, stable, independent existence. The Buddha understood that nothing can exist on its own, defined by its own essence, but that everything inter-is, every thing is tied up with all the rest. There is, for example, no plant essence, no self that is this plant on my desk. Rather, the plant was made from soil, water, sun, and oxygen. It cannot exist on its own. It relies on everything else.

To get a clearer picture of this notion of emptiness, let's explore a thought experiment from an early Buddhist text called Milinda's Questions, which is a dialogue between a sharp and curious King named Milinda and a clever Buddhist monk named Nagasena.

When the King arrived to Nagasena's hermitage to resolve his questions about Buddhism, Nagasena greeted the King by acknowledging that Nagasena was his name, but that his name is only a designation—there is actually no permanent individual "Nagasena" that could be found here or anywhere else.

The King laughed and said, "Who is it, then, who wears robes and takes food? If there is no Nagasena, who receives karma? If there is no Nagasena, then couldn't someone kill you and there would be no murder? It seems," the King said, "with this view of no-self, Nagasena is nothing more than a sound."

"Great points," Nagasena replied. "Let me answer you with a question?"

"Okay," said the King.

"How did you come to this hermitage, on foot or by horseback?"

"I came in a chariot," said the King.

"But what is a chariot?" Nagasena asked. "Is it the wheels, or the axles, or the reigns, or the frame, or the seat? Is it a combination of these elements? Or is it found outside these elements?"

The King answered no to each question.

"Then there is no chariot!" Nagasena said.

The King acknowledged that the designation "chariot" depended on these constituent parts, but that "chariot" itself is just a designation—a concept, a mere name.

"Just so," said Nagasena, "'Nagasena' is a concept, a mere name.

When the constituent parts are present, we call it a chariot. And when the five skandhas—form, sensation, perception, volition, and consciousness—are present, we call it a being." [Note: This chariot simile by the nun and disciple of the Buddha Vajira in an earlier text, the Vajira Sutta (Pali Sutta-pitaka, Samyutta Nikaya 5:10). In the Vajira Sutta, though, she was speaking to the demon, Mara.]

You can also consider this thought experiment by imagining taking the chariot apart. At what point in the disassembly does the chariot cease to be a chariot? When we take off the wheels? When we remove the seats? When we pry off the axle?

Any judgment we make is subjective. You may argue that a pile of chariot parts is still a chariot, just not an assembled one. The point, though, is that "chariot" is nothing more than a concept we project onto the constituent parts. But there is no "chariot" essence that somehow dwells within the parts. The "self" too is nothing more than a concept we project onto constituent parts or processes, each of which can further be broken down and found to be selfless in turn.[32]

A few more examples of emptiness or no-self include things like the Big Dipper. Is there really a Big Dipper in the night sky? Or do we just cast a concept over this collection of stars? What about a storm? Is there really such thing as a storm? Or do we just use this concept when there is rain, wind, lightning, and thunder? A rainbow? You get the picture...

Nothing exists alone, independently, apart from all the rest. All things are made up of everything else. A flower is made up of entirely non-flower elements—soil, rain, air, sun, the birds and bees, etc. You too are made up of entirely non-you parts—your parents, siblings, and teachers; your environment, culture, and language; the earth, space, and time. There are no dividing lines anywhere, except in the stories we tell ourselves, except in thought. But when we really look, we see that thoughts too are not as rigid and defined as we may have thought. They are just passings wisps of energy in the mind, arising and fading in the same continuous ocean of awareness.

The astronaut Peggy Whitson, who has spent 665 days in space, knows the inter-connected nature of all things perhaps better than anyone. From the window of her aluminum castle, some 250 miles above (or below?) the earth, she doesn't see boundaries between nations. She sees the earth as a single organism, a single, interconnected system. She can watch as the winds carry dust from the Sahara Desert across the Atlantic Ocean to the Amazon basin, where it dumps twenty-seven million tons of rock and minerals every year. And thanks to a fertilizer that is carried in that dust, the trees in the

Amazon can flourish. They then suck up water from their roots and release moisture into the air, creating a flying river that flows to the Andes. And as these clouds hit the mountains, releasing rain and snow, the water and ice erode the rock, which is eventually carried into the ocean.

There, waiting for the minerals in that sediment, are organisms called diatoms—single-celled organisms that put more oxygen into the atmosphere than any other source on earth. And if this isn't enough to show you that all things are connected, just consider that when these little creatures die, they fall like snow and create graveyards on the ocean floors. And over tens and hundreds of millions of years, as the earth's tectonic plates shift, seabeds rise, and ocean levels fall, some of these graveyards turn into salty deserts, just like the Sahara. Yeah, that special fertilizer I mentioned above—it's diatom corpses![33]

You can play this world-is-connected game all you want. Seriously, try to separate anything. No matter how hard you try, you'll see that nothing can exist apart from the rest, defined by its own essence. As the famous naturalist John Muir said, "When we try to pick out anything by itself, we find it hitched to everything else in the Universe." The ultimate truth is that the world is one. In the words of the late Tibetan Buddhist lama Kalu Rinpoche, "You live in illusion of the appearance of things. There is a Reality. You are that Reality. When you understand this, you will see that you are nothing. And in being nothing, you are everything."

Don't believe him? Look for yourself.

Who Are You?

We all spend a lot of time thinking about ourselves. We think about what we like and don't like. We think about where we've been, what we've done, and where we're going. We obsess about how people view us, about what we've accomplished, about what titles we hold or possessions we have. We stress over things we should or shouldn't have said or done. And we just continue to accumulate these thoughts, we continue to build out and frame this elaborate story that houses our sense of self.

I wonder, though, what would happen if you actually looked inside. What would you find if you opened the door and looked for your 'self,' if you tried to locate the 'I' who is reaching for the latest phone, the 'I' who needs bigger boobs, the 'I' who is living for likes on social media? Who is this 'I' that worries so much about what other people think? Who are you, really?

Engraved on the entrance to the Temple of Apollo were the words "Know Thyself," a kind of invitation to enter. This invitation I extend to you. Enter the temple of your own being. Know yourself. And remember, no one else can tell you who or what you are. You can't learn this in a book. You cannot discover yourself from outside yourself. To know yourself requires an immediate and intimate kind of knowing, a bare and direct knowing. It requires you to go deep into your own heart and mind. It requires sitting with yourself in stillness and in silence. It requires an intentional, loving, and careful investigation of the unfolding of experience. It requires you to look directly at awareness itself.

So, go ahead, look for yourself. After all, you talk repeatedly about yourself—about 'my' things, 'my' pain, 'my' body. You say, 'I'm' hungry, 'I'm' angry, 'I'm' depressed. But where is this thing you call 'I'? What is it? What is it like? What is its nature?

Because "I" can't be removed from you, because it is essential to you, only you can investigate it for yourself. So, go ahead, take a look. What is this thing you call "I"? Where is it? What is it like? What qualities does it have? What is its nature?

Uhhh...Weird questions? Yeah, I know. "What do you mean, 'What is it?' and 'Where is it?' It's me, duh. I'm right here."

I know. But just humor me for a moment. Try to relax. Maybe take a few deep breaths. And then take a good look at your experience—at whatever there is to be known in this moment. Now, ask yourself: 'What is there to be known? What is here in my ever-changing experience to be noticed? Are there changing sensations in the body? Are there sounds? Are there perceptions? Are there thoughts and feelings?'

Okay. And what about "You"? Where are you in this picture? Where are you in experience? Are you somewhere apart from sounds and sensations, apart from thoughts and feelings? Are you somewhere behind your face, somewhere at the center of experience, or maybe at its edge, directing attention at what there is to be known—at perceptions, thoughts, and feelings?

If you think so, what happens when you turn attention around, when you follow your gaze or a sound or a bodily sensation back to the place where you seem to be directing attention from? Can you find your self? Can you find the "I"? Is there anything stable and unchanging?

You might have to tune-up your concentration a bit to do what I'm asking, but it's possible to witness something transformational here. When you look for the "I", when you turn attention around and follow an object back to the place where "you" seem to be directing attention from, you won't find your "self," you won't find the "I".

Rather, what's there to be noticed in each moment is the wide-open space of awareness—the single unbounded space of knowing; the continuous flow of the ever-changing contents of awareness arising and disappearing, like waves into the ocean. And the feeling that you are behind your face directing attention out at the world or into your mind or body is just another content of awareness. It is a kind of contraction of energy, often in your head or emotional heart—that feeling of space getting a lot smaller. But this too arises and is known in the wide-open field of awareness. Otherwise, how could it be known? How could it feel like something to be you if it is not felt in awareness?

Who or what is this faceless, formless, all-pervasive witness of experience? Again, who or what are you? What is this thing you call "I"?

So many of us take ourselves for granted. We never stop to take a real interest in our own true nature. But once we do, once we try to find and understand the "I," we realize that this feeling we call "I" is, as the philosopher, neuroscientist, and meditation teacher Sam Harris often points out, just the result of thinking without knowing we're thinking, dreaming without knowing we're dreaming. It's what it feels like when the no-thing that simply knows—that is, awareness—has lost itself in its contents, when awareness identifies with what is arising.

But no content of your experience, no object of your awareness, no thought, feeling, or perception, can be who or what "You" are. The dream vapors of experience vanish almost the moment they're known. So, how can this next thought, whatever its content, be who you are? It can't. Awareness is always perfectly open, unformed, unborn, undying, untainted. It just is. All that we know, have known, or will ever know arises from and fades into it.

"You," then, are no thing, though you know, encompass, and compose all things. You and I are as continuous with the universe as a wave is continuous with the ocean. There is no separation in existence. The world is whole. So, how can you be anything less than *It*, than *This*—Love, God, the Cosmos, Awareness, Mind, or whatever else you want to call that which knows, encompasses, and composes all things.

This wholeness, this connection, this completion, is always there for you to notice, right on the surface. But because we have been conditioned to orient from our thoughts, from the ego, from the little problem solver in our heads, it will take time to unwind this old habit. It is going to take time to get through the thick cloud of thoughts and concepts that obscure our true unbounded nature.

That's why we will now turn to a 2,500-year-old Buddhist meditation practice called vipassana, which seeks to cultivate this wisdom directly, as a matter of raw experience. It is a practice of looking directly at your own mind through the power of mindfulness—to witness the mind's selfless, ever-changing, interconnected nature, again and again, and to let this direct insight change your subjective, felt, lived experienced. It is a practice I highly recommend you keep in your repertoire. It is a tool I encourage you to always keep sharp.

If you do practice, I'm confident the time you spend traversing the open, formless, and awake space of existence, will be well worth it. After all, worth, value, and meaning—all arise here, in the mind. Your entire life is, in some sense, made of mind. Mind is the substance and context of all things. You and me...our values, interests, dreams, and aspirations...truth, beauty, goodness...our deeds and our art, our relationships, our lives, our experience—all arise and unfold in it. There is only one place to know anything at all. And that is in the mind, in awareness. It makes sense, then, to take an interest in it, to explore and examine it, to try truly and humbly to understand the awe-inspiring miracle that You are.

What is Vipassana?

Now, to be clear, vipassana is an entirely secular practice. It doesn't require you to adopt any dogmatic beliefs. The only requirement is that you're human, that the light of awareness is on, that the awe-inspiring space of experience stands before you, with all its majesty and mystery. Vipassana, or insight meditation, is merely a means for investigating the nature of one's own mind, a means for cultivating mindfulness and wisdom. The Dalai Lama himself said, "Buddhist teachings are not a religion, they are a science of the mind."

The Buddha was not a god but a human being who saw suffering in the world and was compelled to understand and relieve it. In the end, after an unyielding commitment and devotion to this problem, he not only discovered a lasting peace, but he experienced some fascinating insights about the nature of the human mind, which once grasped, not conceptually or as an idea, but once witnessed directly in one's own mind, leads to a radical transformation of one's own subjective experience. This wisdom—these teachings and insights—have now been passed down, explored, tested, and expanded for 2,500 years. And they are now even being corroborated with the rigorous methods of Western science, in psychology, neuroscience, medicine, and psychotherapy.

Okay, well now that I've hopefully assuaged any concerns, now that you know you're not being inducted into a cult or anything like that, let me build out a bit of a framework, so you have a conceptual structure to sit in when we begin our first practice. Perhaps the first thing to address is the philosophical understanding we have already explored, which sits at the root of both Eastern and Western philosophy—the difference between concepts and reality itself.

In vipassana, we move from the level of concepts to the level of direct experience. To understand this, sit quietly for a few moments as you let your feet rest on the floor. Then, consider what you experience. Most of us will say, I feel my feet. Or some of us will have a mental image of our feet resting on the floor. But if we move to the level of direct experience, we will find that there is no experience called "foot." Foot is just a concept. It doesn't really exist anywhere. Rather, what is actually here to notice is an open field of ever-changing sensations—pressure, warmth, tingling, vibration, and so on. There is no border or boundary anywhere. Each of these sensations is simply arising out of and disappearing into this vast open, empty space all on their own, like waves in an ocean.

This shift will take some time, so no worries if you are a bit frustrated. Your understanding of this distinction will unfold in time. It is enough right now to understand that knowing something conceptually, or as a matter of theory, is much different from knowing something directly, as a matter of raw experience.

"Knowing what something is is different
from knowing how something feels"
- The Giver

Just consider that a child may have some theoretical idea of a romantic relationship. But until the child goes through puberty and meets the direct fiery rush of mixed emotions—lust, infatuation, fear, confusion—then the child's understanding is limited to the dry theoretical realm. We can call a sunset a sunset, but the actual sunset—the direct experience of it—is whatever it ineffably is. It's not the idea or the concept of it. It's just it—unique, new, original, changing, a total mystery. "The finger that points to the moon," as they say in Zen, "is not the moon."

Vipassana, or insight meditation, is a practice of looking beyond the world of appearances. It is a practice of looking directly at experience. It is sometimes translated as "clear knowing" or "bare knowing," which I think is a useful way to think about it—to observe, to feel, to see clearly and directly the raw data of experience, to see things not as concepts or ideas but to know them directly and intimately. It asks us to see experience without our biases and judgments clouding the raw data of it. It invites us to step into the foundational wonder of all things.

But the practice doesn't stop here. The deeper aim of the practice is wisdom, to live in harmony with reality, to align ourselves with the truth of the moment's experience—its selfless, ever-changing, interconnected nature. So, another way to think about the practice is to think about it as a path of opening, of opening to the world and to all its dimensions, including the mind-body process, and then to step into these truths and rhythms, to be at one and at ease with them.[34]

We learn to open to the body, to its constant flow of energy. We learn to open to any areas of tension or tightness, to accept them, to relax into them, and to free them. We learn to open to and refine our senses. When the mind placates, when it gets quieter and more focused with practice, we open to an increasingly brighter and more vivid world. We realize that we had been asleep to so much of the beauty around and within us. We also learn to open to our wounds and traumas, to be with them in a loving way, which allows us to open to the full complexity of our feelings and emotions, the depth and richness of this precious human experience.

We learn to open to the seasons, to the seasons of the world and to the seasons of life, to its ups and downs—to pleasure and pain, gain and loss, praise and blame, joy and sorrow. We also learn to open to our intuition, intuitive realms that don't involve discursive thinking, intuitive systems that evolved long before the thinker in our head had evolved. And so, we learn to trust ourselves more.

And after the mind grows stable with practice, we also learn to open to our thoughts, not only as ideas, concepts, and convictions, but as a matter of direct experience, as passing waves of energy in the mind. This allows us to see and relate to our thoughts in a different way. We can observe them from an open and spacious awareness, which allows us to see their insubstantial and ever-changing nature, rather than collapse into them, rather than identify ourselves so readily with them. This then allows us to be less reactive. It gives us freedom to discern with wisdom which thoughts to engage and which thoughts to leave alone. Finally, and perhaps the pinnacle of the practice, is to open to and discover ourselves, our true and authentic selves, to be at peace with and at home with ourselves.

What is Mindfulness?

Now that we've talked about vipassana, or insight meditation, let's turn our focus to mindfulness, which the practice seeks to cultivate. So, what is mindfulness? Well, the short answer is that it is a direct, open, interested, undistracted, non-reactive, loving awareness, an awareness that doesn't get lost in thought but rather occupies the wide-open space of mind, the wide-open space of knowing in which everything arises, is known, and eventually disappears all on its own. Now, there's a lot packed into this short description, so let's go ahead and unpack it.

Perhaps the first thing to clarify is what I mean by a direct knowing, or a present, intimate, and raw knowing. Most often, we get a direct impression of experience, but then our cognitive faculties quickly build out a conceptual framework around the direct impression in an interpretative or analytic way. So, the mind receives the raw experience free from concepts, ideas, preferences, and biases only briefly before the original experience is clouded by these layers of thoughts and precepts. It's like seeing the moon through a thick layer of clouds.

The Buddha called this process papañca—elaboration, embellishment, or conceptual proliferation. Papañca doesn't really allow us to see experience as it is, directly, but only at arm's length. We see experience through a sticky layer of concepts or mental imagery. Deluded by ignorance, not seeing clearly the selfless, interconnected, ever-changing nature of experience, we paint these embellishments—our projections, biases, prejudices, judgments, comparisons, etc.—onto the objects of experience as if they actually belonged there. And then we use this arbitrary hodgepodge of embellishments as the basis for our values, plans, and actions, rather than the original untainted experience itself.[35]

To correct this distortion, we need wisdom. We need to see nature as it is—selfless, ever-changing, and interconnected. But for wisdom to do its work, it needs direct, undistracted access to experience. It needs to be able to penetrate the clouds of papañca. This is where mindfulness comes in. Mindfulness brings to light the raw data of experience, revealing experience as it is before it has been stenciled and colored over by concepts, stories, meaning, biases, and prejudices. So, unlike our typical way of knowing, knowing about this-that-and-the-other-thing, mindfulness is a knowing that isn't conceptual. It's a knowing that can't be carried into the future, remembered from the past, written in a book, or contained in a thought. It is direct—right here with the truth of the moment's experience.

In a way, then, when we practice mindfulness, we are doing less than we normally do. It's a kind of unknowing. We are ceasing to interfere with experience. We are ceasing to manipulate it or dominate it or control it. We are ceasing to be distracted by thought, ceasing to collapse into some idea or image of who or what we are. We are no longer getting carried away by the incessant stream of judgments, comparisons, worries, concepts, and other fictions that arise in the mind, which end up moving us through the world, causing us to react automatically, to be slaves to our conditioning.

With mindfulness, we learn to simply remain open and receptive to the ever-changing flow of life, of energy, of experience. It is to live in the question, what is *This*? But without the need for an answer. It is to embody the fundamental mystery of existence. It's the difference between an open and closed fist. When we are mindful, we let the raw data of experience land on our hand like a bird, allowing it to come and go all on its own. Or it may be helpful to imagine water pouring over your open hand, just letting it to flow through your fingers. When we give up the fight in this way, when we give up our deep-seated need for control, and simply note experience as it is, you'll find that mindfulness begins to loosen all the knots we've created in our physical bodies and emotional hearts by trying to assert our 'selves' into experience in some way. It brings space and a sense of ease to our being.

To briefly recap, we've seen that mindfulness requires us to refrain from collapsing into our mental embellishments. It asks that we see (or experience) experience clearly, without our biases and prejudices colored all over it. It asks us not to get lost in memories of the past or distracted by thoughts of the future. And it even requires that we let go of the present and meet reality directly—its original, new, and always changing nature. So, is this it? No. There are a couple more dimensions we need to explore.

First, to demonstrate why this kind of direct or bare knowing is not enough, I will turn to an example often used by Joseph Goldstein,[36] one of the grandfathers of Buddhism in the West, who asks us to consider a black lab. Now, a black lab is certainly right up close and personal with experience, not at arm's length. It's not lost in thought, it's not thinking about the future, it's not planning its day, or remembering some interaction from the past. It's doubtful there are clouds of papañca covering its experience. No, a black lab is fully immersed in the present moment, fully immersed in its sense of smell, interested in its surroundings, and happy to be with you. But is a black lab really that mindful? Probably not.

Okay, so what else do we need? Well, another dimension of mindfulness is what scientists call metacognition or meta-awareness—an awareness of awareness itself, knowing that you are knowing.[37] In all states of awareness, even during REM sleep, experience is happening—the lights are on. But there is not always an awareness of the process of awareness itself. This, it seems, is unique to humans. And even still, we are only beginning to wake up to the awareness side. Most of the time, like the black lab, many of us are only aware of the contents of awareness. We are not turning attention around and opening awareness to awareness itself.

Just consider the times you found yourself opening the fridge for the third time without any real awareness of what you were doing. We all know what it feels like to be lost in thought, lost in a trance or a dream. In instances like this, experience is happening—the lights are on—but we aren't really aware of awareness itself. It's like when we get so lost in a movie, so absorbed in the story, that we forget we are just seeing pixels of light on a screen.[38]

To see this from another angle, it may be useful to distinguish attention from awareness. Attention is like the spotlight of the mind. It is that feeling of shining a floodlight from behind your face onto the object of your attention, whether it's an object out in the world or in your own being. Attention narrows our view. So, very often, when we're not mindful, our greater awareness collapses into the object of our attention. And it is this feeling of attention, the spotlight of the mind, that we so often take ourselves to be.

The psychologist and meditation teacher Tara Brach tells a story that may shed some more light here.[39] A student once asked her teacher the great philosophical question, "Who am I?" So, the teacher grabbed an empty sheet of paper, drew a small v on it, and asked the students what they saw.

"A flying bird," most of them said.

"No," he responded, "it's a picture of the sky with a bird flying through it."

Focusing on the bird is like paying attention to what is most obvious in our mind—the contents of awareness. When we do this, our sense of self collapses into the field of attention. But when we open to the greater awareness, we embody the sky. We open to that unbounded space that holds all contents. We open to that formless, alive, and awake space in which everything is appearing and being known, to that space which holds all of life and experience, including our small, ever-shifting sense of self that arises anew with each thought. Mindfulness requires that we don't collapse into our attention, that we don't collapse into the contents of consciousness, but that we remain entirely aware of the unbounded sky, from and as the unbounded sky. It asks us to embody awareness itself, to be entirely open and free, entirely at peace.

There's another little fable that captures this well. It's about two younger fish who swim past an older fish. As they pass each other, the older fish says to the two, "Enjoying the water?" The two fish nod their heads and keep swimming. Once they are far enough away from the older fish, they look at each other and say, "What the hell is water?"

I love these stories because it really points to the power of attention and how it shapes our experience. The father of psychology, William James, captured this when he said, "My experience is what I agree to attend to."[40] And the philosopher Ortega Gasset also spoke to this when he said, "Nothing characterizes us as much as our field of attention...Tell me where your attention lies, and I will tell you who you are."[41] So, in a way, mindfulness is a training of attention. It trains our attention to remain open, holding both awareness and its objects, both the knowing and the known.

Awareness simply is. And it's always here. It's just that we are usually unaware of the empty knowing aspect of it because we're distracted by its contents. We understandably haven't trained our minds to become aware of that which has no shape or form or color. We haven't tuned up our faith in that invisible force that embraces, composes, and knows all things. The Trappist monk Thomas Merton captured this well when he said:

> "Christianity is a religion of the Word. The Word is Love. But we sometimes forget that the Word emerges first of all from silence. When there is no silence, then the One Word which God speaks is not truly heard as Love. Then only 'words' are heard. 'Words' are not Love, for they are many and Love is One. Where there are many words, we lose consciousness of the fact that there is really only One Word."[42]

Well, so far we've seen that mindfulness requires a raw, direct knowing, as well as an awareness of awareness itself—metacognition. Is there anything else? Yes, and it is an extremely important and powerful aspect of mindfulness, but one that can be easily obscured by the language we use to capture it. So, I'm going to approach it from two angles: first, by expressing what it is not, and then by clarifying what it is.

As you may have already noticed, the word mindfulness is often used interchangeably with awareness, which is a big word in English, and can sometimes create confusion. And I too will often use these words interchangeably. So, to hopefully prevent any confusion, let me clarify a bit what I mean when I use these words. To be aware, or to be mindful, of some aspect of experience can be easily interpreted to mean we simply acknowledge the object. When anger arises, for example, and we lose our cool, we can be aware that anger is present and that we have lost our cool. But this is not mindfulness, as it is used in the Buddhist framework.

Mindfulness requires more. It requires a kind of posture in the mind—an attitude or moral dimension.[43] It requires that we don't look at experience through the lens of greed or aversion, that we don't grasp at the pleasant or push the unpleasant away. But rather that we find equanimity— an evenness, coolness, or composure of mind that holds every piece of experience fully and intimately but without reacting to it. It asks us to remain completely open and receptive to each object of experience, whether pleasant or unpleasant.

Now, if you really explore the nature of awareness itself, as a matter of direct experience, I think you'll find that this is how awareness is. It allows everything in without exception, both the pleasant and unpleasant. It is all-embracing, always wide open, perfectly still, and at peace. Just think, any sense or signature you may have of wanting something, or wanting something to go away, is itself arising and being known in the greater space of awareness. Otherwise, how else would you know it? It, then, is not and cannot be what awareness is itself.

This is the aspect of mindfulness I refer to as Love since it is willing and able to accept and hold everything exactly as it is, without conditions, with a sincere interest to understand it. So, again, when we are mindful, we simply become space for the world, we become the space and substance for everything to be—to exist and be known. We give up our biases and prejudices, our likes and dislikes, and simply open to the truth of the moment's experience, whether it's pain, grief, sorrow, anger, frustration, fear, worry, anxiety, stress, desire, hatred, compassion, or joy. We connect with the feeling or emotion fully, but without reacting to it. We hold it like a newborn baby, eager to love and understand it, shining the light of mindfulness on it as long as it needs before it fades back into the open empty space of awareness all on its own.

Now, to be clear, this is not the same thing as being indifferent to experience. Indifference is the near enemy of this quality of mindfulness. Rather than 'numbing out' or becoming indifferent to experience, this loving or equanimous aspect of mindfulness asks us not only to step into and embody the wide-open space in which everything is arising and disappearing but also to embody experience itself, to become intimate with it. You are not just the witness, sitting on a rock watching the river go by. You are also river.

Just as quantum mechanics has come to show us that light functions both as a particle and a wave, well, so too does our existence have both a wave-like and a particle-like dimension—the absolute and personal. This is referred to in some traditions as the Two Truths, or non-dualism.[44] The ultimate and the relative, the absolute and the personal, knowing and being, are two sides of the same coin.

Not-Two

I have emphasized our empty, selfless, interconnected nature quite a bit now. And this is crucial for spiritual life, but it is not the whole story. You are, after all, still a person in the world. You have relationships to foster and maintain. You have work and other duties. You have passions, interests, goals, dreams, and aspirations. You have a tender human heart—emotions and feelings, joys and sorrows, pleasures and pains. You have the rest of your life. That is why if you tell a Zen master everything is an illusion, that everything is empty, she will take her stick, whack you over the head, and ask, "Was that an illusion?"[45]

Spirituality is not something separate from your quotidian and ordinary life. It is recognizing in each moment, however ordinary or profound, that you are both a no-self and a small self (or even many selves or parts), harmonizing the two, and then living with and from that direct understanding.

A school of Vedanta Hinduism known as "Advaita" literally means "not-two." In the Advaita tradition, Brahman (the ultimate reality) appears as the world (the relative world) through its infinite creative potential, like waves continually arising out of and disappearing into the ocean, each wave distinct but not separate from the ocean. The experiencing self or small self (jīva) and the transcendental Self (ātman) are actually the same—both are Brahman.

The famous Sufi poet and mystic Rumi captured this concisely when he said, "Live in the nowhere you come from even though you have an address here."[46] In Christianity, we can get a taste of this too. In God, said St. John of the Cross, we find that the All and the Nothing encounter one another and are the Same.[47] The Christian mystics often say that in the beginning, you pray to God. But after your transformation, after your own personal at-one-ment, you pray through God, from God, as God. As Meister Eckhart said, "Let us pray to God that we may be free of God."[48] If you try to understand Eckhart here using only logic, it won't make sense. It takes a direct understanding, a bare knowing, of non-dual consciousness, of the personal and absolute. "The eye with which I see God," Eckhart says, "is the same eye with which God sees me: my eye and God's eye are one eye, one seeing, one knowing and one love."[49]

We see this in Japanese Zen too, a non-dual Buddhist tradition that evolved out of Taoism. Zen recognizes that because logic operates dualistically—is or is not, yes or no, 0 or 1—it traps us in a prison of our own making. It limits us: if yes, then not no; if 0, then not 1. In other words, if we hold only the self or the particular, we lose the whole. And similarly, if we hold only the whole, then we lose the particular, we lose ourselves and our life story; we turn into a monistic blob. So, Zen realizes that you are and you are not and you are both—you are the yin, yang, and the Tao that holds and transcends them both.

We are not-two. We are spiritual beings, unbound and unformed, incarnated into precious human form. We need to remember our address here as well as our transcendent nature. As Zen so often points out, each of us is a walking paradox of suchness and emptiness, of beingness and openness, of immanence and transcendence. To be whole, we must honor and stand in both truths equally. We must feel the full range, complexity, and intensity of our particular human experience while remaining connected to our transcendent, open, formless, interconnected, undying nature. As Sri Nisargadatta put it, "Love says, 'I am everything.' Wisdom says, 'I am nothing.' Between these two my life flows."

Exercises & Reflections

To get a better picture of what I have been talking about, take a look at the room with a wide-open gaze. And as you sit here, consider how many different thoughts you can have about the space around you. Various objects will arise and pass away as different thoughts flow through you. You can even take one object in the room and, with thought, break it into more pieces. Behind your thoughts, though, there is simply experience. There's just *This*—whatever *This* ineffably is.

Try it out for yourself, but I think you'll find it tremendously beneficial to notice this fracturing—to pay attention to how you are slicing up the Whole and relating the pieces to one another without losing sight of the Whole. As all who have traveled the spiritual path know, and as the core tenets of all the world's religions demonstrate, the spiritual life truly begins only after you have oriented yourself towards the Divine—to God, the Cosmos, the Eternal, Awareness, Universal Consciousness, or whatever else you want to call that which knows, encompasses, and composes all things.

I invite you to keep systematically investigating your "self." Who is it? What is it? Where is it? What is it like? Starting with the body, ask, "Am I the skin, the hair, the muscles and bones, the organs or the blood? Am I this body?" Modern science tells us that the cells of the body are replaced completely every seven years. If you are not the physical elements of this body, then what are "you"? Are you the stream of changing feelings and sensations? Are you the memories and perceptions, the thoughts and concepts, the views and beliefs, that move in and out of awareness? Who or what are "you"?

Keep looking for yourself to see whether there's a persistent carrier of the essence of things. Can you find anything solid, anything to cling to, anything secure? I can't. When I look, I see only a continuous dance of shapes and colors, a seamless voice of poetry, of emotion, desire, and affliction, all of which are choreographed onto the unformed and unbound stage of awareness. When I look directly at my own experience, all I see is Love. What do you see?

4. LOVE

"Your task is not to seek love, but merely
to seek and find all the barriers within
yourself that you have built against it."
– Rumi

"What is essential is invisible to the eye."
– The Little Prince

One of the yummiest parts of my day is found in the company of my family's stillness as we sit around the dinner table just before we eat. "Should we have our moment of silence?" the oldest of our four kids reminds us. The other kids close their eyes, and silence quickly blankets the room.

Of the many forms of prayer we express in our home, there is something unusually special about our dinner prayer. As we sit and listen to the deafening voice of Silence, our busy thoughts are cleansed by Her stillness. Here in the placid waters of mind is that magical moment—that moment when all dividing lines disappear and each of us returns home to the invisible and all-encompassing force in which the foundations of faith are built upon. Here, we commune in Love.

After the waters settle, and my partner and I feel that the room has found its way back home, we tell our kids we love them. As we eat, we ask the kids what they felt in their hearts and minds. Sometimes they express specific things for which they are grateful. At other times, they express their heartfelt wishes for their friends and families. There are other evenings when they talk about how busy their thoughts are, how it was difficult to connect to their experience, welcoming that too with open arms. But very often, the kids express some of the many ways in which they are connected to the rest of the world.

They will, for example, trace the food that sits on their plate back through its journey. They see their food in its fullness, connecting themselves to the soil in which the food was planted, to the sun, air, and rain, to the farmers who cared for the plants, to the truck driver who drove the food to the store, to the cashier who sold the food to us, to me who prepared the food, to their mom who worked hard for the money to buy the food, all the way to the bacteria in their stomach that will help them digest the food and turn it into energy for them to live, laugh, and be.

This is what our family calls wearing our "Love Goggles." The belief—frame, lens, view, or orientation—that we are all interconnected, that there is no separation in existence, that you are not apart from me, is the starting point for me and my family. It is like the exterior framework that holds and houses every other belief we have. It's the glue, container, and substance of all things. It brings a kind of cohesion and harmony to our vast collection of thoughts and beliefs, to our lives and to our being. It is the root motivation for all that we say and do.

Love, though, is not something to take on blind faith. There is a kind of faith involved but it is a faith that comes from your own direct investigation of Love, not from some authority, some scripture or prophet or even me telling you what it is. The word spirit comes from the Latin root *spiritus*, which means breath or wind—that which exists but cannot be seen or grasped. So, the faith I am referring to develops, matures, and strengthens as you become more intimately acquainted with the unseen force of Love.

Seek it out for yourself, of course, out of your own interest, but as my vipassana practice deepens, one thing continues to grow very clear to me—that there is no space between me and what is known. And as this direct insight strengthens, as the barriers between me and the objects of awareness dissolve, as I continually fall back into the single realm of being and knowing, into the glue and container of all things, a quite miraculous feeling of unconditional love continues to expand in my heart and mind.

In Buddhism, this general expression of heart is called metta, or loving-kindness. The feeling can happen quite suddenly upon directly recognizing our interconnected and interdependent nature, as it sometimes does when we are in nature or when we take an entheogen like MDMA or magic mushrooms. But really, for many of us, it is going to take time to cultivate and stabilize since the clouds of papañca are so thick—that is, since we have been conditioned to orient from the thinker who breaks reality into self and other. But I am confident the more you recognize as a matter of direct experience that your life, that your suffering and wellbeing, are not apart from everyone and everything around you, the more natural metta will become.

But again, because it can take time for the clouds of papañca to dissipate and the light of mindfulness and wisdom to shine through, to help prepare the soil, we can also make metta and its three related states, compassion (karuna in Pali), sympathetic joy (mudita), and equanimity (upekkha), a practice of their own. Together, these are known as the Divine Abodes—wholesome sanctuaries for our minds to rest, sanctuaries that are entirely without borders or limits. Each is an expression of love, but this unconditional love takes different shapes depending on the circumstances. Let's go ahead and explore each of them in turn.

Metta | Loving-Kindness

When the famously loving Buddhist practitioner and teacher Dipa Ma was asked whether to practice metta or mindfulness, she replied, "From my experience, there is no difference. Love and awareness are one. When you are fully loving, aren't you also mindful? And when you are fully mindful, is this also not the essence of love?"[50]

This framing really captures the practice for me, not just of vipassana and metta but of life. And I find it especially useful for beginners since the framing is so straightforward. Mindfulness, put simply, is a loving and caring attention. It is a kind of posture we take in the mind toward experience, the kind of posture a mother takes to her precious newborn baby. We worship—or give all of ourselves to—what is in front of us, without the need to control the person or thing or judge it or make it be a certain way. We simply love it, exactly as it is, whether pleasant or unpleasant, whether the baby is kicking and screaming or giggling and laughing.

Rather than the Western approach to happiness, where we constantly try to change our environment to fit our desires and wishes, Buddhist psychology recognizes that it is not our external environment or circumstances that lead to happiness but the very quality of the mind itself in each moment. It realizes that there is a much more sustainable approach in an unpredictable world. Just consider the last time something went exactly as you wished. Life, as you know, continues to throw us curveballs. We cannot control other people. We cannot control the weather. We cannot control how we feel. Some days we feel depressed, lethargic, and apathetic, and some days we feel happy, energized, and full of interest. We each experience seasons of pleasure and pain, gain and loss, praise and blame, admiration and disdain.

So again, with the Buddhist approach, rather than try desperately to make everything exactly as we want it to be, we train our minds to rest in a loving, caring awareness. Just as a person wants to be seen, felt, loved, and understood, we learn to see, feel, love, and understand every dimension of our experience, every person, emotion, and feeling. This way, our peace and happiness are not dependent on anything being a certain way. We can remain with this feeling of unconditional love, this warm and expansive feeling that wishes well to ourselves and others, no matter what is arising in our lives and in our experience.

Of course, this is not always easy. But like with any skill, we can improve and stabilize it with practice, which is exactly what many Buddhist frameworks suggest we do.

To begin, let's first familiarize ourselves with the feeling of metta, since it can be easily confused in Western culture with the feeling of love with attachment—a grasping, limited kind of love. Loving-kindness is not extended to us because of who we are (a child, friend, or lover). It's not extended to us because of what we've done or how we look. It's extended to us freely, without conditions. It's extended to us merely because we are—we exist, we are bound up with the whole, inextricably linked to the cosmos, to god, to awareness, or whatever else you want to call that which encompasses, knows, and composes all things. The Persian poet Hafiz captured this beautifully when he said, "Even after all this time, the sun never says to the earth 'you owe me.' Look what happens with a love like that—it lights the whole sky."[51]

Loving-kindness is simply the generosity and openness of heart that wishes well to all beings. And it's exactly this—the selfless, expectation-less, and condition-less nature—that makes the quality of loving-kindness so remarkable. One of the first things to notice about it is that it is always available since it doesn't rely on things being a certain way. You can tune into love, into well-wishing, whenever you want. As the famous Vietnamese monk and peace activist Thich Nhat Hanh reminds us, happiness is available, please help yourselves to it.[52] We just need to remember to change the channel. May you be happy. May you be free from suffering. May you be at peace.

Even in the most difficult situations, metta is available. After 9/11, for example, Joseph Goldstein recalls leading a retreat in which several people from New York were attending. When it came time to practice loving-kindness, spreading it to all beings, the people from New York were understandably hesitant. They simply couldn't wish the Jihadists happiness. After all, these terrorists had just killed some of their closest friends and family. So, rather than wish the terrorists happiness, Goldstein suggested that they reframe their wishes to "May you be free from hatred and cruelty." And almost immediately, the people from New York were able to soften into their hearts once again. They could really stand behind these wishes.[53] So, at times when we are finding it difficult to tap into metta, we may just need to play around with the wording a bit. Is there anyone you wouldn't wish the following to— may you be free from anger, jealousy, resentment, and ill-will?

In making these wishes, however, we need to make sure our general tone or posture is coming from that place of unconditional love. At points in our practice, we will sometimes repeat in our minds the words and phrases "may you be happy, may you be free from suffering," but we are saying them from a place of greed or aversion. That's not the habit we want to cultivate. So, again, it's important to check the underlying tone and motivation. Are we sending metta to someone or some aspect of our experience without conditions? Or are we doing it in order to get something? Are we doing the dishes for our partner because we want recognition or because we think they'll now do the laundry? Are we hoping that if we send metta to our depression or fear or shame that it will go away?

Another quality of metta to explore is its tremendous purity. Whether metta is directed to another person or to our own experience, when the feeling of loving-kindness is present, there isn't room for unwholesome thoughts. And even if a few harmful thoughts remain, they have no real grip on us. Insecurity, hate, fear, shame—each have the support of loving-awareness. They no longer fracture us. The moment is generally one of true purity. There is a natural ease, receptivity, and openness.

Also, unlike conditional love, the feeling of loving-kindness is remarkably stable. In a world that knows only change, love with attachment too often turns into disappointment, resentment, and jealousy when things don't last or go as expected. The feeling of loving-kindness, though, is not easily shaken since it's simply the wish 'may you be happy.' There's a confidence and strength in it. There's never any remorse or regret to well-wishing. And so, the more we abide here, the calmer and more stable we become.

Finally, as you become more familiar with this feeling of loving-kindness, I think you'll find it to be among the most expansive states of mind. Unlike conditional love, where our capacity to love is limited by our time and attention (we can't be best friends or lovers with everyone), metta knows no boundaries. The feeling of loving-kindness, of goodwill, is wide open. It can blanket the whole world. It can encompass and embrace all beings across space and time. It is entirely without boundaries or limits.

One of our kids got a good taste of this the other night. My partner River was having a hard day, so for dinner, instead of doing our regular moment of silence, I asked the kids if we could gather round mom and pour all our love into her as sincerely and fully as we could. After the group hug, our little one pulled away and said, "I tried to pour all my love into you, mama, but I couldn't because it just kept coming."

Incredible, no? When you really take the time to explore the space of possible mind-states, to connect with one that is so free, so stable, and so vast, shows just how special and inspiring loving-kindness is. The Dalai Lama said that if we were aware that we all contain love within us and that we can foster it and develop it, we would certainly give it far more attention than we do.

How can we cultivate loving-kindness? Well, aside from practicing mindfulness, we can be as creative as we want. Once you know and familiarize yourself with the feeling, there's plenty of ways to cultivate it. You can write letters to friends, family, and strangers to wish them well, to remind them of all the love they carry. When you speak with people, you can look them in the eyes, wrap them in your full care and attention, really connect with them, really try to understand them. You can hold a door for someone, pick up some trash on the street, smile at the clerk in the checkout line, count your blessings before you fall to sleep, acknowledge a good deed, etc.

But because we have such deep habits, because so many of us have been conditioned to carry feelings of ill-will or insecurity towards ourselves, because so many of us have been taught to fear and hate others, because so many of us have learned to close our hearts and minds, it's extremely important that we actively build a formal practice of loving-kindness into our lives. It's important we work hard to unwind all the unhealthy habits we've developed over the years and commit ourselves to rewiring all those neural pathways with some love fiber. As the Buddha said, "with dripping drops of water, the jug is filled."

Again, build a practice that works best for you. But here are a couple ways that have helped me grow this feeling of loving-kindness into something quite extraordinary, into something I didn't even know was possible, and which continues to surprise me. First, every morning, I start my vipassana practice by asking myself sincerely and honestly, 'Why am I doing this? Why am I choosing to sit here looking directly at the nature of my mind?'

And right then, when I pose this question, I realize that I keep showing up every morning because I've seen and felt how this practice changes my capacity for experience—it continues to expand, enrich, and enhance it. It has transformed my loneliness and depression into profound feelings of connection—a connection to myself and to my experience, as well as to the world and people around me. It has made me more attentive, composed, and resilient, which makes me better situated in each moment and in each encounter to engage more wisely with the people, feelings, and emotions in front of me. It has opened my heart and mind, filled me with space, made me feel incredibly vast, entirely whole, and at peace. This is not only good for me but it's also good for everyone around me. It's good for my relationships. It's good for my writing and my art. It's good for my being in the world.

I see and feel, then, that my intention for practicing is not merely for myself. It's out of love for everyone, love for my friends, family, neighbors, and coworkers. It's for every encounter I have with others and with the world. I sit here and observe my mind because I want to be a better dad, partner, friend, student, and teacher. I want a more peaceful, loving, and awake world. And, as Sam Harris often reminds me,[54] the mind is all I have to achieve these ends. So, as you can see, my mindfulness practice is itself an expression of loving-kindness, not only to myself but to the world, to experience.

Another way I cultivate loving-kindness is by practicing concentrating on the feeling itself for extended lengths of time. In contrast to vipassana, where I sit in open awareness, not concentrated on any particular thing, in a formal metta practice, my goal is very narrow and directed: I try to spark the feeling of loving-kindness and then hold onto it and enhance it for as long as I can. Traditionally, this is done in phases. Most often, we start by extending loving-kindness to ourselves. Next, we move onto a benefactor, someone for whom it is easy to spark the feeling of loving-kindness. Then, we move to a neutral person, a difficult person, and eventually we extend this feeling to the entire world.[55] (For free meditations, please visit my website at johndriggs.org.)

I think you'll find this beneficial in a couple ways. First, if you make it a habit through practice, I'll bet loving-kindness will increasingly become your natural state of mind. And second, by practicing in this way, you will see your concentration increase, which will increase your capacity for mindfulness, which will increase your capacity for wisdom. And so, your life will just continue to spiral upward. But again, you'll have to see for yourself.

Karuna | Compassion

While love is, compassion does. It is the sensitivity of heart that compels us to respond to suffering from a place of love and wisdom. Unobscured by delusion and ignorance, compassion is our natural response to the world's tears. It begins with empathy—the willingness to get close to suffering, both in ourselves and in others. But rather than get sucked into the emotion, rather than drown in the pain, grief, or sorrow of others, or even our own, compassion grounds itself in metta—in the wide-open, warm, and expansive wish, may you be happy.

This, of course, can be extremely difficult. When we are faced with pain, for many of us, our habit is to turn away or hold it at arm's length. Very few of us take the time to get intimate with it, to genuinely feel into and listen to it. This is not only because we live in a culture of constant distraction, where we never slow down enough to tune into our own hearts and minds, but also because many of us have built defenses to protect our tender open wounds. When we experience trauma as a child or at a time when we are not able to face the trauma with the full love and support we need, our bodies take protective measures. Often, we learn to numb out to our emotions and feelings. We live in a dissociated state, detached from our bodies, detached from the full range and complexity of the human experience.

Now, let me first say that if you are one of these people, I love you. I'm sorry for the pain, distrust, loneliness, depression, and despair you have experienced. No child of this earth should have to endure such abuse, abandonment, or neglect. Thank you for sticking it out, for putting in the work. I have the utmost confidence that, if you continue to investigate your own heart and mind courageously, openly, and honestly, you will discover a profound peace waiting to be embodied. Spiritual practice has, after all, been considered a process of healing since ancient times. And I too have found this to be the case in my own personal journey.

Many people, though, come to spiritual practice hoping to skip over their wounds. They'd rather jump right into the heavenly realms of grace and bliss, free from pain, difficulties, and conflict. Sadly, some spiritual practices actually encourage this. They teach methods of intense concentration that certainly can and do bring about wonderful states of rapture and peace. Now, don't get me wrong, these have their place in a larger, more holistic framework. But taken alone, as soon as you descend from the throne, as soon as you step down from your spiritual high and get back to real life, the wounds will still be there. You will once again face all the unfinished business of your body, heart, and mind. You will still carry all the same habits—habits of thought and behavior, habits of moods and emotions, habits in your relationships, etc.

And even if you were extremely lucky in life and didn't experience any capital T traumas, no one gets through this life unscathed. Everyone eventually must face a period of great difficulty. We might lose our job or a close friend. We may get divorced. We may suddenly be faced with anxiety attacks, confusion, fear, loneliness, or addiction. We might have to live with a difficult person or bear a painful injury or disability. We might face the illness or death of a child or loved one. And no matter what, in the end, each of us must face our own mortality.

No amount of meditation, yoga, prayer, or therapy will make our problems go away. This is the Buddha's first noble truth—life consists of suffering. Or, as Karl Popper framed it, "All life is problem solving."[56] Compassion acknowledges this—that not all suffering can be avoided—and so it opens to the reality of suffering. Compassion allows us to come close to suffering with the caring and equanimous support of mindfulness.

Compassion is a great gift of mindfulness since mindfulness helps open us to our own emotions, as well as our empathetic heart, with a receptive and composed embrace. Mindfulness lets suffering in without drowning in it, without becoming consumed by the difficulty, pain, grief, or sorrow. It allows us to accept and be with the truth of the present moment, not at arms-length but fully and intimately. It enables us to embody the warm, open, and expansive wish—may you be happy, may you be free from suffering, may you be at peace.

The psychologist Viktor Frankl, who wrote the famous book Man's Search for Meaning, was the sole member of his family to survive the Nazi death camps. Despite all his suffering, though, he found a way to heal, to keep his heart soft and open. "We who lived in concentration camps," he wrote, "can remember the men who walked through the huts comforting others, giving away their last piece of bread. They may have been few in number, but they offer sufficient proof that everything can be taken from a man but one thing: the last of the human freedoms—to choose one's attitude in any given set of circumstances..."

As Frankl and so many others have demonstrated, this human freedom is possible under any circumstance. And it is born out of our capacity to work with any energy or difficulty that arises. As Jack Kornfield says, "It's the freedom to enter wisely into all the realms of this world, beautiful and painful realms, realms of war and realms of peace."[57] It is this capacity that so many shamans carry, like the Shipibo maestros and maestras who hold space for us in Ayahuasca ceremonies. When you sit with Ayahuasca and confront all the different realms of mind, realms of war and peace, you want someone who is soft, tender, and compassionate, but who is also strong, composed, and unperturbed. The more we can get purchase on our reactions to the various landscapes of mind, the more freedom we will have to remain in and act out of our hearts.

The next time you confront suffering, pay attention to the mind's reaction. Whether there is pain in the body or an emotion in the heart like boredom, loneliness, fear, or unworthiness, do you open to it or do you pull back? Do you give it a side-glance or distract yourself with a movie, work, sex, or masturbation? Do you repress it or numb out? Do you fall into self-pity? What about when you interact with a difficult person or situation? Or when you experience racial, political, or sexual injustice? Do you withdraw from the person or situation? Do you judge and condemn them? Or do you become interested in what's happening? Do you try to listen to and understand the person? Do you feel into their heart and hold their energy, as well as your own, with the wish, may you be happy?

Again, often the response for so many of us is indifference. Watch out for this. Next time you come across suffering in one of its many forms, see if you can take a moment to really connect with the fear, pain, heartache, or despair. Can your heart stay open? As Joseph Goldstein says, can you diminish the subtle cruelty of indifference and make compassionate responsiveness the default setting?[58]

Now, of course, sometimes the compassionate thing to do is to step away from a person or situation. Compassion does not mean ignoring our own needs. It is finding balance between self and other. So, if we need to set boundaries or walk away, then please do that. It may be skillful to step away, to slow down our heart, to catch our breath, to let our nervous system settle, before we return to the difficult situation. This can also be true for difficulties we experience in the privacy of our own hearts and minds. If you feel overwhelmed by an emotion, it can certainly be skillful to turn to another task, take a walk, or whatever. If we push it too hard, we can end up making the situation worse for ourselves. So, again, it's not always cowardice to step back. The trick is to play right at the boundary of our comfort zone. Maybe just go and peak over the edge.

To prepare us for the bigger difficulties in life, it can also be useful to frame the smaller, everyday difficulties as a part of our practice. This allows us to see how our pains and struggles can become guides in our spiritual journey. When we are sick, for example, can we listen to what our bodies are trying to tell us, and use it to heal? When our kids act out, instead of getting angry at them or shutting them out, can we feel into their deeper needs? When we are struggling with our partner, can we step into their shoes, recognize our own involvement, and see how we can be more loving and supportive, or how we can communicate our own needs or boundaries more appropriately? When we are angry or judgmental, can we look deeper until we find in that anger or judgment a desire for justice, and then discern with wisdom the best way forward? When we feel lonely, rather than run and hide from it, can we explore whether this loneliness is pointing us to something deeper? Is it reminding us to rediscover the wholeness, connectedness, and completeness that already exists within us?

Again, our trials, difficulties, and vulnerabilities are often the very thing we need to open to in order to learn and grow, in order for us to come home to our unbounded hearts. After all, it's only after the shell breaks that the seed can receive light from the sun and transform into something truly remarkable.

> Your pain is the breaking of the shell that encloses your understanding.
> Even as the stone of the fruit must break, that its heart may stand in the sun, so must you know pain.
> And could you keep your heart in wonder at the daily miracles of your life your pain would not seem less wondrous than your joy;
> And you would accept the seasons of your heart, even as you have always accepted the seasons that pass over your fields.
> And you would watch with serenity through the winters of your grief.
> Much of your pain is self-chosen.
> It is the bitter potion by which the physician within you heals your sick self.
> Therefore trust the physician, and drink his remedy in silence and tranquility:
> For his hand, though heavy and hard, is guided by the tender hand of the Unseen,
> And the cup he brings, though it

burn your lips, has been fashioned of
the clay which the Potter has moistened
with His own sacred tears.
-Kahlil Gibran, On Pain

Another thing to remember when faced with suffering is that there is no single response. We in the West tend to be rule-based, or have black-and-white thinking, about our morality. We look at everything, even our compassionate responses, in terms of good and bad. But compassion doesn't work this way. Yes, there are more efficient ways to accomplish specific aims, which the Effective Altruism movement is trying to capture.[59] If you want your dollar to save the most lives, then you might consider donating money to buy mosquito nets in Africa rather than give your dollars to the Boy Scouts. But the field of compassion is wide open. It can take on any number of an infinite set of forms. If one person's heart moves her to sit in a cave and meditate on the nature of mind and suffering for decades, it's unhelpful to judge her compassionate response or compare it to another's. Maybe one of her few students becomes the next Thich Nhat Hanh, a great peace activist in the world.

Again, the field of compassion is limitless. There is no single prescription for what we should do, no hierarchy of compassionate action. There is space for each of us to find our own way, through the natural and spontaneous expression of heart that is free from self-reference, free from greed, free from hatred, free from delusion. As I said earlier, compassion is the natural activity of a free and liberated heart. It is the expression of wisdom, the result of witnessing directly the selfless, interconnected, and interdependent nature of being. The more we grow into this direct insight of love and emptiness, the more natural compassion becomes. As Dilgo Khyentse Rinpoche said, when we recognize the empty, selfless nature of phenomenon, "the energy to bring about the good of others dawns uncontrived and effortless."[60]

Though I believe this to be true, I would like to add two caveats. First, we've all heard the phrase, the road to hell is paved with good intentions. And we know that even the most enlightened teachers can, and indeed do, make mistakes. In fact, entire cultures have customs that are not conducive to the wellbeing of the people living in them. Sam Harris gives a great example of this when he tells the story of one of his own teachers, Anagarika Shri Munindra from India. Munindra, who no doubt had reached deep stages of awakening, did something most of us in the West would consider unethical. When it was time for his niece to get married, he took a picture of her, lightened her skin with an editing software, and put the photo on the internet to attract potential suitors, as if she were simply property for sale.[61]

Again, I tell this story to make the point that awakening to our true nature is not enough. We need more. Our compassionate responses—our words, actions, livelihoods, politics, ethics—need to be grounded in a tradition of reason. True compassion requires critical feedback. It requires a marriage of Eastern and Western philosophy. So, as I said in chapter 2, we need to continually put our aims, values, intentions, and behaviors under scrutiny. We need to discuss them openly, honestly, and critically, so that we may move ever so nearer to truth. If Munindra is committed to the wellbeing of conscious entities, as his beliefs point to, we could apply critical pressure to see if he was achieving his aim effectively and efficiently—does prizing lighter skin add to the world's wellbeing? Does advertising our women for marriage proposals, rather than allowing them the freedom to explore their own hearts and relationships, increase or reduce suffering?

The second caveat I would like to add is captured by another common saying—actions speak louder than words. Anyone who has ever set a New Year's resolution knows it is much harder to follow through on our intention than it is to simply set it. The truth is, we are habitual creatures. Inertia is real. It takes effort and perseverance to change our deeply conditioned habits. So, yes, when we are aware of our selfless nature, the more natural compassion will be. But it is going to take a lot of practice to stabilize this realization. There is no quick fix.

Something I recommend to help move us in this direction is to open more and more to our motivations and intentions. Tibetan Buddhist say that everything rests on the tip of motivation. It is, after all, the fuel that drives us. Without it, we wouldn't do anything. This is why Tibetan Buddhists suggest that we set our intentions first thing in the morning, and then feel into their underlying motivations. Are my intentions grounded in kindness, compassion, and wisdom or are they grounded in greed, anger, and delusion? This way, we train our mind to abide in these compassionate intentions and motivations. As the Buddha said, "What we think and ponder becomes the natural tendency of mind." To further build this habit, we can also do this every time we shift tasks—every time we get up from our desk, every time we get into our car, every time we step into a conversation, etc.

The importance and effect our motivations have on our wellbeing can't be overstated. It is our motivations and intentions that set our moods and mold our postures and attitudes for the day, or for the specific task we are performing. They also focus our attention. They shape and coordinate what we think, how we feel, and what we say and do. Someone who is motivated out of greed or hatred will see, relate, and move through the world very differently from someone who is motivated out of loving-kindness or compassion.

Research has shown that, compared to those with ego-centric goals, those who have compassionate goals are less likely to be depressed and anxious, and they are also more likely to have good relationships and feel a sense of meaning in their life.[62] Our motives, life goals, and the kind of person we want to be influence tremendously how we navigate our lives. When we intentionally put ourselves in service to compassionate motives like supporting, encouraging, and caring for ourselves and other people, and even the earth at large, it has far-reaching consequences.

This insight has been around for thousands of years and is common to many religions. In Mahayana Buddhism, compassion is seen as the catalyst of transformation that shifts us from a self-centered life to an earth- or cosmic-centered life, a life focused on service to the whole. This is expressed in the Bodhisattva's aspiration of bodhicitta—the awakened heart-mind that is committed to freeing all beings from suffering. This aspiration is captured beautifully by the eighth century Indian monk Shantideva in his perennial work The Way of the Bodhisattva:

> For all those ailing in the world,
> Until their every sickness has been healed,
> May I myself become for them
> The doctor, nurse, the medicine itself.
> Raining down a flood of food and drink,
> May I dispel the ills of thirst and famine.
> And in the ages marked by scarcity and want,
> May I myself appear as drink and sustenance.
> For sentient beings, poor and destitute,
> May I become a treasure ever plentiful,
> And lie before them closely in their reach,
> A varied source of all that they might need.
> My body, thus, and all my goods besides,
> And all my merits gained and to be gained,
> I give them all away withholding nothing,
> To bring about the benefit of beings...
> Like the earth and the pervading elements,

Enduring like the sky itself endures,
For boundless multitudes of living beings,
May I be their ground and sustenance.
Thus, for everything that lives,
As far as the limits of the sky,
May I provide their livelihood and nourishment
Until they pass beyond the bonds of suffering.

No doubt, this aspiration requires great humility and patience. But really, it's not as intimidating as it seems. Rather than view it as some unrealistic and far-off state, we can connect to and embody this intention every time we are mindful. Rather than hold it in thought, rather than stuff our whole future into a bag we have to carry around on our shoulders, we can witness directly in this moment the suffering and dis-ease in the mind and transform it with Love.

Mudita | Sympathetic Joy

Mudita is, I believe, one of the most overlooked mind-states, especially here in the West. It contains so much treasure and yet we don't even have a word for it in English. But it is what loving-kindness feels like in the presence of joy. It is taking joy in the joy of others, understanding that their joy is not apart from your own. It's what grandparents do best with their grandkids.

My kids absolutely love mudita, and they love to recognize it everywhere—in themselves and in other people, in their books, movies, and shows. This is especially true around the winter holidays since our monthly virtue for December is—you guessed it—mudita. My partner and I thought December would be a perfect time to wrap our attention around mudita since December is the season of gifts. As you know, especially if you have kids, this can be a dangerous time to get trapped in the wanting mind, trapped in greed and expectation. We see others get a gift, and we are anxious to receive our own. Or we even compare what we have been given to what others have received, and then get jealous or start feeling sorry for ourselves. So, again, we choose to focus on mudita in December since it is a direct antidote to this kind of suffering.

To give an example, this last holiday season, we went to a family party where one of the aunts prepared a game for the kids. In this game, each kid had the opportunity to win several gifts. Unfortunately, one of my kids was striking out every turn, and so he just continued to watch his siblings and cousins accumulate more gifts. This understandably made him grow frustrated and somewhat jealous. Seeing this, I took him aside and reminded him of the power of mudita. Almost immediately, this switched a flip in him. He went right back to the game with a new attitude, happy to see his sisters and cousins enjoying their prizes. Then, as it turned out, on his next turn, he won a prize. Recognizing that his younger cousin was interested in the prize he had just won, his one and only prize, he gave it to her. Seeing how happy this made her, my son's entire being was suddenly filled with the utmost joy. And this joy stayed with him for several days, especially since we like to point out recent examples of our virtue when discussing it in our morning devotional.

When we really pay attention to the different mind states, we discover that the wanting mind is actually quite irritating. It agitates, contracts, and tightens the whole system. We feel incomplete, like there's a giant hole in us. And so, we try to fill this hole with anything and everything, only to find out that the hole can never really be filled. Yet, for some reason, we keep trying to fill it with food, sex, likes on social media, Amazon purchases, or whatever, and then watch the satisfaction disappear almost immediately.

When we tune into mudita, though, a sense of ease opens for us. There's no wanting or expectation. People like to be around us because they know our joy is tied up with their own. We spend less time in our heads worrying, scheming, and planning. So, the joy is much more rewarding and sustainable than the quick hit of pleasure we get from satisfying our own selfish desires. There's a beautiful example of this in Kahlil Gibran's book Jesus, The Son of Man, where a young man who had been walking for some time with Jesus recounts their walk:

> On a day when He and I were alone walking in a field, we were both hungry, and we came to a wild apple tree.
>
> There were only two apples hanging on the bough. And He held the trunk of the tree with His arm and shook it, and the two apples fell down.
>
> He picked them both up and gave one to me. The other He held in His hand.
>
> In my hunger I ate the apple, and I ate it fast.
>
> Then I looked at Him and I saw that He still held the other apple in His hand.

And He gave it to me saying, "Eat this also."

And I took the apple, and in my shameless hunger I ate it.

And as we walked on I looked upon His face.

But how shall I tell you of what I saw?

A night where candles burn in space,

A dream beyond our reaching;

A noon where all shepherds are at peace and happy that their flock are grazing;

An eventide, and a stillness, and a homecoming;

Then a sleep and a dream.

All these things I saw in His face.

He had given me the two apples. And I knew He was hungry even as I was hungry.

But I now know that in giving them to me He had been satisfied. He Himself ate of other fruit from another tree.

I would tell you more of Him, but how shall I? When love becomes vast love becomes wordless. And when memory is overladen it seeks the silent deep.

Some people naturally have this quality of mudita, like Jesus, but... we're not all Jesus. For many of us, it requires systematic training. This can be for several reasons. Often, we may meet mudita with resistance because we hold various assumptions, beliefs, or frameworks that need to be challenged and ultimately dissolved in order to really turn up the pressure to this wellspring of joy.

A prevalent and pernicious framework in the West is the comparing mind—the thief of joy. We compare anything and everything. She's smarter, he's stronger, I'm uglier. We compare foods—this coffee isn't as good as that one. We compare people—Lupita Nyong'o is prettier than Zoë Kravitz. We compare ourselves, our talents, our gifts, our weaknesses, to others. The comparing mind is ceaseless. And for what? What value does it bring you?

Why not just say what you like or value about someone or something? Simply state its qualities. Let it speak for itself. I get that contrast can be useful to help describe things, or to help us decide which pair of hiking boots to buy. But most often, it is entirely unnecessary. Again, if it is not helping you to make a decision, see if you can simply let people and things stand on their own. Tell me about it—whatever it is—rather than compare it to someone or something else. "This coffee is deliciously full in taste." "Lupita Nyong has an enchantingly beautiful smile." "River has such a strong imagination. That's something I'd like to improve in myself."

We even see the comparing mind in the questions we ask each other: What's your favorite movie? What's your favorite candy? Who do you like more, x or z? Now, of course, we are often just trying to learn more about each other. Our motivation is pure here. But try to be aware of the fact that when we do this, we are immediately putting someone or something beneath another. And like I said, this attitude starts to bleed into all our frameworks, into the subtlety of our thoughts. They sometimes even end up bleeding into our relationships—e.g., favorite parent, favorite friend, favorite kid. Over time, the critic and judge in our minds grow, harming ourselves and others.

Some similar frameworks to watch out for are the competitive mind and scarcity mind. Both share the similar idea that there is not enough joy, praise, success, or good fortune to go around. Now, it's true, sometimes there is only one job opening, one scholarship, one piece of cake, or whatever. But much of the time, we forget that this isn't really a win-or-lose situation, especially when it comes to joy. So, again, it's important to be mindful of and challenge these assumptions when they arise—the ways we withhold, the ways we compare, the ways we needlessly compete, the ways we feel that our lives are empty and always will be.

Another thing to look out for is our negative attentional bias. Though some of us tend to focus on what we like and love about everything, many of us tend to focus on the negative, on what is wrong, broken, ugly, disgusting, or imperfect. And of course, not everything is good and beautiful in the world. There is much that is unacceptable. And to be the adult in the room, we can't live with rose-tinted glasses. We must acknowledge the ugly. When we cultivate joy and mudita, though, we learn that the bad, ugly, and heartbreaking in life live side by side with the good, beautiful, and heartwarming.

There will always be things in our lives that need our care and attention, but that doesn't erase all that is good and well. If you explore your body, heart, and mind right now, there may be places of discomfort and pain, objects that are unpleasant. But there are also probably many places that are pleasant or at ease. For me, the whole house can be perfectly clean except for someone's dish in the sink, and the dish will consume me. I have so many other things to take delight in—the clean laundry, the mopped floors, the beautifully organized living room and bedroom—but I choose to dwell in misery over the tiniest dirty dish.

So, really, joy and mudita are a training of attention. We can learn to spend less time fixating on the negative, on what we don't have, on the bad, ugly, and heartbreaking, and more time on the positive, on what we do have, on the good, beautiful, and heartwarming. Building up our gratitude muscle helps. A simple journal where we list three to five gratitudes a day can go a long way. And they can be as simple as your morning coffee, the lungs that allow you to breath, or the heart that keeps your blood flowing. Again, what we think and ponder becomes the tendency of our minds.

Another place we can train to keep our attention is on the absence or waning of suffering. As Thich said, we always notice when we have a toothache, but why do we forget to enjoy all the moments when we don't have a toothache.[63] The Buddha also pointed out quite directly where to find joy—in the subsiding of what are called the hindrances or afflictive qualities of mind: desire, aversion, lethargy, restlessness, and doubt. See if, the Buddha asks us, being freed from the grip of desire is like being released from a debt; see if being freed from aversion feels like recovering from an illness; see if being freed from lethargy feels like being released from a dark prison cell; see if escaping anxiety and worry feels like being emancipated from slavery; and see if making it through doubt is like getting out of a desert alive. As a bonus, when we pay closer attention to the subsiding of the hindrances, we become less likely to get captured in them. We learn, for example, that we can simply let this desire or worry pass, and instead we can be with the greater ease that comes from renunciation.

There is one last shift in framing I suggest, which I've been dancing around this whole time. I encourage you to think of joy not as something that happens to us when all the stars align, not something we have to wait to receive, but something that we can offer as a gift to the world at any time. When we see directly for ourselves that we have the capacity to generate joy internally, it changes our relationship with the world. We stop pursuing so desperately external things to make us happy. This, of course, doesn't mean we stop appreciating all that is good and lovely in the world. We can still enjoy sex with our partner. We can still delight in the taste of coffee or the warmth of our shower. But our joy is no longer hostage to external conditions.

Upekkha | Equanimity

Equanimity is what makes love, compassion, mudita, and freedom possible. It is the balance and evenness of mind we cultivate in mindfulness practice—the capacity of mind to allow all things in without being controlled or consumed by them. So, it is not only the fertile ground for wisdom, but it is also the great defender of the divine abodes since it allows us to "stay on the log," as my kids say. It is what allows us to not get lured by desire or pushed away by aversion. It is one of the surest signs of spiritual maturity. And when it is well-cultivated, it gives rise to an extraordinary sense of peace—a peace that is not only felt internally but which others can feel in our presence. The Buddha described a mind filled with equanimity as abundant, exalted, immeasurable, without hostility, and without ill-will.[64]

Equanimity is translated from two Pali words—upekkha and tatramajjhattata. Upekkha, the more common term, means "to look over" and refers to the equanimity that arises from the power of pure observation—the ability to see without being caught by what we see. In India, the word was sometimes used in common speech to mean "to see with patience." And tatramajjhattata is a long compound of simple Pali words. The first, tatra, means "there." Majjha means "middle." And tata means "to stand or to pose." Together, then, the word means "to stand there in the middle."[65] It is to remain balanced, to be with whatever is happening, to not lean forward or pull away but to stay on top of your feet, open to what is here.

This balancing function has two specific applications that are relevant to our discussion. The first applies to our practice of dwelling in the divine abodes—loving-kindness (metta), compassion (karuna), sympathetic joy (mudita). And the second applies to maintaining composure against what are called the great vicissitudes of life, or the Eight Worldly Winds—pleasure and pain, praise and blame, success and failure, fame and disrepute.

With the first balancing function, equanimity is crucial because it helps us hold a balanced view of conscious beings, an unbiased impartiality, a mind without attachment or hostility, which is necessary to remain in the divine abodes. This practice carries the potential to veer off into what is called the "near enemies of the divine abodes". Loving-kindness can easily get mixed up with desire and attachment. Compassion can easily turn into pity, where we hold a subtle superiority over the person we pity instead of honoring, understanding, and respecting them. And mudita, when we're not careful, can fall into automatic pleasantry, or what is sometimes called toxic positivity—a kind of attachment to frivolous joys, or an unwillingness to be real about the truth of sorrow in our lives and in the lives of those around us. So, we need equanimity to act as the fulcrum, to balance self and other equally, and to balance the different energies that arise within ourselves as well.

To practice, then, we need to work with our natural tendencies to grasp at those we love, reject those we do not like, and ignore those who fall through the cracks. One simple way to work with our tendency to grasp at those we love, especially our partner or spouse or kids, is by asking the simple question, "How can I love this person more without asking for anything in return." Do this, and I bet you'll be surprised how often your love is tied up with some condition or expectation.

Let me hover over the relationships we have with our kids for a moment, an area in our lives where this balance tends to be particularly difficult. We carry so many conscious and unconscious demands and expectations for our kids. Many of us try to force our interests, hobbies, and beliefs on them, and then get hurt or frustrated when they don't take. A common theme I see not only in the Mormon culture but in all the Abrahamic religions, as well as in Hinduism, is the priority many parents give to their religion over their kids. Many parents of the world's faiths are simply unwilling to accept or come to terms with their children's decision to leave the faith, and so they end up holding their love hostage. This is not the god I know—unconditional love. So, watch out for this. As Kahlil Gibran says in his poem On Children:

> Your children are not your children.
> They are the sons and daughters of Life's
> longing for itself.
> They come through you but not from you,
> And though they are with you yet they
> belong not to you.
> You may give them your love but not your
> thoughts,
> For they have their own thoughts.
> You may house their bodies but not their
> souls,
> For their souls dwell in the house of to-
> morrow, which you cannot visit, not even in
> your dreams.
> You may strive to be like them, but seek
> not to make them like you.
> For life goes not backward nor tarries with

yesterday.

You are the bows from which your children as living arrows are sent forth.

The archer sees the mark upon the path of the infinite, and He bends you with His might that His arrows may go swift and far.

Let your bending in the archer's hand be for gladness;

For even as He loves the arrow that flies, so He loves also the bow that is stable.

Switching now to the difficult people in our lives, it can be useful to reframe our relationship with them by viewing them as our teachers. It is easy to be loving and mindful when everything is going along smoothly. But there's no real growth in this. Character is wrought by pain. It is only because of our difficulties, including the difficult people in our lives, that we can deepen our practice. So, the next time you interact with a difficult person, whether it's your boss, a parent, a neighbor, or whatever, see if you can take it as an opportunity to practice.

The Buddha set a high standard when he said, "Even if robbers and murderers saw through our limbs and joints, let us not give away to anger. Undisturbed shall our minds remain, with hearts full of love, free from any hidden malice, penetrating that person with loving thoughts; wide, deep, and boundless, freed from anger and hatred."[66] Now, of course, I'm not asking you to take it this far. But maybe see if you can recognize the pain behind this difficult person's face, recognize all the circumstances and hardships that brought this person to where they are, and then meet him or her with the wish, "may you be free from suffering, may you be free from anger, hatred, and cruelty, may you be at peace." You can even imagine this person as a young child if it helps.

In doing this, however, keep close the wisdom of "no." Remember, it's okay to say "no" to cruelty, it's okay to say "no" to abuse, to say "no" to racism, to say "no" to violence. As Jack Kornfield said, "There is a yes in compassion, and there is also a no, said with the same courage of heart."[67] This is known in Buddhism as the fierce sword of compassion. It is the powerful "no" of leaving a cruel and destructive family, it is the agonizing "no" of allowing an addict to feel the consequences of their actions without it taking over our own lives, it is the heart-wrenching "no" that removes ourselves and our precious children from abusive partners.

Sharon Salzberg, a famous practitioner of metta and grandmother of mindfulness in the West, tells a story of her time in India that really captures the wisdom of no. One night, she and her friend were on their way back to the monastery, when a man aggressively robbed them. Once they made it back to the monastery, they told their teacher all about the incident. The teacher listened intently and, when they were done speaking, said something like, "Oh my goodness, I'm so sorry. I'm glad you are all right. You should have taken your umbrella and hit that man with all the love in your heart!"[68]

This is an important lesson, especially in today's times. There are many parents I know of who have swung too far in the other direction from our parents' generation, who were a bit too strict and demanding. But love often requires sternness. Can you imagine if we never said no to our little children. What a nightmare that would be. So, again, saying no is an important part of the spiritual journey. We need to know our boundaries and we need to know how to communicate and defend them. We just need to make sure we are doing it from a place of love and wisdom. When I use my low stern voice with our dogs, after they have torn up toilet paper or gone potty in the house, I turn to my kids and wink at them. It's responding from a place of love, not from a place of hatred or anger.

Spiritual practice often emphasizes acceptance—accept things as they are—but, again, you don't have to go along with anything and everything. In fact, please don't. Equanimity does not mean passivity. It means understanding the situation clearly, so we can respond from a place of wisdom rather than react automatically, or habitually. I think James Baldwin captures this balance beautifully in his essay "Notes of a Native Son:"

> It began to seem that one would have to hold in the mind forever two ideas which seemed to be in opposition. The first idea was acceptance, the acceptance, totally without rancor, of life as it is, and men as they are: in the light of this idea, it goes without saying that injustice is a commonplace. But this did not mean that one could be complacent, for the second idea was of equal power: that one must never, in one's own life, accept these injustices as commonplace but must fight them with all one's strength. This fight begins, however, in the heart and it now had been laid to my charge to keep my own heart free of hatred and despair.

Finally, with neutral people, to break the habit of being indifferent towards them, we can simply acknowledge them. When we take a walk or drive in the car or stand in the checkout line, we we can ask ourselves if we genuinely want them to have a good day, if we genuinely want them to get where they are going safely. We can see if we want them to have someone in their life who loves and cares for them. Look and see if you really do hold these wishes for them. Most of us, most of the time, if we are merely willing to look, really do want others to be happy, to be safe and secure, to be free from suffering. Often though, we just need this quality of equanimity—this balanced and unbiased impartiality—to help open us to the whole field of conscious entities.

There's a great example of this in the movie Her (2013) by Spike Jonze. As the two main characters Theodore and Samantha are enjoying a night out together, they try to put stories to the people around them. After Samantha talks about a couple eating pizza with whom Samantha believes to be their kids, Theodore responds, "I don't think they're his kids. He's a little formal with them. I think it's a new relationship. I love how he looks at her and how relaxed she is with him. Ya know, she's only dated fucking pricks. And now she's finally met this guy who is so sweet. I mean, look at him. He's like the sweetest guy in the world. I kind of want to spoon him."

Samantha responds, "That's a good skill you have. You're very perceptive."

"Yeah," says Theodore, "you know, sometimes I look at people and make myself try and feel them as more than just a random person walking by. I imagine how deeply they've fallen in love or how much heartbreak they've all been through."

"Mm," says Samantha, "I can feel that in your writing."

This is a great way to balance out the indifference we feel toward strangers. When we realize that they have the exact same capacity for joy and sorrow as we do, when we realize that awareness sits at their foundation just as it does our own, when we realize that every experience is arising within the same unbounded ocean of awareness, then we can begin to even out our biases and prejudices and open to the entire field of experience, of suchness, of beingness.

If we don't practice, our love and compassion will likely remain limited. We will tend to think only about ourselves and those close to us and miss the potential to feel a much bigger love, a boundless love. Now, of course, this is perfectly normal. Evolution didn't carve out the impulse to love and protect strangers but rather to protect those closest to us. But as we grow more mindful, as our meta-awareness increases, we can imagine and cultivate much grander possibilities—infinite possibilities. We can cover the entire world with the wish, may you be happy.

Let's switch now to the second application of equanimity, which involves what are called the eight worldly winds or vicissitudes, the polarities of experience that are unavoidable in life—pleasure and pain, praise and blame, success and failure, fame and disrepute. Because these winds are forever blowing and changing, they create uncertainty at every step in our journey. We simply don't know what is around the next corner. When we cultivate equanimity, though, we remain balanced. We stand there in the middleness of it all. We learn to be at ease with these winds by understanding that they are transient, that they will pass. Again, Gibran captures this beautifully in his poem titled On Joy and Sorrow:

> Your joy is your sorrow unmasked.
> And the selfsame well from which your laughter rises was oftentimes filled with your tears.
> And how else can it be?
> The deeper that sorrow carves into your being, the more joy you can contain.
> Is not the cup that holds your wine the very cup that was burned in the potter's oven?
> And is not the lute that soothes your spirit, the very wood that was hollowed with knives?
> When you are joyous, look deep into your heart and you shall find it is only that which has given you sorrow that is giving you joy.
> When you are sorrowful look again in your heart, and you shall see that in truth you are weeping for that which has been your delight.
> Some of you say, "Joy is greater than sorrow," and others say, "Nay, sorrow is the greater."
> But I say unto you, they are inseparable.
> Together they come, and when one sits

alone with you at your board, remember that
the other is asleep upon your bed.
　　Verily you are suspended like scales
between your sorrow and your joy.
　　Only when you are empty are you at
standstill and balanced.
　　When the treasure-keeper lifts you to
weigh his gold and his silver, needs must your
joy or your sorrow rise or fall.

By embracing both joy and sorrow, we grow our capacity to be with either. Being able to openly enjoy pleasure, knowing full well that it will fade, is what also allows us to stay open to pain, since we know that it too will fade all on its own. There's no need to struggle. We can delight in the joy of warm sand between our toes at the beach, without desperately hanging onto the moment, and we can fully be with the grief of losing a loved one, seeing them both with wisdom. Of course, equanimity doesn't make the pain go away, but it helps us to understand that resisting the pain or contracting around it only makes the pain worse.

The wise grandmother is often used as a symbol of equanimity. For equanimity looks upon the whole project of our lives like a grandmother watches her grandchildren grow and develop. She sees them experience the highest highs and lowest lows with a collected and loving composure. She feels deeply and strongly for each of them but, because she has a much bigger perspective, she can take appropriate action—laugh with them, cry with them, correct their mistakes, nudge them in a particular direction, and discipline them when she needs—with a sense of ease. She has been on this rollercoaster for a long time and has seen her own children on this ride for some time now too, and so she has learned to relax into it.

So, how do we become more like grandma? Or, to look at the question from upside down—what is it that prevents us from abiding in equanimity? Well, often, it is our framing, our beliefs. When things don't go our way, when our expectations are upset, when our wishes don't come true, then we tend to judge, condemn, and blame reality for how it is. Fyodor Dostoyevsky said the best definition of man is, "ungrateful and walks on hind legs."[69] Sadly, this is all too true for so many of us, much of the time. We expect the entire world to revolve around us and our wishes, and then we're miserable to be around when the world inevitably doesn't go our way. This is the opposite of wisdom. It is the direct path to suffering—resisting, judging, condemning, and blaming Life, Reality, the Dharma.

Again, equanimity doesn't mean that we like or are happy about what happened. Many things in life are unfair or cruel, and it's okay to recognize that. Sometimes the most innocent are harmed, the most generous lose everything, and the most loving are hated and protested. Kids get cancer. Black men and boys in some parts of the U.S. have to worry about the very people who are supposed to protect them. Women are treated like second class citizens across the world. And on and on. Again, equanimity doesn't deny all this. It simply allows us to weather the storm, to plant our roots deep into the earth, into the soil of wisdom. It asks us to open to and unconditionally accept the truth of the moment's experience—the anger, pain, embarrassment, remorse, or boredom. And then, from that clarity, we can respond wisely, lovingly, skillfully, and appropriately.

A great way to start practicing is by applying equanimity to the very reactivity we are trying to diminish. When we react rather than respond with equanimity to pain, disgust, or whatever it may be, we can learn to tolerate and accept our reactions with kindness. We can even do this in our meditation practice when we judge ourselves after we realize we had been captured by thought. Rather than double down on the reaction by condemning or judging ourselves for reacting, we can work on being tolerant and accepting of our conditioned habits or reactions. This way, rather than getting stuck in a loop of reactivity, we learn to step back into a more spacious perspective and meet our reaction with the warm, welcoming radiance of equanimity.

Another way to practice cultivating equanimity is by becoming a student of the many ways we get caught. Rather than pursue some ideal of equanimity, we can note how "we fall off the log." We can explore our triggers. This is where having a good dharma friend comes in handy. We can ask them, or our partner or even a therapist, to keep us sharp, humble, and honest—to call us on our shit. We can let them be a mirror for us to see our reflections clearly. Then, when we can better see and understand our obstacles and triggers, the causes and conditions at play, we can work more skillfully to remove them or prevent them from arising in the first place.

Finally, the Buddha tells us that the key to cultivating equanimity is wise attention—being continually mindful from moment to moment, without losing the thread. If we are aware of the selfless, insubstantial, ever-changing, interconnected nature of being, not centered anywhere but instead embodied in the all-pervasive space of knowing, where our perspective is wide open and our hearts are connected, this becomes the cause for the next moment of equanimity.

Let me leave you with the Buddha's words, his own spontaneous expression of love, a prayer we memorize in our home and work hard to live up to:

May you be skilled in goodness. May you be able, honest, and upright; straightforward and gentle in speech; humble, modest, and simple in living. May you remain composed and calm, not proud and demanding in nature. May you do nothing the wise would reprove.

May you wish in gladness and in safety that all beings be at ease, that they be happy, safe, and secure. Whatever living creatures there be, without exception, strong or weak, omitting none, the short, tall, big, and small, whether seen or unseen, living near or far, born or unborn, may all beings be happy. May none deceive or despise another. May none through anger or aversion, through hatred or resentment, wish harm on another being.

As a mother protects with her life her child, her only child, so with a boundless heart may you cherish all beings. Radiating goodwill and kindness over the entire world, spreading upward to the skies, and downward to the depths, outward and unbounded, freed from hatred and ill-will, whether standing or walking, seated or lying down, free from drowsiness, may you sustain this recollection.

With virtue, vision, and purity of heart, holding no longer to selfish or crooked views, and being released from all sensual desires, may you be free from suffering. May you truly be at peace.

Exercises & Reflections

Tonglen is a Tibetan word that means "taking and sending." "Tong" means "sending out" or "letting go," and "len" means "receiving" or "accepting." This practice originated in India and was brought to Tibet in the eleventh century by the Indian master Atisha. It is part of The Seven Points of Mind Training and is a core meditation practice within each of the main Tibetan Buddhist lineages.[70]

The practice involves taking in the suffering and pain of others and sending them joy, well-being, and peace. When we see or feel suffering, we breathe it in, fully feeling, accepting, and transforming it. Then, we breathe out loving-kindness, release, and openness.

Many people shudder at this idea, thinking things are already bad enough without taking on the suffering of others. Our normal tendency is to hold onto the good and keep away from the bad. But Tonglen reverses this tendency—we give away the good and welcome the bad.[71]

Though we might initially think this is harmful, when we take on the suffering of others, especially those we do not like, we are not really taking on their suffering in a literal sense. Instead, we are confronting our own resistances and aversions. We acknowledge the immense energy associated with resistance and aversion, and we gradually reclaim this lost energy. By doing so, we break down the walls between ourselves and life around us, allowing our hearts to open and become more responsive to the suffering of others. This is the true essence of the practice.[72]

The underlying principle of tonglen is that our problems are not caused by difficult emotions or troublesome people and situations, but by how we react to these things—how we shut them out of our minds and hearts. Tonglen helps us become more aware of how our mind closes down and contracts when we push things away, whether people or emotions, and how this reaction makes us suffer.

Recall the last time you saw someone you did not like and feel your body instinctively tense up. With tonglen, we actively open to this discomfort and resistance, drawing it toward us by breathing it in, rather than following the normal pattern of closing down and pushing it away. Then, we open outward with kindness and spaciousness as we breathe out. In this way, we work directly with the mind's tendency to contract inwardly, shut down, and disconnect from the flow of life.[73]

Go ahead. Give it a try.

5. TRANSFORMATION

"If you let go a little, you'll have a little
happiness. If you let go a lot, you'll have a
lot of happiness. If you let go completely
. . . you'll be completely happy."
– Ajahn Chah

It rather terrifies me to think about where I would be today if I was never introduced to vipassana, or insight meditation. It has been and continues to be central to my life. Every moment of every day, I try to make it my practice. The quality of attention it cultivates determines the quality of everything else I do. It determines the quality of my life. It shapes my words and my actions. It shapes my attitude and experience. It shapes my relationships, my work, and my art. It holds my entire life with a loving, tender, and caring attention.

I first encountered the practice around the age of twenty-two, after being diagnosed with obsessive-compulsive disorder (OCD). For the decade prior, I had struggled with suicidal ideation, with a growing intensity over the years until, finally, I hit rock bottom in my first year of law school. Nearly every day, I would find myself on top of the law school building, seven stories up, waiting for the impulse that would send me plummeting to my death.

My thoughts became so frequent, intense, and aggressive that I got to the point where I didn't sleep for three days straight. Every time I came close to falling asleep, an electric shock would ripple through my head, sending my heart and mind racing. Something had to break.

It did. On the fourth night of no sleep, as I laid in bed, I fell into a wake-initiated lucid dream, or a WILD, something that was entirely unknown to me at the time. But there I was, suddenly in front of an old, leafless tree, with many thick branches stemming from its center. The sky was dark and cloudy. It felt extremely cold. I was shivering uncontrollably. And there, on a branch, hung a noose. I turned away from the tree to look around and saw only darkness. But when I turned back to face the tree, there was my entire family, standing with their eyes closed. Suddenly, in unison, their eyes opened, which glowed pure white. And again, all at once, they pointed to the noose.

There it went—the electric shock moved violently through my head and dropped down into my heart. I jumped up immediately and began to puke all over my sheets. I spent the rest of the night in my bathroom, some 1,500 miles away from my family and friends, dry heaving.

The next day, I was able to get into a psychiatrist, who introduced me to something that would transform my life—vipassana, or insight meditation. At the time, though, she didn't introduce it as such. Rather, she presented it as a kind of stress ball to calm my thoughts, which was great. It really did help to settle my heart and mind. It helped me to step back from the cruel bombardment of thoughts.

But the real transformational power came only after I put the full philosophical and historical context behind the practice. For the next few years, after marrying the philosophy to my practice and really putting in the work, the suicidal thoughts slowly faded, along with their intensity. They never disappeared completely. But the practice gave them the unconditional space they needed. It allowed them to arise without forcing my "self" onto them. It allowed them to be here, without struggle. Even now, they arise from time to time. And that's okay. Whenever they do, I simply say, "Hey, old friend. It's been a minute." I don't need to fight them or be annoyed that they are here. I can simply wish them well. I can love them unconditionally. I can still dwell in the divine abodes.

In any case, as my practice continued to strengthen and my conceptual and experiential understanding continued to deepen, behind that dark cloud of thoughts opened a clarity and spaciousness, as well as an immense gratitude and thirst for life! My mind continued to reach profound levels of peace and joy. My heart remained open. My eyes wide and interested. Everything within and around me became brighter and more vivid. New levels of concentration and mindfulness led to an incredible sense of rapture and joy in my heart and mind. I felt lighter and more alive. It's like I got to experience the world as a child again, with the same kind of play and wonder, but with the intelligence of an adult.

I remember vividly, in the early years of my practice, when I would smile naturally, the mindfulness was so bright and vivid that it would create a 'hall of mirrors' effect—I would notice the smile with that polished attention, and so the smile would grow bigger, which I noticed, and so it grew even bigger. Even the experience of stubbing my toe was profound and uplifting. To have the mindfulness present at the moment I stubbed my toe, and to not react or become identified with the pain, felt so rewarding and encouraging. I couldn't help but smile. Once, after ten 18-hour days of vipassana and another three days of metta practice, I felt a gratitude for my parents that was so intense I thought my body was going to explode. It was pushing outward on every wall of my being, choking me as it moved up my throat, trying to escape.

The practice, I came to quickly understand, was much more than a stress ball. It provided a door into the deepest insights of my true nature. It radically transformed who I took myself to be, which in turn transformed my direct felt experience in profound ways. The transformational power of mindfulness is simply astonishing. For the rest of the book, then, I would like to explore the Buddha's greater philosophical framework in which vipassana is but a piece.

The Truth of Suffering

Essentially everyone who steps foot on a spiritual path discovers the need for a profound personal healing. A wise spiritual practice asks us to discover the depth of our wounds, to address the pains and conflicts in our lives, the breaks and fractures, so we can tend to them with loving awareness. As the Thai Forest Master Ajahn Chah said, "If you haven't cried deeply a number of times, your meditation hasn't really begun."[74] The Buddha himself was quite explicit that he taught only suffering and its end, which is expressed in the Four Noble Truths, the indispensable foundation embraced by all Buddhist lineages, no matter how far their metaphysics and methodologies diverge.

That brings us to the Buddha's First Noble Truth—life is made of suffering. At first glance, this may seem both obvious and, at the same time, too strong. I'm sure I don't need to convince you that suffering exists and is a part of the human condition (and even the whole of conscious life). You are likely intimately familiar with it. But you might hesitate to concede that all life is composed of suffering, that suffering is an essential mark of existence. And I think you'd be right. So, let me take a step back and clarify my terms here.

The word "suffering" is a translation from the Pali word "dukkha," but to translate dukkha as merely suffering would be misleading and incomplete. Dukkha encompasses much more than suffering alone. The problem with the translation here is that modern English words can be too specialized, too limited, and too strong. So, we can't capture the full meaning of dukkha with a single word. We'll need to call in some other concepts to help point us to the actual felt experience of dukkha itself. From here you can then begin to build out your own direct understanding.

If we look at the word etymologically, we can break it into two parts: the prefix "du," which means "bad" or "difficult," and the root "kha," which generally means "empty" but can more specifically mean "the empty axle hole of a wheel."[75] So, if we put these two words together, we can begin to feel more viscerally what is meant by dukkha—just imagine riding in a cart that has a poor fitting axle. It's going to be a bumpy ride. We can think of dukkha, then, as the bumps and agitations, the ups and downs, the felt experiences of our journey through life. This dramatically changes and enlarges our understanding of the First Noble Truth.

But let's not stop here. Let's look at the more general meaning of "kha," empty, to add another dimension to our understanding. When we look at dukkha from this angle, we can think of it as anything that is ultimately empty of lasting satisfaction. We can translate dukkha more generally, then, not as 'suffering' but as that which is ultimately unsatisfying or unreliable, which is all things in a world of constant change.

> "Birth is suffering; aging is suffering;
> sickness is suffering; death is suffering;
> sorrow and lamentation, pain, grief and
> despair are suffering; association with the
> unpleasant is suffering; dissociation from
> the pleasant is suffering; not to get what
> one wants is suffering..." – the Buddha[76]

Now that we hopefully have a clearer understanding of dukkha, let's consider how it is applicable to our own lives. Perhaps the first thing to say is, we can't be freed from dukkha until we witness directly the dukkha in our own life so that we can transform it. Understanding dukkha, as a matter of direct experience, is not only the gateway to liberation, to freedom, to the highest peace, but it is also a direct path to compassion—the heart-felt desire to free ourselves and others from suffering. It is precisely our deepening understanding—that is, our deepening felt experience—of dukkha that opens and moves us to compassion.

So, how can we start opening to dukkha? With mindfulness. It is mindfulness that allows us to open to life, to dukkha. It is mindfulness that allows us to get close to it, to let it in. It is mindfulness—the wide open and all-encompassing heart of awareness—that listens to dukkha, that tries to understand it, that strives to love it. It is mindfulness that opens us to the direct experience of the First Noble Truth.

Let's start by listening to the obvious dukkha, the obvious pain and suffering we experience in our lives, like breaking a bone, getting hit on the head with a stick from your Zen master, living with a physical disability, chronic illness, etc. This kind of pain hurts, full stop. The way we relate to this pain, however, determines whether we add unnecessarily to it. When asked to describe how a wise person responds to pain, the Buddha gave an analogy of someone shot by an arrow:

> When an ordinary person experiences a painful bodily feeling they worry, agonize, and feel distraught. Then they feel two types of pain, one physical and one mental. It's as if this person were pierced by an arrow, and then immediately afterward by a second arrow, and they experience the pain of two arrows.[77]

I'm sure you know what this feels like. We experience some pain, and then we experience more pain from thinking about our pain. Sometimes our thoughts get so overwhelming that our original pain has subsided, but our thoughts are still piercing us, one arrow after the next. You may have seen this with a young kid who falls and scrapes their knee or something. Often, if you simply watch without interacting, the kid will get up and be on their way. But if a parent freaks out—"Oh my god! Are you okay?"—then the kid, seeing their parent's reaction, immediately gets pierced by the second arrow. The pain gets extended by this stream of thoughts. We adults are not much different.

Sometimes, the mere anticipation of pain, the mere thought of it, is enough to make us suffer. I see this all the time with the cold—one of my greatest teachers. When I turn the shower to the coldest setting in the morning (a mental practice I do, which is also showing some promising benefits for physical health),[78] I often immediately contract, even though the cold water hasn't hit my skin. When I can drop the story, though, and enter into beginner's mind, it is much easier to be with the changing sensations we call "cold." Just consider kids' relationship with the cold versus us adults. Adults have created an incredibly strong conviction, a story, around the cold. We closed ourselves off to it long ago. Some of us wake up and see the snow outside and we're immediately struck by arrows, even though we're still in our warm bed. My kids, on the other hand, go out into the snow in their undies without the slightest bother. They remain open and receptive to what is here, not collapsed into their thoughts about it.

Now, of course, the cold is unpleasant. We don't need to deny that. The Buddha himself said that a wise person will still experience the first arrow—pain is just a part of the deal when you have a human body. But he adds:

> When a wise person experiences a painful bodily feeling, they don't worry, agonize, and feel distraught. They feel physical pain but not mental pain. It's as if this person were pierced by an arrow, but a second arrow didn't follow it, so they only experience the pain of a single arrow.[79]

In other words, the wise person stays mindful. They experience the pain clearly, seeing it as an impermanent and ever-changing pattern of energy in the body, recognizing the arising and fading of the unpleasant feeling tones. But they don't collapse into stories about the pain, perpetuating and magnifying it. They don't make it personal. So, the difference is in how we respond to pain, not in whether we can make the pain go away. Again, by the Buddha:

> Having been touched by the painful feeling [of the first arrow], an ordinary person resists and resents it. They harbor aversion to it, and this underlying tendency of resistance and resentment toward that painful feeling comes to obsess the mind.[80]

You'll have to explore this in yourself, of course, but from my own

89

experience, it is no doubt the resistance I have toward pain that leads to true agony. On the other hand, when I am able to open to the pain, to feel into its fluid and ever-changing nature, and then meet it with love, kindness, and tenderness, it's much easier to remain at ease. There's a spaciousness and a support that makes the pain more bearable.

It's important to remember, however, that there is often a message contained in our pain which requires us to respond—to go to the doctor, to remove ourselves from a situation, to take appropriate medicine, etc. When we're bit by a poisonous snake, we don't just sit there noting, "pain...pain... pain." No, we take the steps necessary to keep ourselves healthy. Joseph Goldstein captures this in his book The Experience of Insight, where he says that elephants would often be walking down the road as he and his fellow meditators, in India, were going to town. "When we saw the elephant coming down the road we did not just stand there saying 'seeing, seeing,' we moved out of the way. Use the thought process when appropriate."[81]

At other times, however, when we experience pain, there isn't any action we need to take. It is common among meditators to experience what is called "dharma pain." Dharma pain comes to us when we start to sit still with ourselves and open to our bodies. Each of us, over the years, carry habitual tensions in certain parts of our bodies—our jaws, back, shoulders, fists, forehead, etc.—from all the many stresses and traumas we have faced. We create energetic knots that need to be untied. So, with this kind of pain, we simply need to learn to open to them, to accept them, to relax into them.

For some people, it takes years for these knots to unwind. And that's okay. The more we practice, the lighter our bodies will become. Now, of course, this isn't a perfect upward trajectory. And there is no guarantee, especially as we age, that our pain will unwind. But the equanimity we build in our mindfulness practice allows us to be with our pain with a bit more patience and ease. We learn to not contract around the pain.

So, how do we know if it's dharma pain? Well, to know whether we are experiencing dharma pain or a pain we need to respond to, we can often just get up and move around. If the pain subsides, it's probably dharma pain. If it lingers, we need to readjust our posture, take a break, walk around, or maybe even see a doctor if necessary.

Another form of dukkha to explore is our emotional trauma. Unacknowledged and unhealed traumas from our lived experiences of abuse, abandonment, or neglect, or even from our own mistakes, become powerful forces in our lives—habitual energies that repeat themselves. Very often, these harmful habits, or energetic imprints, show up in our relationships. It's especially important, then, to look out for this form of dukkha in our lives so that these habits don't hinder us from connecting with our loved ones, as well as ourselves. Very often, this will require the help of a spiritual teacher or licensed therapist since many of these habits are so deeply entwined in our being that we may not be aware of the full impact they have on us. In any case, as we open to this kind of dukkha in our lives, it is extremely important in the healing process to cultivate compassion, patience, and respect for ourselves. It's important that we allow ourselves to be human, to be imperfect and vulnerable and afraid, without judgment... even of our self-judgments. It's important we learn to hold ourselves with loving awareness.

Unfortunately, this is not a norm we have established in many of the world's cultures. In the West, for example, particularly in the U.S., we are taught to repress our emotions and vulnerabilities. We are taught that we are weak or even sinful for having them. So, we beat them into submission. We build up our inner critic, that nasty voice in our mind that tells us we are not good enough or worthy enough, that voice that shames us or denies parts of ourselves. It is this same voice that can keep us addicted to drugs or alcohol or sex and that also projects itself onto others, seeing only the bad and ugly in everyone and everything.

Sadly, this attitude stems largely from many of our spiritual traditions, which believe the physical human form itself is evil or sinful. To take an example, the protestant reformer John Calvin said:

> For our nature is not only utterly devoid
> of goodness, but so prolific in all kinds
> of evil, that it can never be idle ... The
> whole man, from the crown of the head
> to the sole of the foot, is so deluged, as it
> were, that no part remains exempt from
> sin, and, therefore, everything which pro-
> ceeds from him is imputed as sin.[82]

Protestants and Evangelists have carried some version of this for centuries now, heavily impacting U.S. culture. Catholics too have their own version of "Original Sin," which has impacted the rest of the West. And even my parents' faith, the Mormon Church, holds a similar disdain for what they call "the natural man."

In 1989, at one of the first international Buddhist teacher conferences, the Western teachers brought up the pervasive problem of shame, unworthiness, and self-criticism that they were seeing not only in their students but in themselves as well. The Dalai Lama and other Asian teachers didn't understand. It took the Dalai Lama ten minutes of talking with his translator to even comprehend the concept. Then he turned and asked how many teachers experienced this in themselves and in their students. Essentially all of them said they had. Genuinely shocked, the Dalai Lama replied, "But that's a mistake. Every being is precious!"[83]

In Buddhism, there is no equivalent concept of sin. As you'll discover shortly, when we move into the second noble truth, Buddhism teaches that we suffer not because we have sinned but because we remain asleep to our selfless, interconnected nature. There is no blame put on us. The idea of blame is totally incoherent against the truth of emptiness. Agency, or freewill (the notion that we could have done otherwise), no longer has a place. The mind, the body, the world, each abide by natural laws. This does not make the world devoid of meaning. Nor does it relieve us of responsibility. In fact, quite the opposite.

When we witness that we are not-two, when we see both our empty, selfless, interconnected nature, as well as our personal, immanent, felt experience, then love and compassion are the natural responses. Meaning comes into the world not through the plan of some omnipotent male creator but through each of us—how we understand ourselves, the world, and our place in it. As I said at the beginning, everything unfolds from understanding. Understanding is the cause and condition for love and compassion to arise.

When we see ourselves in everyone and everyone in us, all held together and composed of the same tapestry, we naturally begin to approach our difficulties with a tenderness and openness of heart. This is how healing takes place, by understanding, not by controlling, suppressing, or manhandling our shadows, wounds, and vulnerabilities. The more awareness we bring to ourselves and our connection to the earth and all its creatures, the more love and compassion will arise. Mindfulness, then, is essential to the healing process since it is mindfulness that leads to love and wisdom.

Let me note, however, that in the early stages of our practice, it may seem like suffering increases or is intensified. But this is because we no longer hide from our shadows, we no longer try to push away the unpleasant dimensions of our experience. Again, sadly, this approach stands in stark contrast to our culture's typical strategy of avoidance and distraction. Just consider how many of us find it damned-near impossible to sit still with ourselves. The moment we are forced to wait in line, stop at a traffic light, or pause even for a second, we reach into our pocket and start scrolling through social media, checking our email, or whatever else people do on their phones. We constantly distract ourselves with food, music, shows, movies, drugs, alcohol, endless activity, and even pointless conversation. And we do all of this simply because we can't be with ourselves. We are too afraid to look under the bed because we think that's where the boogeyman lives. But really, what are we so afraid of? What is it we think we'll find when all the distractions are stripped away? Boredom? Remorse? Fear? Death? Emptiness? What?

Avoidance and distraction simply don't lead to a life of peace, meaning, and freedom. Avoidance and distraction are counter to wisdom. Wisdom, remember, is the project of aligning ourselves with truth, with reality, with nature. And the truth is, life is full. Pain, suffering, grief, and sorrow are all a part of it. "Your joy is your sorrow unmasked. And the selfsame well from which your laughter rises was oftentimes filled with your tears."[84] So, if you are hoping to find a spiritual practice that skips over your wounds and difficulties, good luck. But you'll find no quick fix here, no pill to swallow that will remove all your suffering.

Again, a genuine spiritual path does not avoid difficulties or mistakes but holds them with the transformative power of heart. When we set out to love, to awaken, to become free, we are inevitably confronted with our own human limitations. The Tibetan master Lama Trungpa Rinpoche, who suffered from alcohol addiction, said that spiritual progress from the ego's point of view is "one insult after another." If we frame this instead as "one mistake after another," we can view spiritual practice as one opportunity after the next to show humility, learn, and grow. To live life, to be human, is to be imperfect. When we really understand this, we can be more forgiving to ourselves, allowing a sense of ease to settle in. We can learn to be patient with and laugh at ourselves, to not take ourselves so seriously, and to provide the grace for others to be human as well.

The Cause of Suffering

Once we start opening to dukkha, we begin to see that it, like everything else, is brought about by causes and conditions, which brings us to the Second Noble Truth—grasping is the cause of dukkha. The Pali word for grasping is tanhā, which is more directly translated as "thirst," but can also be thought of as desire, craving, longing, or identification.

No matter how you'd like to think about it with concepts, tanhā happens when we lose sight of the selfless, ever-changing, inter-connected nature of experience. Now, if you've ever practiced meditation, you'd know how often this happens, even over the duration of a few breaths. Suddenly, we find ourselves behind our face, looking down at the breath or out at the world of seemingly concrete things, grasping at or hooked onto an object of experience, identified with some thought or emotion. Awareness collapses into its objects, and so we lose sight that it is—that we are—entirely whole, without border, shape, or boundary.

This grasping is like reaching your hand into a river and trying to grab onto it. We try to grasp onto our youth. We try to grasp onto our health. We try to grasp onto our life. We identify with our body and senses, with our beliefs and worldviews, with our likes and dislikes, with our prejudices and biases. We hold onto our grief, pain, and sorrow. We cling to lust, cling to anger, cling to material possessions. We get snagged by our comforts and expectations. But if we try to hold onto something that by its very nature changes, we will inevitably suffer.

So, rather than clench our fist, holding tightly to the world of ostensible things, rather than stand in opposition to the way the world is, we can instead hold everything with an open hand. We can let the bird land on our palm and stay as long as it likes, while we take a loving interest in it. We all know what this feels like, when everything is running along smoothly, without effort. We may be lost in our art or work, we might be playing sports, or listening to music. There's no grasping at or controlling experience. There's no bumps or agitations. There's no struggle at all. Everything is simply unfolding on its own. We're in a natural flow.

If you open awareness to the breath right now, you can see this—breathing is happening all on its own. There's no need to control it. There's no need to make it a certain way. You can simply receive it. The same is true for sounds... and sensations... and feelings... and emotions... and even thoughts, which include our volitions and intentions. Pay close attention, and you will see that you are not the author of your experience. Everything is simply arising and being known all on its own and in its own place. You aren't producing any of this, and you're not producing your awareness of it either.

Now, to get a taste of dukkha, notice what it's like when you try to focus on the breath. Notice how this efforting arises from time to time as you try to remain mindful. Notice how you lose the flow. Everything becomes bumpy, scruffy, jagged. It's like you are leaning into the next breath, trying to capture it, instead of being settled back and simply receiving it. The energy is frenetic. It's tight, closed, contracted. The little thinker in our heads, the meditator, feels like it has to do something in order to be aware of the breath. It feels like it has to work so hard to live this life. This subtle contraction around the breath is dukkha.

Again, if you pay close attention to your moment-to-moment experience, you will see that you are not the author of your experience. Everything is arising and being known all on its own and in its own place. You aren't producing any of your senses, thoughts, feelings, or emotions, and you aren't producing your awareness of them either.

So, rather than thinking about the cause of dukkha as grasping, we can also think about it in terms of delusion, since it is only when we are deluded, when we are not seeing with wisdom, that we mistakenly identify ourselves with objects of mind. We mistake ourselves, or some part of ourselves, as the flame, forgetting that we are the Everlasting Fire.

To see this mistaken identification, in Buddhist training, as well as in wisdom traditions like Advaita, we intentionally and continually put our identity under scrutiny, discovering a closet full of many masks we put on, until finally they dissipate through the gradual and systematic training of mindfulness. We also see this in the contemplative traditions of Christianity with monks like Thomas Merton, who said:

> Learning to be oneself means learning to die in order to live. It means discovering in the ground of one's being a 'self' which is ultimate and indestructible, which not only survives the destruction of all other more superficial selves but finds its identity affirmed and clarified by their destruction.[85]

Now, of course, as both Buddhist and Western psychology recognize, it is natural to develop a sense of self, and even important to develop a healthy one. We need it to maintain self-integrity, to hold and defend certain values, and to have aims and aspirations. Our identity, which is closely connected to our motivations, allows us to coherently organize our minds. Without an identity, it would be impossible to know what to think, what to value, or what to do in any situation. We would be chaotic, unpredictable, and destructive. To have any purpose or meaning, to live an intentional life, we must know who we are and what we are in service to.

What's interesting, though, is that none of us have a single identity. Like I said, we put on many masks—employer, employee, parent, child, sibling, friend, spouse, lover, teacher, student, athlete, meditator, citizen, artist, musician, Democrat or Republican, patient, customer, neighbor, philosopher, Buddhist, spiritual practitioner, etc. And we shift back and forth among these masks depending on the circumstances. To live healthy, happy lives, we need to be able to wear each of these masks with full awareness and compassion. Where we run into trouble, though, is when we cling to any one of them, when we are not able to let them go. The boss needs to drop her role as boss when she is with her friends. The teacher needs to drop his role when he is with his husband and kids, who need a spouse and dad, not a teacher. And so on. We can be free only if we can remember who we truly are underneath all these temporary roles, which is entirely open and free. As the Buddha reminded us, make sure to always keep one hand in reality.

Another aspect of our experience in which we cling to or identify with is our shadow parts—fearful parts, lustful parts, ashamed parts, judging parts, critical parts, doubting parts, angry parts, cruel parts, perverted parts, etc. What is so difficult about these parts is that they are so entangled in our being that we don't realize how identified with them we really are and, therefore, how much they control our lives. So, the first step or challenge is to simply name them when they arise. We need to bring them to our mindful, equanimous attention.

When anger arises, for example, we simply note, "This is a mind filled with anger." Note how it feels narrow, tense, and closed off, like a clenched fist. Note how thoughts continue to feed it, how they play with and shape the emotion. Note all the unpleasant feeling tones that arise and fade. And note too the pleasant feelings, if any, like the pleasant feelings associated with thoughts of justice, redemption, or revenge. Simply watch all this with our loving attention until it fades away. In this spacious, non-reactive, and fully awake space of awareness, understanding grows naturally. As we become more familiar with each part, we can notice what brings it about and how to respond to it more skillfully, ultimately unlocking and freeing the valuable energy that is bound up in it.

This has been practiced across cultures since ancient times. Shamans learned that when we name our difficult parts, when we name what we fear, we can begin to work skillfully with them. The Sufis call these parts Nafs. The Christian Desert Fathers of ancient Egypt and Syria called them demons. In Buddhism, these inner forces are traditionally personified as Mara, the god of delusion, and are also called the hindrances—desire, aversion, restlessness, lethargy, and doubt. In some Hindu traditions, the ego is viewed as working for the god Maya, whose goal is to keep us chasing material things and sensual pleasures. She is considered a temptress like the Christian Satan, who keeps us attached to the external world of illusion.

Today, however, Richard Schwartz's Internal Family Systems[86] has become a popular and skillful model for working with the various pieces of ourselves. IFS thinks of each human as a family composed of many different parts or members, each of whom are trying their best to protect us. So, rather than think of them as bad or evil, we simply need to bring all the hurt, scared, ashamed, embarrassed, and angry members out of isolation. We need to let them know that we—loving awareness—are here for them, that we see and support them. We need to thank them for working so hard to protect us, no matter how misguided their efforts may have been. And as we gain their trust, we need to let them know that they can let go of the heavy burdens they carry—the emotions, memories, and responsibilities created from past traumas. We need to let them know that we, loving awareness, are okay.

There are many different protectors, each shaped by our trials and traumas. Some are constantly on guard, keeping watch for danger, to the point of exhaustion. Some make us believe we have to work tirelessly to avoid losing our money, car, and home. Some puff up their chest, act hard, and are easily angered because they don't want us to appear weak and vulnerable. Some make us take downers like alcohol and narcotics or cause us to dissociate to make sure we don't feel physical and/or emotional pain. Some ruthlessly criticize us and push us to perfection because they want us to be worthy or admired. Some make us think that, to be beautiful, we need to be skinny, so they cause us to binge or starve ourselves. Some parts make us repress and hide any flaws because our families believe they need to present the perfect image to the outside world. This one is a huge in Abrahamic and Hindu cultures, and even in Hollywood and the Woke Left culture. Another common part of us that often stems from the world's religions is the part that shames us for our sexuality, in all its forms. It constantly reminds us that we need to stay clean, pure, virtuous, or else we will not be worthy of god's love.

If you have any of these protectors from past traumas, I highly encourage you to work with a licensed psychotherapist who is familiar with IFS. And if you prefer to explore these parts on your own, I suggest you read two of Schwartz's books—Introduction to Internal Family Systems and No Bad Parts: Healing Trauma and Restoring Wholeness with Internal Family Systems Model. I also highly recommend the psychotherapist and meditation teacher Loch Kelly's meditation app Glimpses. But in the meantime, just see if you can start to note the different pieces of yourself as they arise. How are they trying to serve you? Why do they feel they have to protect you? What do they fear would happen if they didn't? Recognize your own non-dual nature—the limitless love that you are—and, from here, hold these precious pieces of yourself as you tell them they will always have your unconditional support. Your true nature is always okay—it is unborn, undying, untainted, undisturbed, entirely at peace.

Okay, well, another way to think about the cause of dukkha is in terms of desire. This translation, however, can be a bit tricky. In English, we sometimes use the word "desire" to simply state our intention to do something (e.g., I desire to study astronomy in college), which is not tanha or grasping. Desire in this way is not the root of suffering. In fact, it's necessary. We need desires to move us through the world. We need desires to live and learn and grow. You wouldn't be reading this now if you didn't have some desire to do so. "Desire" in a Buddhist context is narrower. We must look deeper into the desire to see if it is rooted in greed, hatred, or delusion or whether it is rooted in generosity, loving-kindness, and wisdom.

Now, this too can create some confusion, so let me take a quick detour and briefly share some relevant aspects of the Buddha's own journey. As a young prince, Siddhartha Gautama (the pre-enlightened Buddha) enjoyed all the worldly pleasures of a prince. But after encountering sickness, aging, and death one day in the streets of his kingdom, Siddhartha realized that worldly pleasures were unstable and unsatisfying, and so he left home in search of the end of suffering. For years, he studied with the ascetics, who believed they must renounce everything to become enlightened. Eventually, though, after having grown weak and fallen ill, Siddhartha realized that this was not the way. So finally, he came upon what he called "the middle way"—avoiding the extremes of indulgence and asceticism.

I share this story to make the point that it is okay to eat and enjoy a piece of cake. It is not selfish to do so. There is a middle way between self-indulgence and self-mortification. So, when I say we need to look deeper into our desire to see if it is rooted in greed, hatred, or delusion, I am not suggesting that every act we do for ourselves is selfish. Remember, equanimity harmonizes the self with other. So, a useful reframe here, which comes from Goldstein, is to look at our desires in terms of addiction. Which desires can we simply enjoy in the moment, without grasping at them? And which desires imprison and compel us?[87]

To explore where desire shows up in your own life, the Buddha created three useful categories to explore: (1) the desire for sense pleasures, (2) the desire for existence or becoming, and (3) the desire for non-existence or non-becoming. Let's look at each of these in turn.

With the desire for sense pleasure, it's important to first note that, in the Buddhist frame, the mind is considered the sixth sense. So, all mind-states and emotions are included here as objects of our desire—rapture, excitement, concentration, calm, thinking, daydreaming, fantasizing, planning, etc. Now, if you take a moment to think about where you find gratification in your life and in the world, I bet you will discover that most of your time and effort is spent seeking gratification here, in the realm of sense pleasure. This is certainly true of most people. It's been the standard operating procedure for some time now. We constantly try to fulfill ourselves through sex, food, movies, shows, music, esteem, drugs, and even 'peak' spiritual experiences. Many people go their whole lives seeking one hit of pleasure after the next, and then they die. This road has been tried and tried with little success, yet where do so many of us continue to seek our own gratification?

I'm certainly not immune from this. This is largely because we have been given no alternative. The Buddha himself said that, even if we see the drawbacks of chasing sense pleasures—their fleeting and, thus, ultimately unreliable and unsatisfactory nature—the mind will still chase them if it is not given an alternative. So, what is the alternative?

As our mindfulness grows with practice, as we get better at watching desires arise and fade without reacting to them, it is important that we pay close attention to the quality of mind as the desire subsides. What is this transition like? Does it feel as if you have been let out of the grip of something? Does the fiery, frenetic energy of desire turn into a soft, open, easefulness? Again, see for yourself, of course, but I bet the more you pay attention to this transition, the more naturally you will move toward the peace of renunciation, a mind without clinging.

Now, you may hear this and think, "No thanks! Renunciation does not sound peaceful. It sounds terrible. It reminds me of things like repression, lack, deprivation, and scarcity." I hear you. Many of us, especially in the West, naturally meet it with resistance. But again, what we're really trying to capture is living without addiction. The Buddha called the blessing of renunciation a cleansing of the mind. It's like going to rehab or fasting to clear the body of toxins and contaminants. Renunciation brings a purity, clarity, simplicity, and contentment to the mind. It releases all the noise and clutter, the constant nagging of desire and lack in our everyday life.

What sense desires do you find yourself chasing in your daily life? And how hard, I wonder, would it be to let each of them go? To widen your lens, let me throw a few out there for you to consider. In addition to habits around food, sex, masturbation, alcohol, drugs, movies, and music, also consider your habitual desires around comfort, work, wealth, power, cleanliness, and control. What about your phone, email, and social media? Can you put those down? What about the desire to please everyone all the time or to be the peacemaker? What about moods, mind-states, or emotions? Are you addicted to calm, excitement, rapture, or even to fear, the thrill of watching a scary movie or going to a haunted house? Are you addicted to your meditation being a certain way? Do you get grumpy if it's interrupted or if you're not able to fit it into your schedule? Can you renounce proliferating thoughts, particularly thoughts of I, me, or mine, and instead come back to the simplicity of the moment—to the interconnected and ever-changing field of sounds, sensations, perceptions, feelings, thoughts, and emotions? Also consider if you're addicted to wanting itself. Do you find yourself scrolling through Amazon or Etsy, or walking through Target, though there's nothing you need? You're not alone. We all find enjoyment in wanting. The wanting is what gives us a hit of dopamine.

Again, look at your habitual patterns for the day—your email, social media, phone, coffee, and emotional habits—and see what it would take to change those habits. You might be surprised at how hard it is to skip your hot shower, say, or your morning coffee. But go ahead and practice letting it go. See if it opens some space in the mind. As Goldstein says, renunciation aerates our lives and our habits. It allows for the biodegradation of those habits that no longer serve us, clears the space, and provides the energy necessary for new growth.[88]

The wisdom of "no" that we explored in Chapter 4 is also applicable here. When we say no from a place of love and wisdom, we're not being oppressive or avoidant. We're not pushing things away or denying their presence. We're not casting judgments or having aversion to what's arising. With the wisdom of no, we are discerning skillfully, with clear comprehension, what leads onward to peace and what leads to suffering. We turn away from those things that add to suffering, not out of hate but out of love. It's like saying "no" to our kid who is about to do something harmful. It's a "no" of care and concern. Again, as Goldstein reminds us, each of us at times needs to be a parent to our inner two-year-old.[89]

Let's move on now to the desire for existence or becoming. This dimension of craving is a strong one in the West. There is so much pressure in our culture to become someone, to do something great and meaningful with our lives. It's as if our worth is entirely dependent on what we produce, on who we become, on what titles we acquire, on what job we get, on what car or house we buy.

It's always go, go, go, do, do, do. And so, we often get stuck in the planning mind, where we obsessively plan and try to control and map out everything. We obsess over future versions of ourselves, we obsess over our projects, and so we are never really able to arrive here, in the moment. It's as if we are always leaning into the next moment, the next experience, the next feat, the next thing.

Goldstein calls this "the in-order-to mind." We are with this moment in order to get to the next. I'm going to school in order to get a well-paying job. I'm at this job in order to get a nicer car and home. I'm going to church or following these rules in order to get into heaven. You can also think of it as the if-then mind. If only I had this much money, then I'd happy. If only I had a better body, then I'd be satisfied. If only x, y, or z, then I'll be complete. Can you see how this is a problem? We can't hang our happiness out in front of us, always just out of reach, like a carrot tied to a bunny.

On the other side of the desire for existence, we also experience the desire for non-existence, which can be thought of as aversion—a pushing away from something or wishing that it would go away, that it would not be. We see this, for example, when we experience certain moods and emotions like loneliness or depression—e.g., life is so lonely, I don't want to be alive. But what is important to note here is that this kind of desire is still rooted in the sense of self. The ego builds itself up by identifying with or attaching to the unpleasant. Look closer, though, and explore who or what is experiencing these unpleasant feelings. Is there someone on the other side of these fleeting sensations and feelings? Who or what is it that doesn't want to exist? Now, of course, it's important to tenderly and affectionately acknowledge painful feelings and emotions. We need to take care of our precious human hearts. With grief, for example, when we lose someone dear to us, it's as if we have lost a large piece of ourselves. And often, we don't want to let go of the grief since it is, in some sense, all that remains of that person. So, we cling desperately to it. It's a constant battle, drowning in the grief at times, coming up for a moment of air, and then sinking right back down. In times like these, the best we can do is be patient with ourselves.

To finish the chapter, I just want to say that we are alive at a crucial moment in history. We, as an entire culture, seem to be united in grief. With our technological power, nuclear weapons, artificial intelligence, biotechnology, rapid spread of misinformation, as well as the population explosion, climate change, and the rapid decline of forests and biodiversity, the need for a critical mass of Self-awareness has never been so urgent. The Earth herself is hurting. And though she continues to give us signs that she is not happy or healthy, many of us are too disconnected to hear her, to feel her viscerally, even though we may have some vague feeling that something is wrong. It's time we start to listen. And that begins by listening to our Self, discovering within ourselves our interconnected and interdependent nature.

Exercises & Reflections

As you go about your week, I invite you to track your desires in a journal. And in particular, try to notice how much of your time and attention is oriented around sensual desires. When a desire arises, don't hide or distract yourself from it, but rather really bore into it—examine the raw experience of it. Explore every inch of it with compassion and interest, with a real eagerness to understand it. And if you're able to observe a desire without reacting to it, pay careful attention to that moment when the desire subsides? What is that moment like? Write about this experience in your journal.

And if you do end up getting pulled in by an unskillful desire or end up acting on one, no worries. There's no need to judge yourself. Remember, judgment is just another thought. Instead, open awareness again to the present moment's experience, try to note how your mind and body feel, apologize if necessary, and consider whether the desire delivered on its promise. Again, write about this experience in your journal.

Remember, what we are really seeking to cultivate here is wisdom—we want to know from our own direct investigation what leads onward to peace, happiness, and freedom, and what does not.

6. WORLDVIEW

"Believe your life is worth living and
your belief will help create the fact."
– Henry David Thoreau

Recently, as my family and I hiked through a dense aspen grove in the Wasatch Range, one of my kids said, "Aspens are such great teachers of Love. They remind us that we are all one."

"Yeah!" one of their siblings quickly chimed in, "Even though we appear separate, like each of these trees, at our root, we are all connected."

The kids are right. There really is no teacher like nature. I've hiked over a thousand miles along this mountain range, and it continues to share its wisdom with me—the composure and resilience of the mountains, the cyclical nature of the seasons, the delicate harmony and necessity of biodiversity. But perhaps the most apparent lesson is this lesson of the interconnected nature of all things.

When we get away from the concrete jungle, get away from the straight lines and boxes that surround us in the city—our box houses, box offices, box beds, box cars, box ovens, box microwaves, box fridges, and box thinking—and instead surround ourselves with nature, something profound begins to happen. Our entire being begins to open. We start to feel vast and connected. The wind murmuring through trees, the water racing down rocks, the sway of bough and leaves—loosen up the straight lines and boxes that imprison our minds. There is an organic flow to experience, rather than a rigidity or stiffness. Our senses come alive. We smell the dirt, herbs, and fresh air. We sense the sun on our face. We feel the textures of grass, shrub, and bark on our arms and legs. We come into our body and feel its relationship with the earth as we traverse the uneven ground at our feet.

But in the city, we lose touch of all this. We keep our bodies comfortable with our chairs, couches, and cushions. We walk on flat floors. We control the temperature of our air and water. We drive in our box cars, take our box elevators, and wait for Amazon to deliver our things...in boxes. We wander the digital space on our box phones and box televisions for hours on end. The hard truth is, we spend most of our time in self-created boxes. We are tragically disconnected from our bodies, senses, and the earth.

We live almost entirely in our heads, identified with the thinker—that faculty which takes the seamless, interconnected whole of existence and dices it into pieces, into subject and objects, putting our self on one side and everything else on the other, seeing objects in terms of what they can do for us. And before we know it, without meta-awareness and critical pressure, we take this ego, the thinker, to be who we are. It's no wonder we have a spiritual urgency in our culture. Too many of us feel cut off from our roots, from nature, god, awareness. Too many of us feel isolated and alone.

To heal the isolation and loneliness, to bring a deep and meaningful connection back into our lives, I believe it's important we challenge openly and critically the way we view ourselves, the world, and our place in it. We must look at ourselves both intellectually and experientially, with reason and mindfulness, with humility and courage. Are you really apart from me? Are we not-two? Again, when you really feel into and examine yourself, I think you'll discover that the ultimate and relational reality are each two sides of the same coin, that nothing is isolated or cut off from the rest of existence, that everything inter-is. Everything, each of us, has loving awareness at our backs.

The Possibility of Wellbeing

To help open us further to this understanding, to help us embody our non-dual nature, in this chapter I'd like to explore the rest of the Buddha's Four Noble Truths. Once we see that grasping, delusion, and misidentification lead to disconnection, dis-ease, and unnecessary suffering in our lives, we can see that a life of peace, harmony, and connection is possible. This is the Buddha's Third Noble Truth.

Of course, for a philosophy to be any good, for it to be meaningful or useful, it needs more than words. The words must be made flesh. They must be embodied, felt, and experienced. Wisdom is lived. This is what sets the Buddha apart from so many philosophers. Rather than talk the talk, he walked the walk. Examining the cause of dukkha and the various ways

104

it presents itself in our lives, the Buddha created and fine-tuned a toolkit to move us away from disharmony and discontent. He created a map that navigates us wisely through our lives. That brings us to the Fourth Noble Truth—there is a path that leads away from suffering, namely, the Noble Eightfold Path.

Now, before we explore the Eightfold Path, let me quickly hover over the word "path" since it can be a bit misleading. "Path" makes the Eightfold Path seem linear, which it isn't. On this path, there is no beginning or end. Instead, each of the eight "folds" work in conjunction with and support all the rest. So, it might be more helpful to think of the Eightfold Path as a wheel that carries us smoothly through all the terrains of life, with each fold considered as a spoke on that wheel.[90]

Or if you find it more useful, you can think of the Eightfold Path as a training program that is broken into three arenas. The first arena is a training in wisdom, which includes workouts that shape our thoughts, intentions, and worldview. In the second arena of training, we train ourselves in virtue, we sculpt our words, and actions. The third and final arena of training is a training of the mind, which includes workouts that sharpen our cognitive faculties—our focus, mindfulness, and viriya (a Pali word that has no great translation in English, but can be thought of as energy, courage, strength, and perseverance of heart and mind).

In this Chapter, however, we will focus only on the first arena of training, training in wisdom. Everything, as I've said, unfolds from understanding. How we view ourselves and our relation to the world determines everything we do. Everything! Every bit of information we take in is processed through this lens. If someone views himself as a separate entity, disconnected from the world, then his intentions, motivations, behaviors, and even his felt experience will take very different shape from someone who views herself as inextricably linked to, entirely at one with, the world.

To narrow our exploration even further in this chapter, I'd like to focus on three important dimensions of our worldview. First, we will explore the law of cause and effect or the law of inter-relation, which will hopefully expand the boundary of what we take to be our "self." Second, I'd like to explore the role of perception in forming our worldview, which is an element of experience we often cling to or too easily identify with. My hope here is that our exploration of perception will help to loosen this stronghold of self, ultimately bringing much more space to experience, connecting you to your unbound nature. And finally, I'd like to explore the role thoughts have on our worldview—i.e., on our operating system—and, therefore, why it is so important that we not only guard them with mindfulness but that we systematically train our thoughts.

Cause & Effect or Inter-Relation

To start, let me just emphasize once again that we humans need a worldview to move anywhere or do anything at all. The way we understand ourselves and our relation to the world acts as our operating system. It is what navigates us through the terrains of existence. It is what moves our lips and our limbs. It is what filters not only our external inputs but our internal inputs as well, that is, our innate desires and impulses. It is our worldview that shapes our entire lives, it is what shapes our entire experience. Therefore, it is central to our spiritual journey.

And at the core of any operating system, as any software or computer engineer knows, is the law of cause and effect, or karma. In our inter-related world, it's important we understand that what we say and do has consequences in space and time. What we do over here affects them over there. And what they do over there affects us over here. We can see the law of cause and effect everywhere—in accounting, biology, epidemiology, physics, chemistry, climatology, economics, sports, art, music, and in our own personal relationships. As Newton said, for every action there is an equal and opposite reaction. The first law of thermodynamics expresses this truth as the conservation of energy—energy can neither be added to nor destroyed, but only transformed.

This knowledge isn't new. The Buddha and many others understood this long ago. The Buddha, however, emphasized that not only do our actions have consequences out in the world but that they have consequences on our *own* hearts and minds. More specifically, he highlighted that the seeds of these internal consequences lie in the motivation of each action. When our intentions are motivated out of generosity, loving-kindness, and wisdom, the karmic fruit is sweet—our hearts and minds feel inner peace, love, joy, and connection. And on the other hand, when our intentions are motivated by greed, hatred, and delusion, our karmic fruit is sour and bitter—our hearts and minds feel discontented, dis-eased, and disconnected.

Again, see for yourself, but the more you see in your direct experience that your inner fruits stem from your motivational seeds, the more this karmic framework will become a part of your worldview. And so, hopefully, more of your actions will stem from motivations of goodwill. This, of course, is a practice that lasts a lifetime. But it's important to remember that each step brings peace, love, and joy.

There's another advantage here. Bringing this understanding into our moment-to-moment experience will also begin to open us to the ultimate reality. The more we can see this causal chain play out in our lives, the more our ostensibly perceived dividing lines will disappear. Our eye of wisdom will continue to open its perspective until, finally, it becomes all-encompassing. At this point, we will see beyond ourselves, beyond the chain of karma, beyond the relative world, beyond the world of concepts. We will penetrate the ultimate nature of reality itself. Here, there exists only a seamless and interconnected whole, a constant stream of changing energy in which there is no-thing that can reliably be called "self," "me," "I," or "mine." Here, the world is—*you* are—without beginning or end, unborn and unformed. Here, we come home to our divine, unborn, and undying nature. Here, we reach what has been described as the highest peace—nibbana (nirvana in Sanskrit).

When we finally get our first glimpse of this, we see that the world of things is just an appearance, a chimera that arises when attention collapses into thought. We realize that we are not behind our face somewhere. We dissolve the duality of subject and objects. We witness directly this centerless, open space of awareness.

Now, of course, it takes time to open our eye of wisdom since we have been so deeply conditioned to orient from our small sense of self. So, don't be discouraged if this direct insight doesn't stick around for long at the early stages of your practice. We will likely collapse back into our small sense of self quickly and often. And you can be sure that this will continue to happen for the rest of your life. But the good news at this point is that we can now make non-dual awareness our practice. We can experientially merge our relative lens with our ultimate lens. We can put on our bifocals of being-ness and emptiness, of love and wisdom.

And to be clear, I don't mean we go chasing after the euphoric feeling of oneness that often arises when we first penetrate the clouds of papañca. This is a common trap for meditators, which can last many years if we're not careful. Spiritual practice, again, is not about gaining anything. It's about letting go. Rather, what I mean is that, in our practice and in our lives, we try to orient from this centerless, open awareness instead of occupying the thinker. It's like ringing a bell. We ring it, and when the sound disappears (when we fall back into our dualistic view), we ring it again. And we do this over and over again to stabilize our new non-dual view.

The Buddha invites us to ground ourselves in this worldview—that we are not-two—and to live from this direct understanding of interbeing and emptiness. This is seeing and living with wisdom. And it is this—the eye of wisdom—that leads to the liberation of suffering. It is this that allows us to become living expressions of love, joy, compassion, and peace. It is this eye of wisdom that intimately shapes the relationships we have with ourselves, others, and the world. As the eighth century monk Padmasambhava said, though my view is as vast as the sky, my attention to the law of karma is as fine as a single grain of barley flour.

If you are interested in peace and freedom, I invite you to start examining directly in your own life the internal and external consequences of the motivations and intentions for each of your actions and words. Witness them again and again, and see whether it becomes intuitive, like driving a car. I bet the more you witness directly that each of your words and actions have consequences, and that each of these words and actions are preceded by an intention and motivation, the more you will act naturally out of generosity, kindness, and wisdom, bringing more peace and harmony into Being.

Perception

When I was a kid, I used to lay on the bed with my siblings and look up at the plaster on the ceiling. We would see all kinds of shapes in the patterns—animals, faces, landscapes, monsters, all kinds of things. I'm sure you've done something like this—looked up at the clouds or stars, which told you endless stories.

This is our perception at work. The faculty of perception takes sensory data—in this case, light waves—and constructs them into distinct percepts. It organizes the data into like-patterns, creating a useful and coherent model for us to navigate the world. Without perception, we wouldn't be able to distinguish the world of things, let alone have thoughts about them.

The neurologist and physician Oliver Sacks tells a story of a patient whose vision he was able to restore, which really captures the point I'm trying to make here. Right after the procedure, Dr. Sacks asked the patient, "Well...what do you see?" The patient paused in confusion. As it turns out, the patient's visual field was restored but all he could see was a chaotic soup of shifting lights, colors, and shadows. He had not yet developed a perceptual visual map of the world.[91]

So, how do we accomplish this incredible feat of building perception? Like any knowledge-creating process, it happens through a continuous process of trial and the elimination of error. Our faculty of perception creates a collection of percepts, which are continuously refined by feedback from both genetic impulses and external sensory data. As Dr. Sacks says:

> "The rest of us, born sighted, can scarcely imagine such confusion. For we, born with a full complement of senses, and correlating these, one with the other, create a sight world from the start, a world of visual objects and concepts and meanings. When we open our eyes each morning, it is upon a world we have spent a lifetime learning to see. We are not given the world: we make our world through incessant experience, categorization, memory, reconnection. But when Virgil opened his eye, after being blind for forty-five years—having had little more than an infant's visual experience, and this long forgotten—there were no visual memories to support a perception, there was no world of experience and meaning awaiting him. He saw, but what he saw had no coherence. His retina and optic nerve were active, transmitting impulses, but his brain could make no sense of them; he was, as neurologists say, agnosic."[92]

What this story also highlights about perception is that each of us makes our own model of the world. Because our causes and conditions are unique to us, none of us share the same perceptual model of the world. Each of us is shaped by the family, community, and environment we were born into; the language, norms, laws, beliefs, and culture of our upbringing; the trends, styles, and preferences of our generation; the books we read and the movies we watch; the friend groups we hang out with; our prior experiences; our interests and impulses; our genetic makeup; and so on.[93]

There's a famous parable from India that captures this well. It is said that a king gathered up several blind people and presented an elephant to them. To one, the king presented the ear. To another, the tusk... another, the trunk... the leg... the tuft... and so on. Then, when asked what each had felt, each responded differently. The person who was presented the ear thought it was a large leaf. The other who was presented the tusk thought it was a plough. The trunk, a hose... the leg, a post... the tuft, the end of a broom... and so on. Comparing these limited views to the views of various brahmans and recluses, the Buddha said, "Even so, bhikkhus,[94] are those wanderers of various sects blind, unseeing... saying, 'Dhamma is like this!... Dhamma is like that!'... Some recluses and brahmans, so called, are deeply attached to their own views. People who only see one side of things engage in quarrels and disputes."[95]

To take this further, even our moment-to-moment perception can change on a dime, depending on the lens we are viewing it through. My partner recently shared a story with me that is applicable here. When she and her ex-husband were on their honeymoon in Europe, they stayed in a hotel that smelled terribly rotten. It bothered them immensely. After a couple days, though, when they were walking near their hotel, they saw a fromagerie, or cheese shop, connected to their hotel. From this point on, the smell no longer bothered them but, in fact, delighted them. To take another example, you may like eating one or two Oreos, but how would you enjoy your 15th or 100th Oreo? What about hearing a beautiful bird sing while hiking compared to hearing it all night long while you're trying to sleep?

Another thing to consider is the perception of other animals. Snakes, for example, experience the world of vision in infrared. Bats experience a visual representation of the world through sound waves, and dogs see, in some sense, with their olfactory system. Do we have the correct perception of the world, or do one of these other animals? As Oscar Wilde said, "Experience is the name everyone gives to their mistakes." Similar to our conceptual ideas, our perceptual experience is like a net we cast over an infinitely small portion of ultimate reality. We can never say, with perception, that we have come to the (capital T) Truth.

The Space of Possibility is open and unbounded. How much of the world can we keep opening to? How far can our creativity bring us? Just think, soon I imagine we'll be able to add attachments to our perception. We'll be able to upgrade our consciousness to see in infrared, say, or in ultra-violet. Or maybe we'll be able to experience the world through some yet-to-be-created perception! Again, the Space of Possibility is endless.

Now, although perception is entirely open, and although it is creative, and although we each wear our own particular lens, again, this does not deny us of objectivity. There are still objective relational laws that are born out of the undivided whole, out of inter-relations. Just consider a jigsaw puzzle. We can slice up a picture in an infinite number of ways. But no matter how we slice it up, we can't just place the pieces anywhere. There is still structure and order there. We need to see how each piece relates to the others and fits into the whole. There is still the world behind appearances. And it is one way, not another. Our perception, as well as the perception of all the animals, has evolved—through trial and error—to align itself the best it can with this ever-changing, always evolving, inter-connected reality. If it hadn't, we and the other animals would not be alive today.

To finish, I just want to bring it back to freedom from unnecessary suffering. I want to stress once again that when we simply rely on perception uncritically, we fail to see the impermanent and insubstantial nature of all things. We get trapped in the illusion of the stability of things. This then solidifies our surface-level view of the world, including our sense of self.

So, what is the remedy? First and foremost, mindfulness. Mindfulness allows us to see the selfless, ever-changing, interconnected field of being, which prevents us from collapsing into any percept or concept. Second, a remedy I caution you to explore with reverence, but which has been of tremendous value to me in my own journey, is psychedelics. Taking magic mushrooms, Ayahuasca, or lysergic acid diethylamide (LSD or acid) have the potential to cut directly through this illusion we carry. It immediately demonstrates that what we took to be solid, all those things out in the word, are in fact fluid and changing. They humbly bring into question what we thought to be true, what we took to be certain. This opens space for us to develop a new worldview, which can be particularly helpful for those of us who have strong conditioning in a particular religious worldview, say, or who are stuck in a past trauma. Just tread carefully and responsibly, please. Remember, spiritual life is not about chasing peak experiences. It is about letting go. It's about finding peace in this moment, here, now, no matter what is arising.

Further, taking psychedelics on their own won't provide anything of lasting benefit. We still need to actively build a new worldview. This won't simply come to you by dropping acid. In fact, I hesitated to include this suggestion because I see too many people using psychedelics and entheogens as a form of spiritual bypassing or simply to get high. But I ultimately decided to leave it in because of the tremendous benefit they do carry. You can meditate for weeks or even months without finding anything of value or significance, (since you may just sit and think the whole time, lost in the content of thought without seeing its empty nature). But sit with ayahuasca and you can almost guarantee that the worldview you once held will come into question.

Okay, well, with the final section of this chapter, I want to explore how we can use thought to help us build a worldview that is grounded in wisdom.

Thought

Thought, together with perception, produces everything. It provides a space, a home, a roof, for our sense of self to create, express, live, and love. It takes the seamless and interconnected whole of existence and breaks it into pieces, which can then come into relation to one another. It is in thought that 'you' and 'I' come alive, where 'you' and 'I' can relate, where 'we' can exist in relation to the world. Thought is where time and space begin. It is what separates birth from death. Relations, knowledge, opinions, judgments, and understanding—are all impossible without it.

Sadly though, the ego often gets a bad rap in spiritual circles because it can—and certainly does—cause a lot of problems for us. As Mark Twain said, "I have known a great many troubles in my life, most of which never happened."[96] Like Twain, we all know what this feels like to crank out problem after problem in our own minds, most of which have no real bearing on our lives. I encountered a recent example of this when I took a group to Peru to participate in a traditional Ayahuasca ceremony with the Shipibo people. Before our first ceremony, one of the guys in the group had been expressing a problem he was having—'Why is life worth living now that I no longer believe in god or an afterlife?'

As you can see, the little thinker in his head had created a problem of meaning, which sent him into a nihilistic view of the world, stripping him of all his passion and vitality. This is a problem many of us face in the West, a problem that is becoming more common as people leave their faith behind. If you too face this problem, you are not alone. Since Nietzsche[97] and even long before, all the way back to the ancient Greeks,[98] many have stood right where you are, feeling the ache of this emptiness.

Luckily though, it is more often just a steppingstone on the path. But to see if I can push you along a little bit, let's explore how your religious beliefs unnecessarily conditioned this meaning into your life. To start, consider whether the other animals worry about meaning? Are the owls staying up at night because they are worried there is no afterlife, no owl paradise to go when they die? No, of course not. What about when you were a toddler or young child? Did you stress about going to heaven? Again, no. As you grew up, an outside source—a prophet, scripture, family, community—told you where to find meaning. They told you to how to live and what for, to live for god so that you may go to heaven. This is not freedom. Nor is it where you will find true meaning or satisfaction in your life. Meaning must come from within your own heart and mind.

When I told this to the participant, it settled his nerves for the moment. But as the first ceremony approached, he began to spin out again. This time, I used no words. Instead, I cupped the back of his head with my right hand, pulled his forehead to mine, and just stood with him, bathing in love. Rather than me holding him, however, it felt as if we were both being held. It was as if the whole Cosmos was saying, "Do you feel that? What more do you need, my sweet boys? Everything, all the meaning in the world, is right here." Meaning, again, comes from the creative power of mind, the expressive power of loving awareness. It is love embodied.

Now, despite the ego's tendency to create many problems in our lives, like the problem of meaning, we could never understand, embody, and express Love without it. If you grew up in a Christian frame, it may be useful to think of it in terms of the fall of Adam and Eve, a necessary part of the human journey. Before a child is born out of the oblivion of oneness, it is entirely unaware both of itself and of Love or God. And even until about the age of two, until a child first becomes self-conscious, she remains with God, at one with God. To know God, she must fall from heaven, she must fall from grace, and into the world of 'me,' 'myself,' and 'I', into the world of desire, aversion, and delusion, into the world of fractured thought.

Only after Eve falls from grace can she make her way back to God with full awareness of God, herself, and their at-one-ment. That is, only after her fall can she come to learn the Two Truths, that we are not-two. Without this fall, there would be no Adam and Eve, no yin and yang, no self and other, no world of things. Without the fall of Adam and Eve, there would be no relational world. There would be no hard stone (the self) to sharpen up all the concepts and images in the relative (or relational) world. We wouldn't comprehend anything. We would live in a monistic oblivion.

We shouldn't condemn the thinker, then. We want to make it our friend. We just need to make sure loving awareness doesn't become obscured by the fractured pieces of thought, by the clouds that block out the wide open sky. We don't want the thinker to feel isolated and alone. We want it to know how much we appreciate it, how much we depend on it. We want it to know we need it to live this life. We want it to know we need it to embody Love.

To bring this back to the Noble Eightfold Path, the Buddha asked us to stay awake to our thinker, to clearly comprehend how it is relating to the world. Are we seeing through the lens of mindfulness or are we seeing and relating to things through desire, aversion, and delusion? Are we wearing the "shopping lens," the "comparing lens," the "Tinder lens," or the "pity lens"?

Or are we seeing everything through the lens of love and wisdom, allowing it to shape our actions and attitudes in the world?

How awake are you to the lenses through which you view the world? Were you aware of even a single frame today? Or was your conditioning, your mindless worldview, thoughts, and automatic behaviors driving your every observation and action? Are you clearly comprehending your aims and motivations and whether each word, action, or omission you take is achieving those aims skillfully and efficiently? Clear comprehension brings the relative side of the coin into sharp view, which is necessary to keep us on the path of liberation.

> "When going forward and returning one acts clearly knowing; when looking ahead and looking away one acts clearly knowing; when flexing and extending one's limbs one acts clearly knowing . . . when eating, drinking, consuming food, and tasting one acts clearly knowing; when defecating and urinating one acts clearly knowing; when walking, standing, sitting, falling asleep, waking up, talking, and keeping silent one acts clearly knowing."[99]

As you can see, it is this element of clear comprehension that extends our practice beyond the cushion and into our everyday lives. It's the difference between living an awake, examined life and sleepwalking to our grave. It is the understanding that our life is our practice. As Ajahn Chaa said, "Some people think the longer you can sit, the wiser you must be. I have seen chickens sitting on their nests for days on end. Wisdom comes from being mindful at all times."[100]

To finish the chapter, let me leave you with a quote from Sam Harris, which eloquently captures the necessity of thought in spiritual life:

> "It is obvious that knowledge... has real power. If we ever cure cancer, it will be based on understanding something about the biology of disease. And this understanding is different from our present state of relative ignorance. But ignorance and confusion have power too. And they account for most of what is wrong in our world. Our world isn't filled with bad people, intentionally doing bad things. There are some people like this. But it is far more common to find good people... doing bad things while under the

sway of bad ideas. And once you see this, you recognize that there's no force on earth more powerful than human thought. Apart from an immediate asteroid impact, ideas are the most powerful forces of nature we ever encounter. Each of us comes into the world, having inherited the cultural artifacts and assumptions of our ancestors. They built this place. They canonized certain norms of behaviors. They wrote the laws and built the institutions. They fought the wars. They filled the reservoirs of grievance between disparate peoples. What we have beneath all of this, all of culture, are words. There is language under the pavement. Civilization is a word predicated on the meanings of other words—freedom, art, science, reason, justice, democracy. All we can do is seek to persuade one another with better concepts and ideas. And our ability to identify problems and to solve them and to identify and solve new and hopefully more subtle problems is entirely the product of thought. So, there's nothing about the practice of meditation that denies the power of ideas. The question from the point of view of practice is whether one needs to be identified with thought, confused by it, ruled by it, made to suffer by it, in each moment. And the answer to that question is no. Recognizing thought as thought, truly as a transitory appearance in consciousness, isn't just another thought. But neither is it a substitute for thinking when thinking is required. So, there's no need to denigrate thought. It's almost everything. Almost.[101]

Questions & Exercises

Grab a pen and a pad and, without thinking about it, write down the first five things that come to mind to describe the world as you know it.

Now, take a look at what you've written. Do you think it's possible your comments tell you more about yourself than they do about the world? How are you structuring the world and relating to it? Can you love or hate something about another person or the world unless it is already a part of you?

Try to be conscious of this possibility moving forward. Try considering that every comment or judgment you make about the world, about another person, about an event, or about life, is a projection of yourself, of your own interior landscape.

What if you lived as if others are simply reflections of yourself, as if everything in the world is no more than a shiny mirror for you to see yourself clearly?

7. COMMUNICATION

"Devotion to truthful speech is a matter
of taking our stand in reality rather than
illusion."
– Bhikkhu Bodhi

In the Buddha's second arena of training—training in virtue (or *sila* in Pali)—we work to choreograph our thoughts, intentions, and understanding onto the world stage through our words and actions. But before we jump into the details, let's step back for a minute to get some perspective. Let's see how this arena of training fits into the greater context of the Buddha's philosophy and hopefully clear a potential misunderstanding.

Because our focus here is on doing and not doing certain things, it can seem dogmatic and authoritative—just another someone or something telling me how I should live my life. But to understand our training in this way would be misleading and incomplete. Yes, there is a "moral code," but the code is not a dogmatic prescription to action. Rather, it is a map or toolkit to help establish peace and harmony in our lives, hearts, and minds.

So, to see our training in a more complete way, it may be useful to shine some light on the translation of the Pali word *sila* into "morality" or "virtue." In English, "morality" and "virtue" carry an historical and theistic context that don't track well with Buddhism. They suggest a sense of obedience that is absent from the Buddhist concept of sila.

The Buddhist framework is non-theistic. It grounds its morality not in the Word of God or in any other authority, but in harmony, in wholeness, in love and wisdom. Sometimes, sila is even translated into "cooperation" and "coordination." So, virtue in the Buddhist framework means to cooperate and live in harmony with life, to live with love and care for the world and its creatures, including ourselves. And again, not out of dogma or authority, but to purify the heart and mind, to become free from suffering, to find lasting peace.

There are no demands along this path. Only invitations. Come and see for yourself, the Buddha says, if establishing virtue allows your spiritual life to flourish. Come and see if speaking and acting with love and harmony calms the heart and opens the mind. See if it brings about more concentration and wisdom. See for yourself if it leads onward to freedom.

With this in mind, let's go ahead and move into the substance. Training in virtue, as I said, is about training our beings in the world. And the way we show up in the world is through our words and our bodies. So, our training will consist of exercises in speech and action. And because so much of our speech and actions are tied up with our careers, we will give it its own consideration. In this Chapter, however, we will explore only our speech, which we will turn to now.

Four Measures of Speech

There is a story about a wise master who was asked to heal a sick child through words of prayer. As the master began, a skeptic in the crowd yelled out, expressing doubts about such a superstitious way of healing. So, the master turned to the skeptic and said sharply, "You know nothing of healing, you ignorant fool!" The skeptic was very offended. He grew red in the face and shook with anger. And before he could gather himself to reply, the master spoke again softly, asking, "When one word has the power to make you hot and angry, why should not another word have the power to heal?"

Our words are powerful. They can be used to start wars and spark revolutions. They can incite mobs to violence or gather thousands to march for peace. They can fill libraries with useful knowledge or they can flood our social media and news channels with fear, deception, and misinformation. They can bring us closer to our families, friends, and neighbors, or they can be used to tear us apart. Words condition our hearts and minds. They condition our moods and emotions, our likes and dislikes. They shape our sense of self, our stories, our identities, values, and aims. The words we use matter.

How awake are you to the words and frameworks you use in your life? How are you using your language, naming, framing, and storytelling to set us and others free? If you're anything like me, I'm sure there's room for improvement. To help open us to our speech, then, let's explore the four elements of speech the Buddha invited us to continually put under the magnifying glass, which are typically framed as abstentions, but I will reframe them as questions.

1. Is your speech honest?
2. Is your speech beneficial?
3. Is your speech kind?
4. Is your speech skillful?

Is Your Speech Honest?

"Avoid false speech and abstain from it. Be devoted to truth. Speak the truth. Be reliable and worthy of people's confidence, not dishonest or deceptive." – The Buddha

When asked what I believe, or to condense my own philosophy into a few words, my reply is usually the same: I believe in honesty. Honesty is foundational. It is a commitment to reality. In a way, it transcends morality, it transcends our pursuit of freedom, or any other endeavor, because nothing has a basis without it. As the Buddhist scholar and long-time practitioner Bhikkhu Bodhi said, "Truthful speech establishes a correspondence between our inner being and the true nature of phenomena. Thus, much more than just an ethical principle, devotion to truthful speech is a matter of taking our stand in reality rather than illusion."[102]

Attaining and embodying wisdom is impossible without a commitment to honesty. Because wisdom seeks the realization and embodiment of truth, because its aim is to come into harmony with the way reality is, we must resolve to take a stand in reality. And we must make this resolve not only internally but also externally, with our speech and communication with others.

So, before you speak, try making it a practice to ask yourself, "Is this true?" And don't stop here. There's too much hearsay and misinformation flooding our world to stop here. Ask the follow up, "How do I know this to be true?" This way you won't add to the noise, confusion, distrust, and the damage it is causing across the world. Remove yourself from the problem. Be careful what you say or share on social media. Have a genuine sense of humility about what you know and don't know. State your sources clearly.

And when you don't know whether something is true based on your own experience, or you are not sure your sources are reliable, be clear about that. The world is in dire need of honest and humble communicators.

Now, it's worth pointing out that honesty goes beyond merely speaking the truth and refraining from speaking what is not true. Real honesty requires that we open to and see clearly the motivations and intentions behind our words. William Blake wrote, "A truth told with bad intent beats all the lies you can invent." He has a point—just because something is true is not, in itself, a reason to say it. And I would add here that a lie told with good intent can be more honest, in many ways, than a truth that leads to harm.

In Yoga's ethical code, the Yamas and Niyamas, which mean restraints and duties, the second yama, truthfulness, should always bend its knee to the first yama, non-harm. It's okay to lie to the Jihadists at your door who are looking for the Jews or infidels in your basement. Again, examining whether speech is true or false on its face is not enough. We need to look at the shadows of our speech, at our motivations and their effects.

Now, when I say that truthfulness should always bend its knee to non-harm, I do not mean that we should withhold things simply because we believe it would upset someone. If, for example, you do something that would upset your partner and don't tell her, because you know it will hurt her, this is not honest. I have heard from several women in my life who have told me that their partners use this as an excuse—"I didn't want to tell you because I knew it would upset you." Well, no shit, man. Texting your ex behind your partner's back is obviously going to hurt her. Again, this is not honesty. What's the real root motivation here? Are you doing this out of love and respect or are you just being deceitful or cowardice?

Something else we discover when we examine our motivational roots is that our false speech can take many different forms, each of which lead to specific consequences, internally and externally. When our false speech is motivated by greed, for example, it often dresses up as cleverness and deception. "Oh, the cleverness of me!"[103] Watch out for that cleverness. It's a double-edge sword. It can be our best friend or our worst enemy if we're not careful. The cleverer we are, the easier it can be to manipulate ourselves and others in our selfish pursuits.

Where are you performing intellectual gymnastics in your life? To whom do you bend and twist your words to justify your actions? Are you fooling yourself? Don't let your words become illusions, smoke and mirrors, aimed at self-gain or self-importance. Make sure to constantly ask yourself where cleverness is showing up in your life, in your thoughts, words and deeds. Humility and honesty are rare gems in the world. It's much more attractive, disarming, and relaxing to be around someone who is honest and humble, as opposed to someone who cleverly strings together words. The latter can be exhausting and confusing. We lose trust in them, or sometimes even ourselves. In your spiritual journey, be particularly weary of the prophets and soothsayers, those with much to say.

When, on the other hand, our false speech is motivated by anger or hatred, it often dresses up as some kind of justice warrior. Here, the lies can be tricky. Feeling that we ourselves or another have been wronged, we often inflate the truth, present it narrowly, or don't bother to understand the fuller context in which the anger arose. We see this everywhere on the Far Left right now with the "bleeding heart liberals" who rush to judgment without pausing even for a moment to get grounded in the facts, or to check their sources, or to understand critically the situation. They take a clip from Tik Tok or Twitter or Instagram to be fact and continue to spread it like wildfire.[104]

Of course, it's not just people on the Left who wear this particular garment of lie. On the Far Right, for example, we see Christians eager to go to war with Hamas, not so much because they want to defend liberal, democratic values, but rather because they hold hatred toward Muslims, who they believe have corrupted God's religion.

Watch out for when you feel the righteousness of anger? Watch out for righteousness, period. Let it be a sounding bell to pause for a moment. Sit with the anger or indignation mindfully. Let it cool down before you say or do something stupid. The Buddha described anger with its honeyed tip and poisonous root. There is an energy and a sweet justice to anger. It is an important emotion, largely because it does contain a message of injustice, as well as the energy necessary to do something about the injustice. But when we act out of anger, instead of from love and wisdom, it almost never has positive consequences for us or the people on the receiving end. Take the message and wait to respond from a place of wisdom rather than react automatically. Wait until the flames have cooled and your heart has softened.

Finally, when our false speech stems from a place of delusion, it can take the form of an irrational or compulsive lie, a weird exaggeration, or a sarcastic comment or joke. A friend recently told me that she and her husband had just started taking walks in the evening. And on their first walk, they ran into their daughter's father- and mother-in-law, who asked, "Do you walk through our neighborhood often?"

Immediately, my friend's husband replied, "Oh yeah, all the time."

My friend turned to her husband and said, "My dear, this is the first time we've taken a walk together in years."

In this example, there was no premeditated or intentional lie or omission, probably just some social anxiety that had caused the husband to react quickly. So, the karmic fruit with this kind of false speech is typically not as unsavory as that of an intentional lie or omission. But it still creates dis-ease in our hearts and minds. The husband may have replayed this situation in his mind for days or weeks after, perhaps feeling embarrassed. So, to combat this false speech, we need to stay mindful, which again will allow us to respond rather than react to situations.

Another form of lie rooted in delusion I want to mention is our tendency to exaggerate. Have you ever noticed this in yourself—where you just add a few more numbers to something or dress up the truth in some way? Maybe you meditated for thirty minutes but you tell someone you meditated for forty? You say you ran three miles, though you actually only ran two? These exaggerations not only wear down other people's trust in us but they condition a lack of integrity in ouselves, so watch out for this tendency to exaggerate. Why do we feel we need to exaggerate? Do we think people won't like us as much or think we're not special enough if we don't dress up the truth? What's the underlying root here?

The last form of false speech rooted in delusion I want to explore is sarcasm. I grew up around a lot of sarcasm, which I was told is supposed to be funny. This in itself is funny, since the word is derived from the Greek *sarkazein*, which means "to tear flesh." And even now, the Oxford Dictionary defines it as "the use of irony to mock or convey contempt." Now, of course, a clever and pointed irony can be funny. As the licensed mental health counselor Anthony Smith says, "A little sarcastic wit is like a spicy seasoning. A pinch of it can make food enjoyable, but a serving of the spice itself hurts."[105]

However, I rarely find sarcasm used in a way that adds that perfect amount of spice. More often, it is hostility, frustration, or cowardice disguised as humor. It seems to me that people use sarcasm because they find it difficult to communicate their needs or emotions, like expressing necessary boundaries. That is, they don't know how to have difficult conversations. So, there's often a passive-aggressive element to it that is born out of this fear of confrontation or vulnerability. Passive-aggressive people use sarcasm to protect themselves—the sarcasm allows them to express contempt or frustration in a way that feels safe, since the sarcasm obfuscates the contempt or frustration. If someone challenges the sarcastic comment, the person who "tore flesh" can always say, "I was just kidding. Can't you take a joke?"

Well, sure, it's important that each of us can take a punch without losing our cool. But this is not the real motivation behind sarcasm—to build resilience into people. Again, it is deployed as a defense mechanism. And it most often just creates confusion and more frustration. Just consider the last time someone pointed a sarcastic comment at you. Did you appreciate it? Did it uplift you? I doubt it. It probably felt like a form of bullying.

If you are someone who uses sarcasm, consider whether a little courage is needed to express your honest thoughts and feelings. Do you use sarcasm as a defense mechanism? If you want deeper, more meaningful relationships, I suggest you lay off the sarcasm. Let's be real with each other. And if you have someone in your life who uses sarcasm, be straightforward and gentle with them—tell them softly but sternly that you don't appreciate it. And if they continue, voice to them that you will put up boundaries, like speaking or visiting less often, to protect yourself.

Now that we've explored the different shapes our false speech can take, depending on our root motivation, let's turn to an extremely important dimension of honest speech—the ability to listen mindfully. Our speech isn't honest when it's only one-sided. Speech is something that happens between and among humans, and even the earth and her creatures. If you do not listen and try to understand the person across from you, as well as the mood or energy in the room, what is your speech worth? Very little, I'm afraid.

Listening mindfully is a practice of its own, and it takes time to develop. But the next time you have a conversation, see if you can listen without judging or reacting, just as you listen to sounds or sensations in your meditation practice, where you are entirely open and receptive. As you listen, notice what inner dialogue is going on. Are you thinking about what you're going to say? Are you thinking about how this person is wrong? Are you thinking about how you have a better story? Do you get easily distracted by unrelated thoughts? Or are you giving this person your full, undivided attention?

Once this person is done speaking, take a moment to pause and settle into your own heart before responding. If you need to, you can even tell the person that you need a moment before you are able to respond with your full care and concern. Can you open awareness to the motivation behind the words that are bubbling up to the surface of consciousness before you express them out loud? Are they honest? Beneficial? Affectionate? Skillful?

If you slip and express some form of false speech, no worries. You are human. Just note the false speech and pen to and investigate it. What was the motivation and intention behind it? Did you exaggerate the truth or pretend to be an authority on some matter to sound smarter or to get recognition?

Did you manipulate, equivocate, and twist your words to get something you wanted? Did you stay silent because you feared rejection? Did you lie because you didn't want to sound weak, needy, or jealous? Again, look out for your motivations and intentions every time you open your mouth. And for those of us who speak very quickly, let's try to slow things down, to get on top of our feet, so we're not leaning forward with so much force, creating dangerous conditions for ourselves and others.

Another skillful thing to do to tune up our speech is to really reflect on the consequences of false speech. Contemplate and try to understand why it is important to speak with honesty and integrity. Consider how false speech corrodes our relationships, how it makes our society and institutions inoperable. Consider how dishonesty undermines our ability to cooperate and support each other. Understand that to live together successfully, we need an atmosphere of mutual trust.

Reflect also on the personal consequences of false speech. Consider the nature of your lies to proliferate. When you lie and someone suspects it, do you double down? Do you feel the need to lie again and again to keep face, to paint a consistent picture of events? See for yourself how the process of lying repeats and conditions itself, how the lies continue to stretch, multiply, and connect until, as Bhikkhu Bodhi says, "they lock us into a cage of falsehoods from which it is difficult to escape."[106] This is exhausting. Don't become a victim to your own cleverness and deception. As Mark Twain said, "If you tell the truth, you don't have to remember anything."[107]

On the other side of this, contemplate how honesty leads to more ease in your life, more happiness and freedom. When you embody honesty, see if people find it easier to be around you. See if they tend to confide in and value you. See if they tend to support you. See if honesty allows your heart to become soft, warm, and open. See if it brings more peace, space, and clarity to the mind. See if it enables you to grow more concentrated and focused, and if this allows for more insight and wisdom to unfold. Honesty, when it is embodied, speaks volumes. It is a real treasure in this world. Become this treasure.

Is Your Speech Beneficial?

"Avoid slanderous speech and abstain from it.
What is heard here, do not repeat over there;
and what is heard there, do not repeat here,

so as to cause dissension. Unite those who are divided; and encourage those who are united. Delight and rejoice in concord. Let your words sprout and spread concord." – The Buddha

You know as well as I that we humans are wired to gossip. And no doubt, there's some evolutionary and social utility in it, right? It's useful to know who is up to this-that-or-the-other-thing. We need to keep an eye on the troublemakers, and know who the liars, cheaters, and deceivers are in our circles so we can make wise decisions in our personal, social, and work lives. There is an element of safety couched in gossip.

But when we look at the gossip in our lives, how much of it is really done with pure motivations, a motivation to keep ourselves and our family safe? I'll bet very little. Often, what I find is that gossip is a low hanging fruit. It's easy to gossip when we don't have anything of value or substance to bring to the table. Sometimes we do it because we're simply afraid of the silence. We're uncomfortable being with people without talking.

Another reason people seem to gossip is because it provides a sense of ego gratification, especially when we feel vulnerable or unworthy. Rather than turn inward and deal honestly and humbly with our own problems, we take the easy way out and highlight what's wrong with everyone else. And for a brief moment, this might actually make us feel better about ourselves. We might feel powerful or self-righteous or superior. But in the end, this just adds to the disharmony and agitation in our lives. We hide from ourselves, making it impossible to align ourselves with the dharma, to do what is necessary to embody peace.

Next time you find yourself gossiping, try to take it as feedback. Are you gossiping because you have nothing better to contribute to the conversation? Are you doing it because you are hiding from your own faults, and it's easier to cast shade on others than to confront your own issues? What are your motivations? Are you trying to bring people together or tear people apart? Is there any value at all to this gossip? If there is value, does it outweigh the potential harm?

Another skillful thing to do is to investigate what the mind feels like the next time you are mindful enough to refrain from the impulse to gossip. Is there a sense of peace or relief? Is there more space in the mind? Is there more clarity? I find that when I am mindful enough to catch gossip before it reaches my tongue, a sense of ease washes over me. Just keep a close eye on it because, you might catch it the first time, but I assure you that the impulse will wait for the perfect moment, the moment your mindfulness guards are down.

Gossip, slander, and backbiting are usually meant to create opposition, hostility, and division, to alienate people, to make them feel isolated and alone. And they often stem from unwholesome mind-states like self-doubt, fear, jealousy, resentment, hatred, and aversion. Sometimes, they are even be motivated by cruelty. You might wish harm on another, or you might even find delight in seeing people divided. Or maybe the motivation isn't some form of aversion or cruelty but greed. Again, really try to pay attention to your motivations. Are you trying to gain affection, status, position, or wealth, at the cost of another?

It's important to open to our shadow side but, remember, we also need to be holistic and consider the light too. So, on the other side of this, I also invite you to explore whether your speech is motivated by love and harmony, whether you seek to promote unity, connection, and friendship. Does your speech come from the heart, does it come from an understanding of the interconnected nature of all things, from a mind of loving-kindness, mudita, and compassion?

What does this feel like? Does it lead to deeper and more meaningful relationships in your life? Do people give you their trust and affection? Do they feel they can confide in you without worrying you will use their vulnerabilities or secrets against them? Allow your relationships to act as a mirror in which you can see your own reflection clearly. Really explore what your speech can teach you about yourself. As Ryuho Okawa said, "Words can be a very good indicator of the character of the person who utters them, so examining the kinds of words you have used during the day is a very clear and useful checkpoint for self-reflection."[108]

Okay, let's move on to explore the next dimension of speech the Buddha invited us to investigate in our lives—the kindness, tone, care, and thoughtfulness of our speech.

Is Your Speech Kind?

"Avoid harsh language and abstain from it. Speak words that are gentle, soothing to the ear, loving; words that go to the heart, that are courteous, and friendly." — The Buddha

We all know how unpleasant harsh speech feels, both when we give it and receive it. Yet for some reason, we still do it. Why? Well, usually because we are angry or frustrated. Anger, again, is just too appealing. As I said, it has such a sweetness to it, a sense of justice or self-righteousness that is backed by an empowering energy—the honeyed tip and poisoned root. With its seductive appeal, it can be very difficult to work with anger skillfully, especially for those of us with abusive traumas or generational anger moving through us. But it begins with mindfulness. Only after we bring it into the unconditional field of awareness can we then bring compassion and understanding to it, only then can we transform it back into love.

Harsh speech is almost always intended to hurt someone. It is rooted in cruelty. We can intend to hurt them by scolding, criticizing, or blaming them with the energy of anger, using loud, sharp, aggressive, or bitter words. Or we can intend to hurt them with an insult, by mocking, ridiculing, or scorning them, by assigning them some terrible, offensive, or unattractive quality. Or we can intend to hurt them with sarcasm, by seemingly praising them, though with a tone and an irony that makes it clear we intend to cause pain.

Anger, plain and simple, is not the best mind state for open and productive communication, which really is what our speech is about. When we speak from anger, it cuts away at the peace and harmony in our hearts and in the world around us. Now of course, we don't want to suppress whatever we are feeling. We may need to have a hard conversation. We may need to draw boundaries or say something to prevent present or future harm.

To do this out of anger, though, isn't going to help anyone. It often just magnifies and spreads the anger. So instead, we need to be mindful of the anger and the underlying message contained in it but wait until the anger has moved through us to communicate this message. The goal is to communicate in a way that fosters harmony, connection, and resolve rather than discord, division, and more problems.

The antidote, then, generally is patience. We need to learn to be with our anger, to love and care for it while it is with us. We need to stay mindful of it, we need to hold it with a great deal of equanimity and composure, so that we can listen to it without reacting to it. Thich Nhat Hanh put it this way:

> The Buddhist attitude is to take care of anger. We don't suppress it. We don't run away from it. We just breathe

and hold our anger in our arms with utmost tenderness. Becoming angry at your anger only doubles it and makes you suffer more.

The important thing is to bring out the awareness of your anger to protect and sponsor it. Then the anger is no longer alone, it is with your mindfulness. Anger is like a closed flower in the morning. As the bright sun shines on the flower, the flower will bloom because the sunlight penetrates deep into the flower.

Mindfulness is like that. If you keep breathing and sponsoring your anger, mindfulness particles will infiltrate the anger. When sunshine penetrates a flower, the flower cannot resist. It is bound to open itself and reveal its heart to the sun. If you keep breathing on your anger, shining your compassion and understanding on it, your anger will soon crack and you will be able to look into its depths and see its roots.[109]

Patience is a virtue not to be overlooked. It's a foundational virtue required at every step along the path of freedom. And to work skillfully with anger, patience is essential. To stay calm, composed, balanced, and responsive, we need to learn to tolerate blame and criticism from others, as well as from ourselves. We must learn to sympathize not only with other people's shortcomings but also our own. We need to learn to respect different viewpoints and opinions, and to take punches without the need to retaliate. (Of course, there are times we need to fight but, again, only from a place of metta.) We need to be able to remain open to and interested in life, in all its forms.

Another antidote to anger and harsh speech is forgiveness. Forgiveness can clear away negative energy and open space in our hearts and minds. It allows us to transform our pain and anger into love. So, try to check in when you're holding onto some anger. See if your heart is willing to forgive anyone, including yourself. And if it's not, let your heart know that is okay. Allow it to forgive whatever it is willing to forgive, and then extend patience for what it is still working through.

Anger is one mind-state we need to look out for when it comes to spreading harsh speech, but there are also some less obvious ones—anxiety, restlessness, sleepiness, sickness, and depression. When we're in these states or moods, we are more likely to use, not blatantly harsh speech, but negative speech—speech that doesn't help anyone, speech that signals and spreads a bad attitude. Watch out for that negativity if you're feeling restless, irritated, down or blue. It's okay to ask for help or to let someone know how you are feeling. You don't want them to think they have done something wrong or that you are mad at them. So, let them know where you're at. Just be careful to use a tone and language that doesn't bring yourself or others down but rather uplifts, loves, and supports yourself and those who care for you.

We've explored the negative side to this dimension of speech, but it's also important we explore the positive side. There really is no limit to the amount of joy we can spread with soft, kind, and skillful speech. It is incredibly warming to tell someone, "I appreciate these qualities about you or the hard work you did," "You handled that difficult situation so maturely and beautifully," or "It's such a joy to see you happy and full of light." This kind of affectionate speech warms and uplifts the heart of both the speaker and the person spoken to. "Pleasant words are as an honeycomb, sweet to the soul, and health to the bones." (Proverbs 16:24)

Speaking our praise and appreciation increases the happiness of everyone involved. It helps us make and keep friends. Everyone wants to associate with people whose soft and gentle speech makes them feel safe, relaxed, and comfortable. Soft words help friends and family become closer. They help children flourish and grow up with positive feelings of self-worth and a sense of belonging.

One more thing I want to mention before we explore the final dimension of speech is that harsh speech encompasses not only what we say but also what we don't say. Is there someone in your life or a group of people in your community getting bullied or being discriminated against who you could stand up for? Is there something you can say to someone that could potentially save them or another from harm? What aren't you saying and why? Remember, our silence can be just as harsh as our words.

And this is also true for parts of ourselves. Are there parts of you that you aren't speaking up for? Are there parts of you that feel hurt, scared, and alone, parts of you that need to be voiced? Is there something you value or care about that you're not expressing? Stand up for yourself. Let your own voice be heard.

Okay, let's move onto our final dimension of speech—wise & beneficial speech.

Is Your Speech Skillful?

"Avoid idle chatter and abstain from it. Speak at the right time, in accordance with facts, and only what is useful. Speak of the Dhamma and the discipline. Allow your speech to be like a treasure, uttered at the right moment, accompanied by reason, moderate and full of sense."

— The Buddha

When you consider the wisest people in your life, what distinguishes their speech? I'll bet you they don't speak too often. But when they do, people listen. Why? Because people know that what they are about to say will be skillful, it will carry depth, meaning, and purpose. Their words will be full of treasure.

On the other end of this is what in Pali is called *samphappalāpa*, which means idle chatter, or frivolous chit chat. It is pointless and wasted speech. It lacks purpose, meaning, and depth. Not only that, but it also stirs up restlessness in the mind and distracts us from our aims and intentions.

We see it very often in our face-to-face social situations. It's as if we simply need to say, "I'm here. Notice me." But it also makes an astonishing presence in our digital worlds, in our social media channels, news sources, and entertainment. If we're not careful, samphappalāpa can flood our entire lives, washing it of purpose and meaning. "I don't know what your generation's fascination is with documenting your every thought... but I can assure you, they're not all diamonds. 'Roman is having an OK day and bought a Coke Zero at the gas station. Raise the roof.' Who gives a rat's ass?" (Griffith, Easy A (2010)).

Do your best to avoid the incessant stream of needless information online. Enjoy yourself, of course, but find an appropriate balance. Limit your exposure to distracting entertainment, which leaves your mind passive, barren, and dull. Be sagacious about the social media and digital content you engage in and expose yourself to. You are what you eat.

Equally important, watch the company you keep. We are social creatures. Who we engage with regularly shapes us. And remember, this goes both ways. It means that you yourself must be a noble friend. And to be a noble friend requires a commitment to mindful and skillful speech, on- and off-line. It means you have to put in the work.

Of course, our lives call for small talk with friends and family, and for polite conversations with acquaintances. But don't let these conversations stray too far, where the restless mind grows hungry and desperate for something to feed on. In these situations, don't speak just to be a people-pleaser, don't speak just to say you're here. Speak because what you have to say is true, beneficial, kind, and skillful. And speak it regardless of whether people want to hear it. In other words, speak courageously if it needs to be said.

Again, don't do all this because the Buddha said to, but do it to see for yourself whether it leads to more peace and satisfaction in your life. Do it to see if it keeps you on the path of freedom. Do it to see for yourself how idle and frivolous talk drain you of energy, how samphappalāpa brings nothing of value to your life, how it conditions people to lose interest in and respect for you.

Don't you yourself hold in high regard those people whose speech is deep and full of meaning and utility? Be one of those people. How? With mindfulness. You must first be aware of the impulse to engage in samphappalāpa before you can refrain from it. So, start to open to this tendency within yourself. And make the commitment to refrain from it. When you see the impulse to say something completely useless, practice putting it down. And see if this feels like a little victory. See if it provides more space and peace in the mind. See if people become more interested in what you have to say. And if you are ever uncertain about whether to say (or not say) something, again, just ask:

> Are my words honest?
> Are they beneficial?
> Are they affectionate?
> Are they skillful?

This requires us to become mindful of the impulse to speak. It requires an awareness of the motivation behind our speech. And it requires an awareness of its delivery. This is an incredibly challenging task but one that is immensely rewarding.

When we tune in to our speech, we begin to see the tremendous influence it has over our lives and our sense of well-being. We see the influence it has over our postures, attitudes, and actions in the world, over our moods and emotions. We see its influence over our beliefs and understanding, over our preferences and biases, our likes and dislikes. When we tune in to our

131

speech, we begin to see more clearly how our words can imprison us and, therefore, how we can free ourselves. As Hafiz said, "The words you speak become the house you live in."

In closing, let me once again highlight that our aim here, with training in speech, is to find freedom from suffering. We want to live in harmony with the true nature of things, to be at peace with reality. We want to know our wholeness, to live from the completeness of our body, heart, and mind. We want to express truth, beauty, and goodness, to live with loving-kindness, compassion, and joy. We want to align ourselves with the dharma.

Exercises & Reflections

I invite you to sit across from a friend or loved one and gaze into their eyes for fifteen minutes, without saying anything. Simply radiate metta towards this person in front of you. Then, once you have sat quietly for fifteen minutes, ask this person how you could communicate more effectively with them. Are there areas of my speech that could be more 1) honest, 2) beneficial, 3) affectionate, and/or 4) skillful? Is there anything you are finding difficult to tell me?

Now, as the person responds, try to stay in that place of metta. Listen mindfully, without reacting, without judgment, without even nodding your head or making facial gestures. Again, just receive this person's words with the fullness of your heart. And when they are done, simply say, thank you. Then, if they are willing, reverse places.

8. WISE ACTION

"Do you want to know who you are? Don't
ask. Act! Action will delineate and define you."
– Thomas Jefferson

Together with speech, our actions compose the second arena of training along the Buddha's Noble Eightfold Path—training in virtue (or sila in Pali). Before we get into the substance, however, I want to once again underscore our motivation and clear up some common confusion. As with all the other dimensions of our training, it is important to remember that we are training to liberate our hearts and minds, to free ourselves and others from suffering, to embody lasting peace. This is often misunderstood or forgotten when we turn to training in sila since it can seem dogmatic talking about what we should and shouldn't do. So, let me linger on this point for a moment before we jump into the juice.

In most religions, our actions are judged as good or bad, usually by God or one of his prophets. Buddhists, though, avoid this framing. Good and evil, as we learned in chapter 5, don't even come into the picture. Instead, Buddhists look at actions as either skillful or unskillful means to alleviate suffering in our hearts and minds. So, there's no real authority aside from you and the critical feedback you get from experience, from the inner and outer worlds, from the dhamma. Several times, in fact, the Buddha, when asked by his followers who would lead them after he died, very clearly stated that there should be no authority but the dhamma.

I highlight this because so many of us in the West have been conditioned to think of religious codes as ultimate declarations of good and bad behavior, as prescriptions or recipes to enter heaven or win god's favor. So, again, I just want to encourage you to keep your eye on the ball—at the aim of our practice: to free our hearts and minds from suffering. If freedom is what you want, the Buddhist code is merely an invitation to explore for yourself what actions lead onward to peace and what leads to suffering. There are no hard and fast rules here, only guiding principles to help us along.

Now, no doubt, while some of you may despise any set of rules, others of you may really appreciate the structure and clarity rules provide. My son, for example, who is quite literal, appreciates clearly defined instructions in all arenas of life. There is an element of safety for a lot of people to be given clear directions, whether it be instructions for a school assignment, the recipe for enlightenment, the code to get into heaven, or even how to behave in a specific social setting.

So, let me address both types of people here—those who despise rules and those who appreciate the structure they provide. First, for those who like the structure, the Buddha does offer a clear code of conduct to help prevent unnecessary suffering in our lives. He is one of the clearest and most exhaustive thinkers and communicators I know. He is fastidious and methodical in his investigation. So, there is plenty of structure to keep you grounded and directed.

But—and this 'but' is meant to address those who despise rules—the spirit or idea behind the Buddha's code of conduct goes far beyond any list of dos or don'ts. Again, the rules are not ultimate declarations. They are guiding principles to support you in your pursuit of freedom. So, as we move through this section, keep in mind the wise words of the singer-songwriter Amos Lee: "Keep it loose, keep it tight."

Skillful Precepts

The Buddha's code consists of four precepts:

1. Refrain from killing or causing harm
2. Refrain from sexual misconduct
3. Refrain from taking what is not given
4. Refrain from intoxicants that cloud the heart and mind

Your first reaction to these precepts is likely, "Duh!" And you're right. For most of us, these are no-brainers. They weren't created by the Buddha. You can find them in many of the world's wisdom traditions. But look around. Look at the state of the world. We are still plagued by war, violence, and terrorism. We are gluttonous consumers, taking from the earth without mercy. How many of us still rape and sexually abuse our women, sisters, and children? How many of our loved ones are drowning in drugs and alcohol, desperate for unconditional love and compassion, desperate for forgiveness?

Joseph Goldstein often points out that in spiritual practice we do not simply follow our hearts, we train them. And he's right. As anyone who has looked inward knows, we are a mixed bag of competing and contradictory motivations. Awareness holds it all. We have both generous and greedy impulses. Our hearts contain both love and hatred. Even the purest of children, as they grow, become corrupted by the world, corrupted by fear, corrupted by anger, corrupted by greed, corrupted by pain and suffering. So, again, we need to train our hearts. We need to address the fear, anger, greed, and suffering within each of us and work toward transforming it into love.

How? Well, it begins with mindfulness. We must first open to and accept all the pieces of ourselves. We must understand and accept the hurt, fractured, and isolated pieces of ourselves—the angry, perverted, cruel, prideful, judgmental parts—so we can extend our compassion and forgiveness to them. The bulk of this chapter will be a plea to do just that—to love and forgive yourself. Responding to a question about how we can treat ourselves less harshly, Ram Dass said:

> "Part of it is observing oneself more impersonally... When you go out into the woods and you look at trees, you see all these different trees. And some of them are bent, and some of them are straight, and some of them are evergreens, and some of them are whatever. And you look at the tree and you allow it. You see why it is the way it is. You sort of understand that it didn't get enough light, and so it turned that way. And you don't get all emotional about it. You just allow it. You appreciate the tree. The minute you get near humans, you lose all that. And you are constantly saying, "You're too this, or I'm too this." That judging mind comes in. And so I practice turning people into trees, which means appreciating them just the way they are."

It is mindfulness that gives us the space to do this, to observe ourselves more impersonally. It is mindfulness that opens awareness to our habits and conditioning, not with self-judgment, not from the harsh critic up in our heads, but from the wholeness of our heart—with understanding, compassion, and forgiveness. Only after we become mindful of our harmful

135

patterns can we put in the work to rebuild new ones. Mindfulness is synonymous with freedom. It is what allows us to take a new path. It is what gives us the choice to refrain from our reactivity, to refrain from our conditioning, and to pursue another way, a way that is grounded in love, wisdom, and reason.

Now, because the old habitual energy will often be strong in the beginning, when we first start training, it can be skillful to strictly stick to the precepts. Otherwise, if we're too loose, our clever ego will figure out all kinds of workarounds. We will too easily be pulled back into our old routines.

I often smoke weed at nights and have since I was fifteen. It is one of my oldest and deepest habits. During the day, my personality is a bit buttoned-up and my posture is quite upright. So, I feel that smoking weed at the end of the day creates a nice transition out of my workday. It loosens me and allows my thoughts to run free. I'm less guarded and more playful. But sometimes, my oldest mistress—weed—gets the best of me. So, I try to stay aware of who is in charge of the relationship, me or she. And very often, if I'm being honest with myself, it is she who holds the reigns. When this is the case, I know it's time to take a break. Very often, however, "the cleverness of me" shows up. If I don't strictly abide by my commitment to take a break, I find myself saying, "Well you can have some on Mondays and Thursdays after you go to the gym to help with your appetite," or "It's okay if you smoke on weekends," or "If you visit with friends," or whatever else that witty little shit comes up with. I'm sure you're familiar with something similar. If we're going to break old habits, in the beginning (and sometimes forever), it's often wise to stick strictly to "keep it tight."

Another way to think about this is how young kids need strict rules—Don't run into the street or touch the curling iron or take things from strangers. Kids need this strict structure because it's too hard for them to conceptualize the potential harm. And their curiosity and impulse to act are just too strong. The same is true on our spiritual path. Some of our old habits are like children. They need a strict "no". As kids get older, though, they realize that their parents' rules weren't just dogmas. They existed to prevent them from harm. So, from this point on, the once-child-now-adult no longer needs to strictly stick to the rules. They have a skillful habitual foundation to keep them protected but can now live according to the rules' underlying principle, which sometimes even means breaking the rule.

Let me hover here for a moment, because right now, as a culture, we are quickly moving away from the moral and religious institutions, norms, and traditions that have stood before us for hundreds and thousands of years. We are outgrowing many of the religious outfits of our past, and for good reason. But in times of great cultural change like now, when we start to question old rites, traditions, and institutions, I think it's important we try to articulate what purpose they were meant to serve and to what efficacy they are achieving that purpose before we simply toss them out. Often what I have found is that there is a kernel of truth and value to them. Their framing just needs to be updated and tweaked a bit to fit our modern worldview. And the dogma, authority, and superstition need to be thrown out.

I say this to open you not only to the Buddhist precepts but to all the world's religions and wisdom traditions. I believe there is wisdom in each of them. So, I invite you to explore with fresh critical eyes the norms and ethics of your own cultural upbringing too. Just remember to keep your eye on the ball—is this rite or ritual causing harm or is it leading onward to peace? Stay connected with your personal integrity and responsibility so you don't get lost in the seduction of your desires and impulses or in the confusion, pressure, and fearmongering of the world's authorities, including the authority of popular opinion and the social media mob.

Though the world's religions offer much wisdom, to be honest and holistic, they are also causing tremendous harm. Many atrocities are committed under the name of one god or another. Daughters are being stoned to death by their fathers in the name of Allah. Gays are being publicly hung in the streets of the Middle East under Muslim theocracies. They are prohibited from marrying in many parts of the world. And even here in the West, queers are being kicked out of their homes, denied unconditional love and support. All around the world, women are forced into childbearing, forced into silence, forced to cover their faces and bodies, denied leadership positions, denied the freedom to make decisions about their own bodies, about their own lives. Arranged marriages are still being forced onto our children. And at the root of all this, lies a doctrine from one of the world's religions. Our religious books are far from perfect. In fact, many of them are anciently outdated. So, address them honestly. Throw out and criticize what is harmful. Remember from our chapter on speech, it is also harmful speech when you remain silent and don't stand up for the injustices and harms being committed in the world.

Anyway, I hope my words help you connect to a moral code in your own unique, personal, and meaningful way.

Committing to Non-Harm

"Avoid taking life and abstain from it. Without stick or sword, conscientious, full of sympathy, desire and pursue the welfare of all sentient beings."[110] – The Buddha

Killing and causing harm are easy to see and understand. But this precept goes much deeper. Really, it is about living in harmony with life, about honoring and holding reverence for the earth and all its plants and creatures. So, there are many subtler dimensions to explore than just refraining from hitting, biting, scratching, and clawing. But one thing that is common to all acts of violence, crude or subtle, which I invite you to explore in your own life is that there is almost always an element of fear at its root. Pause to really let this sink in.

Now consider its antidote. What is the antidote to fear? Love. Love sits at the core of non-harm. Where fear creates violence, discord, and harm, love creates support, harmony, and safety. As Jesus said, "Perfect love casts out fear." (1 John 4:18) And this applies not only out in the world but in our own hearts and minds. We need to love all the pieces of ourselves. When we resist loving ourselves, when we judge, condemn, and demoralize parts of ourselves, because some part of us is afraid, we cause all kinds of harm to ourselves and others.

When, for example, like me, you are overly sedulous, tip-toeing the line of a disciplinarian because some piece of you is afraid to feel unworthy if you don't produce something or accomplish something every minute of every day, you will feel the pressure, yes. But others around you will feel the same pressure. If you are overly self-critical and -judgmental, again, everyone will feel the criticism and judgment. But if you are light-hearted, forgiving, and compassionate with yourself, others will feel that same ease, acceptance, and safety when they are around you. A young holocaust victim named Etty Hillesum said, "Ultimately we have just one moral duty: to reclaim large areas of peace in ourselves, more and more peace, and to reflect it towards others. And the more peace there is in us, the more peace there will also be in our troubled world."[111]

One way this commonly shows up is when we try to "help" or "fix" other people. And sure, sometimes this can help us to get out of ourselves. But it is usually only a temporary fix. We get a temporary sense of achievement, pride, or even holiness for "helping." But in the end, it not only pushes our own problems further into our being, but it often ends up hurting the very person we are trying to help.

This can play out in several ways. But let me mention only a couple. First, when we have not done the work to heal ourselves, we aren't really in a position to help others. We need to put on our own oxygen mask first. I see this all the time in healing and spiritual circles. Someone will have got the smallest taste of some kind of healing, or even just a "spiritual high," and then they eagerly jump into the role of "healer" when they are nowhere near prepared. Their own traumas then bleed into the hearts of those they are trying to help, causing more confusion and pain. As Lao Tzu said, "If you want to awaken all of humanity, then awaken all of yourself...Truly, the greatest gift you have to give is that of your own self-transformation."

Moving to the second way this plays out, when we try to "help" or "fix" others, we often think we know what's best for them. I catch myself imposing my values on others all the time, thinking I know what they want or need. But the truth is, I have no idea. I'm not them. I don't know what they like or want or value. Sure, I may point to certain things for them to investigate if they are interested. Or I may open them to a question, which they themselves can then follow. But it is far too easy, when we're not careful, to force our values and beliefs on others, to preach at them, to lecture at them, etc. This has been an extremely important lesson for me to learn. A good teacher or healer does not teach or preach to anyone. Instead, they take a loving interest in people. They try to understand and support them. Khalil Gibran says it beautifully:

> No man can reveal to you aught but that
> which already lies half asleep in the dawning
> of your knowledge.
> The teacher who walks in the shadow
> of the temple, among his followers, gives not
> of his wisdom but rather of his faith and his
> lovingness.
> If he is indeed wise he does not bid you
> enter the house of his wisdom, but rather
> leads you to the threshold of your own
> mind.... For the vision of one man lends not
> its wings to another man.
> And even as each one of you stands
> alone in God's knowledge, so must each one

of you be alone in his knowledge of God and
in his understanding of the earth.[112]

Whenever you have the impulse to "help" or "fix" someone, explore whether you see a reflection of yourself in the other person, a reflection that needs some loving attention. Are you trying to help your kid get better at football or dance because that's what they want? Or is there hurt there, a story that tells you you're not important—that you have no value or worth if you're not good at football or dance? Are you helping your kid become more popular, normal, attractive, or accepted by certain people? Who are you helping? Them or a hurt, embarrassed, or scared part of you? Why do so many of us feel that we need to make people be a certain way, rather than allow each individual to express their own heart, to tell us who *they* are?

Deborah Adele has a useful reframe here, which is to "support" others instead of "help" them.[113] This simple shift in framing naturally avoids the impulse to impose our values and ideas of happiness on other people and, instead, to learn what it is they want and why. Only then, when we understand them, can we truly lend our support, our love and encouragement. When we "help" others, however, we often just end up harming their sense of freedom and independence. We end up as an obstacle in their way rather than the fuel to get them where they are going.

There is an old parable from India that captures this well. As the story goes, one day a passerby saw a monkey holding a fish in a tree. The monkey seemed confused and somewhat put-out as it said to the fish, "But I saved you from drowning!" The monkey, thinking it had saved the fish, had taken the fish to a place that couldn't meet any of the fish's needs. The monkey "helped" the fish, assuming it knew what was best for the fish.

Our commitment to non-harm asks us to trust people, to understand it is only they who can know what is best for them. So, non-harm asks us to have faith in the other, rather than pity, belittle, or control them (the near enemy of compassion). It asks us to trust other people's journeys and to simply extend our love and support to them along their way, even if that means stepping back and allowing them to make their own mistakes. And as Deborah Adele says, if we are genuinely concerned, though we can't bring them into the tree, we can always jump into the water with them.[114]

Are you afraid to love yourself? Why? What do you think would happen if you loved yourself, if you forgave yourself, if you took an interest in yourself, if you cared for yourself, if you were grateful for yourself? If you want to find peace, concentration, and clarity, commit yourself to non-violence. And do this first by making it a practice to be kind to yourself, to fall in love with yourself. Every morning when you wake up, extend some love, attention, and forgiveness to yourself. And every night before you lay your heart to sleep, do the same. Do this and see if everyone else around you feels that love.

Well, so far, we have focused on what we can do to refrain from harm. But let's look at the other side of this. The reality is, many of us are or have been victims of abuse. And it's important we meet this abuse with the utmost care, not only to heal ourselves, but also to prevent more harm from arising in the future. So, if you or a loved one has been a victim of abuse, I'd love to share how I have approached my own.

To begin, let me just say that I have never really thought of myself as naïve or innocent. I was physically and emotionally abused for most of my childhood by an older neighbor who displayed some truly creative cruelty. I was sexually abused by two teenage girls from about eight to ten. My family was a shelter home for abused, abandoned, and neglected children, and so I had a sad window into some hard truths about our neighbors and community. I watched heroin take one of my closest friends in highschool. I've seen the depressing reality for young women and girls in the red-light districts of Thailand. I've been pushed into an unwanted coke deal in Peru by an older teen who had been dragged into gang-life. I was robbed in Ghana when conflict broke out in the Ivory Coast and the borders were closed, overcrowding the dirt roads and slums of Accra. I've spent nights on the streets with the homeless people of Salt Lake City, getting to know their traumas and life-stories. I've seen ugly, in its many forms.

But it has been only in the last several years that, as an adult, I have really gotten close to what I will call "bad actors"—those who on the surface appear to be incredibly fun, loving, vibrant, and sometimes even generous people, but who are in reality dangerously manipulative, emotionally and physically abusive, most particularly to the people closest to them.

Now, let me first say that I am hesitant to use the term "bad actors" because, at bottom, I don't believe any human or creature is fundamentally bad. We all share, at our root, a fundamental goodness—unconditional, loving awareness. So, more often, I think harmful behaviors stem from bad ideas—people have harmful operating systems running, like the belief we should mutilate little boys' and girls' genitals because Yahweh or Allah said so, or to become a martyr for Allah because he promises you virgins in heaven for your noble sacrifice, or that people of dark skin are inferior because they are descendants of Cain, who was cursed by god. Again, I believe "bad"

141

more often stems from the code we have running, our memetic conditioning, not because we are inherently bad.

Another reason I'm hesitant to use "bad actor" is because very often, if we look into the depths of these "bad actors," we will very likely find traumas scarred deeply into them, scars that often reach back for generations. We will see that their sense of safety and freedom, worth and significance, joy and innocence, were stripped from them early in life. We will discover that their foundational neurological pathways were shaped by violence committed on them, and so we will see that the trauma continues to live and move through them.

With this said, though, I'm learning from my mistakes. I have been fooled too many times in recent years. I have unwittingly put my children at risk, carelessly let untrustworthy people stay in my home. I have armed bad actors with a spiritual language they can use to manipulate others. I have stood up to bad behavior, protected the innocent, been gaslighted by it, and helplessly watched as enablers protected the abuser and cowards turned their heads in the name of "peace." My heart has been flooded with sorrow and a deep distrust.

Let me explore just one personal example here, one that is far too common in our world—that is, sexual abuse. Recently, a member of my extended family voiced their many years of sexual abuse committed on them by my grandfather, who had always been held up as a saint, and who always appeared so loving and generous to me. And then a second member voiced her abuse. This news caused the trauma from my own sexual abuse to resurface, and flooded me with a renewed anger, fear, sadness, and deep distrust.

Within all this darkness and pain, however, I have also found immense beauty. I have had the opportunity to connect with the victims, who have displayed so much love, compassion, and wisdom. I've been able to renew and strengthen my trust in River, my partner, and to find an immense love and gratitude for her. I've been able to hold my children with a profound level of appreciation, care, and tenderness. And I've been able to hold my self too with a new kind of compassion, a compassion I don't think would have been possible if this news had not resurfaced my old traumas and allowed me to see them and hold them from the lens of a parent. Seeing my kids, and then seeing myself at their age losing my sense of trust and safety has cracked my heart wide open.

Sadly, I know there are so many of you who can relate. So, how can those of us who have lost our trust in humanity move forward on the spiritual path? How can we live with open hearts and, at the same time, protect ourselves and our loved ones from those who would harm us?

As I said earlier, I've been struggling with these questions for a few years now. The problem first arose when I was introduced with full disclosure to a so-called "bad actor." At the time, to keep myself and those close to me safe, I was encouraged to read up on the literature surrounding sexual, physical, and emotional abuse, narcissistic personality disorder, and antisocial personality disorder (otherwise known as sociopathy).

Sadly, as I read through the literature, I recognized several people in my life who displayed some of the patterns I was learning about. I became aware of the many ways they manipulate the people around them. And as I said earlier, even after reading the literature, I have still been fooled too many times in the past few years. So, I've tightened up my circle. I have sharpened up how I interact with certain people. I've recalibrated and tuned-up my bullshit detector. I am learning how to skillfully apply and enforce boundaries. In short, I'm figuring out my posture to the world.

It's been a long road. But I feel like I'm starting to find a posture that is open, relaxed, and receptive but not too open and relaxed. I'm finding a posture with a strong back, one that is resilient and enduring, but that is also soft and flexible. Instead of reacting from a place of fear, anger, or distrust, I'm getting better at simply recognizing the emotions when they arise, welcoming them into awareness's loving embrace, holding them, listening to them, having compassion for them, trying to understand them, and then—and only then—responding to a person or situation if necessary.

Of course, staying mindful and responding with wisdom is not always easy. When I am "more or less mindful," as Joseph Goldstein calls it, aware but not fully open and receptive, subtly identified, I often try to distract myself from these hard emotions, difficult conversations, or hard decisions, by turning to a movie or to endless productivity or by sleeping more, sleeping in, unwilling to meet the day. That is, I succumb to restlessness or sloth and torpor (which we'll discuss more later).[115]

Thankfully though, the watcher on the wall, the shield that guards the realms of men, mindfulness, eventually blows the horn to alarm me that Mara has penetrated the walls (Mara is the personification of delusion in Buddhism). If the mindfulness still isn't strong enough, however, if I keep running from or getting caught in the emotion and all the thoughts that surround it, to dispel Mara's magic, I will sometimes seek the wisdom of reflection to help reinforce and support the mindfulness, to renew its strength.

The reflections I want to explore are the three marks or dimensions of wisdom—1) the selfless or interconnected nature, 2) the impermanent and ever-changing nature, and 3) the unsatisfactory, bumpy nature of reality (dukkha). And though each of these reflections are really windows into the same insight, which is both the goal and the path of spiritual practice, we can investigate and apply more skillfully certain dimensions of wisdom to help cut through the Gordian Knot of self-illusion and once again open our hearts and minds.

When, for example, anger or indignation arise, when I feel that my innate sense of justice has been violated and I feel the strong impulse to act out of this anger, I will often contemplate the selfless, interconnected nature of reality. I can reflect on this person who has committed the injustice and realize that if I had this person's genes and grew up under this person's circumstances, I would be this person. I would have spoken and acted just as they have.

It's the same reflection Ram Dass asked us to make—seeing people as trees. We understand that some people didn't get enough light, and so they turned this or that way. We don't condemn or hate them. We simply understand that impersonal causes and conditions brought them to where they are. Just as we don't damn the tree, we need not damn the human, cast his soul into eternal hellfire.

When we put on our Love goggles, we can see that there is no soul, no self, no isolated and independent force that gave this person the agency to do what he did, an agency that is removed from the rest of the world and the laws that govern it. Just as the tree is made of soil, water, and air, inextricably linked to the earth and her seasons, her relation to the sun and moon, all governed by universal laws, well, so too is this person. He is made up of non-person parts, each inter-dependent on the rest, all bound by universal laws.

Sometimes this reflection—on the delusion of free-will—makes people feel uncomfortable. This is understandable. So much of our identity, our sense of self, is caught up in our volition. And to be stripped of this idea, deluded as it may be, can throw many of us either into an existential crisis or a nihilistic stupor. But this is to miss the deeper insight—that you are so much more than this small ego-based part. You contain it but, at the same time, transcend it. Again, this is not something to take on faith. It's an invitation for you to look directly for yourself.

Now, another common question that arises here is, "So what? Why is this important or useful? If this is true, then nothing anyone does matters since there's no responsibility. If I don't have free-will, then why does it matter if I lie, cheat, steal, or kill?"

Well, first of all, our intentions still matter, even if it is a total mystery that they do in fact arise, to say nothing about how. It's important to know whether I intended to hit you or whether it was just an accident. When we know that someone carries ill-intent to harm, we do what is necessary to protect the innocent. Consider your posture or attitude towards a tornado that goes ripping through a city, destroying homes and killing people. Do you get angry at the tornado? Do you blame it? No. Now, of course, as Sam Harris points out, "If we could put a hurricane in prison to prevent it from causing harm, we would."[116] But we wouldn't do it with anger or with the intent to punish the hurricane. No, we understand that entirely impersonal causes and conditions came together to bring about the hurricane. Rather than curse it, we learn as much as we can about its causes and conditions, and then do what we can to create warning systems and other forms of protection.

Consider if we carried this same attitude into our criminal and justice systems. Rather than blame people and punish them, we could learn more about the causes and conditions that bring about criminal behavior and work towards solutions that skillfully and compassionately protect all of us. We would move from punitive to rehabilitative and restorative systems.

We can even take this understanding, this reflection of the delusion of free-will, into our homes. Rather than punish our kids for their behaviors, we can work towards understanding all the causes and conditions at play so that we can correct them with compassion and bring more peace into the home. In dealing with sexual abuse, I can still do everything I possibly can to protect my children, but I can do so not out of hatred but with love in my heart.

This reflection, if we are honest with ourselves, allows us to let go of so much needless suffering. When we recognize that everyone and everything is inter-connected, that we all abide by lawful and universal forces, then much of our anger, jealously, blame, hatred, shame, and frustration dissipate. Again, don't take my word for it. Be honest and investigate it for yourself.

Okay, let's move on to fear. When wrestling with fear, there are a few reflections that seem to help me. And you'll just have to play around with them yourself to see which one works for you. You can reflect on the truth of impermanence, investigating directly the ever-changing nature of experience until you find that there is no one there who is afraid, there is no stable, unchanging entity called self. There are sensations, thoughts, feelings, etc—all fading as quickly as they are coming into being, and so we just allow ourselves to settle back into the effortless flow of experience.

This doesn't work for everyone, though. So, another option is to explore and emphasize the knowing aspect of awareness, the deathless, the unborn and unformed, the unperturbable, the untainted, the timeless, the no-thing, that which cannot arise and therefore cannot disappear. That which simply knows.

What I find most useful, however, when in the grip of fear, is to reflect on metta, on loving-kindness, the simple wish that I, that you, that all beings, that all experience, be at ease, that all be at peace, that all be happy, safe, and secure. The Buddha's spontaneous expression of metta that I shared in Chapter 4—"may you be skilled in goodness..."—actually arose in response to a group of monks who expressed their fear to the Buddha. The monks had tried meditating in the forest but couldn't focus because they were afraid. The forest was full not only of dangerous creatures but many of the outcasts and outlaws of society also lived there. So, to find inner peace, the Buddha suggested that the monks reflect on these warm wishes. This has been an incredibly successful strategy for me. Whenever fear drapes me, I repeat the Buddha's words: "May you be skilled in goodness, May you be able, honest, and upright..." The next time you find yourself in the grip of fear, give it a try.

The last emotion I want to explore is distrust. This one has been extremely difficult for me. It has really impaired my ability to open to the world, to establish deep and meaningful relationships, which requires us to expose our precious, tender, vulnerable hearts. Trust works on its own time, much like forgiveness. But what seems to help me is to reflect on my own sila, my own goodwill, to reestablish and connect with my intention to commit no harm. As my humble and noble friend Logan asked me, after I expressed all the distrust I had been facing, "Do you trust yourself?"

"Yes," I replied.

"Good," he said. "Stick with that."

"With others, start by giving them only small tasks to build your trust. If they break it, then there won't be too much harm done. If they show up, if they take responsibility, if they demonstrate trust, then give them a little more. But keep who and what you value close. It'll never hurt to stay skeptical and awake."

And as my love, River, has really helped me to understand through her example, being distrustful does not make us pessimistic misanthropes. Often, it's necessary to be the adult in the room—we need to be skeptical of others to protect ourselves and our children. But there's also room to be optimistic for people. We can understand that many of us are hurt, we are trees who haven't received enough light. Being skeptical is not the same thing as being judgmental. For the adult in the room, skepticism comes from a place of metta, to protect the innocent.

Refrain From Taking What Is Not Given

"Avoid taking what is not given and abstain from it. Do not take away with thievish intent that which another person possesses. And do not take more than what is offered."
– The Buddha

Many of us, especially in the West, tend to view ourselves as the center of the universe. We move through the world looking at it in terms of what it has to offer us, in what it can do for us. Because of our Judeo-Christian underpinnings, which I believe many people have confused and taken literally, there is this deep-seated idea that we were put onto this earth, and that everything was made, in some sense, for us.

But as Alan Watts said, "We do not 'come into' this world; we come out of it, as leaves from a tree."[117] Ask any of the astronauts who have traveled beyond our atmosphere and witnessed directly the majesty of our blue planet in its fullness, and they will confirm this. They will tell you the earth is a single, living organism. There are no divisions anywhere. You and the earth are of one flesh. As Jesus said, "Abide in me, and I in you. As the branch cannot bear fruit of itself, except it abide in the vine; no more can ye, except ye abide in me. I am the vine, ye are the branches: He that abideth in me, and I in him, the same bringeth forth much fruit: for without me ye can do nothing." (John 15:4–5 KJV)

This shift in frame dramatically changes the Buddha's second precept. With this new view, we can see that nothing is ours. Everything belongs to the earth. It belongs to the entire collective. We are only borrowing the earth's resources for a time, including our own bodies. Deborah Adele captures this wonderfully when she says, "We are visitors in the fullest sense of the word. You wouldn't go to a friend's house for dinner, complain about the food, leave your trash lying around, and walk off with the candlesticks because you wanted them. And yet, this is so often how we treat our world."[118]

Non-stealing asks us to live in harmony and reciprocity with the whole of existence. Where stealing or careless consumption and consumerism is an expression of greed or envy, of our egocentricity, non-stealing is the expression of generosity and thoughtfulness, of our fundamental non-duality. So, really, abstaining from taking what is not given implies more than not stealing. It is an inherent understanding that we are in debt to this gift called Life.

When we really understand this, how we view "possession" and "ownership" begins to change. Now of course, there is utility in property law. I went to law school. I understand that we don't want to live in a world where we have no claim to our homes, cars, phones, laptops, and other possessions. That would be a total nightmare. But when we look at the world through the ultimate lens, we understand that we can't really possess anything.

Because, however, we play out our lives on the relative level, we will naturally use language like "my house, my car, my phone." We just need to be careful that our language doesn't distract us from the deeper truth that nothing is really ours. We must remember to keep one hand in the ultimate truth, to hold the relative and ultimate together harmoniously. When we do this, we can start to view everything in our "possession" as something very precious on loan to us, as something we ought to take great care of. We can think of ourselves as stewards of the earth.

When we become fractured by thought and forget our interconnected nature, we too easily succumb to greed. We forget that everything is borrowed, and so we end up stealing in all kinds of ways. You don't have to look far to see how our greed has stolen from other animals. We've dumped plastics into our oceans, destroyed forest upon forest, replaced more and more of the earth's surface with concrete jungles, landfills, and commercial crops that destroy the soil and habitats of so many creatures.

Nor do we need to look too hard to see that we are stealing from the future, from our children and grandchildren. Our consumerism has given us an insatiable appetite for everything. We pull from the earth as if its resources are unlimited. We exist in a giant black hole, which no number of possessions can fill. In ancient Indian religions, there are legendary human-like creatures called pretas, who are inflicted with insatiable appetites. Their extremely large bellies demand more and more, but they are never able to satisfy their bellies because their necks are too long and narrow. This is our situation. Never have we had more. There is excess everywhere—excess on our plates, excess in our bodies, excess in our closets, excess in our schedules, excess in our minds. Yet, we can't fill our bellies. We continue to take and take and take. We've forgotten entirely about tomorrow.

Let's try to change our focus from what we don't have to the abundance that is right in front of us. Let us live in the peace and joy of contentment rather than in the pain and emptiness of lack and want. Let us expand not our possessions but our very beings by getting in touch with our true unbounded nature. Let us live in gratitude—gratitude for the spoils that even kings and queens of old could not have hoped for, gratitude for the gift of life, gratitude for all those who came before us and sacrificed so much, even their lives, so that we could live with more freedom and opportunity.

John Adams, in a letter to Abigail, wrote, "I must study politics and war that my [children] may have liberty to study mathematics and philosophy. Our [children] ought to study mathematics and philosophy...commerce and agriculture in order to give their children a right to study painting, poetry, music, architecture, statuary, tapestry and porcelain." And from Einstein, "A hundred times a day I remind myself that my inner and outer life depend on the labors of other people, living and dead, and that I must exert myself in order to give in the full measure I have received and am still receiving."

In all the instances where we steal, we make the situation about our small, fractured self, not about the Whole. It comes from a place of greed, scarcity, and fear, all of which ironically impoverish our hearts and minds. Another subtle way we see this is when we "one-up" people, when we come behind them with a 'better' story or a 'cooler' party trick, usually to buoy our own sinking ego. Observe how you engage with others. Are you really taking an interest in them or are you just looking for ways to steal attention or boost your own ego? Try to take the time to sink into the other person's story, to really admire their art, project, skill before you jump in with your own. When we just try to one-up each other, there is no real sharing or cooperation involved. There's no bonding or bridge building. There's just selfishness. We just take up space and oxygen.

On the window in front of my desk, I have scribbled onto it, "Be space for others." When we really examine ourselves, when we look directly at our own mind, at bottom, this is what we are—the space in which everyone and everything arises. The mind is what holds all things. So, when we don't pay attention to the people around us, we steal from their existence in a way. Watch out for this especially when it comes to our kids. I can't express how much we steal from our children when we don't give them the attention they need. Not a spoiled attention, but an attention of true love and care, one that contains the wisdom of "no". What a world it would be if each of our children grew up knowing that they were felt, seen, understood, and appreciated.

Another way we steal from ourselves and others is through the comparing mind. By its very nature, with the comparing mind, we step into a dualistic frame, where we intend to put someone or something above or below the other. That is, we take value or worth from someone or something, very often our own. When we compare ourselves to others, we often find scarcity in ourselves, we think we are lacking, which makes us feel cheated. And on the other side, we may find ourselves superior, which leaves us arrogant and makes the other feel lacking. In both cases, though, we are stealing. What's the common saying?—"Comparison is the thief of joy."

Another way in which we steal from ourselves is when we impose an outside image of ourselves onto ourselves. When we do this, we rob ourselves of our true and authentic selves. We take away the precious uniqueness that your relative self has to offer the world. We don't need more people cut from the same cultural cookie cutter as everyone else. Look around at life. It survives and flourishes only because there is so much diversity. Don't let fear warp and stunt the unique blossom of love that desperately wants to bloom from your heart.

Here are some other considerations. Do you steal from yourself when you live in a constant state of hurry and busyness? Is it theft when you don't give yourself time to listen to your heart or digest and assimilate your experiences? Aren't you stealing from yourself when you don't allow yourself time to contemplate, reflect, and rest?

Okay, before we move on to explore our livelihoods, I want to bring up one more powerful antidote to stealing—that is, generosity. Generosity cuts straight to the heart of our spiritual practice and taps into the boundless wellspring of love within each of us. It is the polar opposite to greed. The power of generosity to open, soften, uplift, and expand the heart is so powerful that the Buddha is said to have begun every public discourse with generosity. "If," said the Buddha, "you knew what I know about the power of giving, you would not let a single meal pass without sharing it in some way."[119]

Now, as with all our trainings along the Path, generosity too is a practice. Just like metta or mindfulness, it too can be cultivated, developed, and strengthened. And when we do, you'll have to see for yourself, but it can lead to tremendous landscapes of peace, non-attachment, and ease. This, of course, is not going to be true for everyone, especially in the beginning. If, for example, you have been conditioned to live from a scarcity mindset, you might initially shudder at the idea of giving anything away.

In any case, the first thing to do in cultivating a generous heart is to simply open to it, in ourselves and in the world around us, and then to explore the impact it has on us, whether it brings fear or peace. How does it color our heart and mind? After we watch it with equanimity, observing it, learning about it, we can then begin to cultivate it skillfully.

If you've been conditioned to live from a scarcity mindset, one thing you might consider doing is simply imagine being generous. What would it feel like if you gave something to someone you know would appreciate this thing deeply. You might have an old possession you never really use and consider giving it away. See what this does to your heart and mind, even if in the end you aren't ready to let it go. I bet you'll find some joy by feeling connected to the person on the receiving end, imagining their smile and gratitude. See if it expands and softens your heart.

Another way to practice milder forms of generosity is to *share* your things rather than give them away. Let others share in the enjoyment of your possessions. See what this does to your sense of well-being. Then, as you grow more comfortable with giving, as you eliminate the sense of scarcity within yourself, practice giving freely, and discover the joy in that giving. Of course this doesn't mean you need to give everything away. Equanimity, remember, balances self and other. We need to remember to be compassionate and caring toward ourselves. So, simply give where you can without adding unnecessary stress to your life.

Do this and I can guarantee you will discover an abundance within yourself. Some of the happiest people I've met, people in the Tibetan villages of the high Himalayas, have next to nothing. Continue down this road, and And some of the unhappiest people I've met, people I've worked for who have a billion dollar portfolio, are miserable, and they make everyone around them miserable. I think you'll discover that you don't need a lot of things to be happy. It is our relationship to life, our posture to the dhamma, our attitude, that determines our happiness or sorrow, not the number of possessions we have. It is witnessing that you are already entirely whole.

And last but certainly not least, practice the giving of yourself. As Kahlil Gibran says, "You give but little when you give of your possessions. It is when you give of yourself that you truly give. For what are your possessions but things you keep and guard for fear you may need them tomorrow?"[120]

Wise Livelihood

Work life and spiritual life can often seem like two very separate and even incompatible things. But our work takes a central role in our lives and so it must play a central role in our spiritual journey. For many of us, it occupies more of our time than anything else we do, so it's essential we hold it and relate to it in the context of our deepest aim or aspiration. As Gibran says, "Work is love made visible."

In the context of the Eightfold Path, we want to ground our work in love. We want to stay in concord with life, aligned with our pursuit of wisdom. So, as we navigate our work life, we need to stay in touch with the fact that we are not apart from the rest of the world, that we are not apart from our colleagues, customers, and clients, that we are not apart from the earth and her resources.

> "To you the earth yields her fruit, and you shall not want if you but know how to fill your hands. It is in exchanging the gifts of the earth that you shall find abundance and be satisfied. Yet unless the exchange be in love and kindly justice, it will but lead some to greed and others to hunger."
> - Kahlil Gibran, *On Buying & Selling*[121]

As we go to work, day in and day out, many of us come to feel like we're not contributing in any way to the earth and her creatures, to our friends and neighbors, or to the future. We may even carry some ideal of what it looks like to do work that is "meaningful," to live a life of service, and then end up feeling guilty or worthless at some point because we think our career isn't living up to that ideal.

If you have ever felt like this, let's see if we can shift our frame a bit to help unwind some of this guilt or felt 'lack of meaning.' First, when we consider our work in the context of spiritual life, try to remember that it's not only what we do that matters, but it's *how* we do it.

> "All work is empty save when there is love; and when you work with love you bind yourself to yourself, and to one another, and to God. And what is it to work with love? It is to weave the cloth with threads drawn from your heart, even as if your beloved were to wear that cloth. It is to build a house with affection, even as if your beloved were to dwell in that house. It is to sow seeds with tenderness and reap the harvest with joy, even as if your beloved were to eat the fruit. It is to charge all things you fashion with a breath of your own spirit." — Kahlil Gibran, *On Work*[122]

No matter what work we do—with some exceptions, of course, like sex trafficking—we can bring a posture of service to it. We can give it our full care and loving attention. We can uplift and support our colleagues and customers. We can take a genuine interest in our employees. We can continue to seek out and encourage better business practices—better work-life balance, office culture, environmental sustainability, health- and child-care, etc.

We can also keep close to our hearts the service we are providing for our families, who require the financial support to keep a roof over their heads and food on their plates, to provide them with opportunities to get an education or to learn a trade, to take ballet or art classes, and a thousand other things. Again, if we're not harming anyone with our work, then whatever work we do can be an expression of generosity and loving-kindness.

> "Always you have been told that work is a curse and labor a misfortune. But I say to you that when you work you fulfil a part of earth's furthest dream, assigned to you when that dream was born. And in keeping yourself with labor you are in truth loving life. And to love life through labor is to be intimate with life's inmost secret." — Kahlil Gibran, *On Work*[123]

Another important element I want to explore is how we hold and relate to wealth in spiritual life. Some people, across many religions and even in Buddhist circles, make wealth out to be some kind of villain. This view helps no one and it even carries a kind of superiority conceit. In the Buddha's teachings, wealth gained with integrity is seen as a blessing that can be used for the benefit and welfare of others. And in fact, two frequently mentioned people in the Buddhist scriptures, Visakha and Anathapindika, used their wealth to support the Sangha and to provide aid, medicines, and other resources to those in need. We still see this today with many of our charitable organizations—they rely on wealthy donors.

It is not unwholesome or unskillful to acquire wealth. Wealth can be a tremendous power for good in the world. Just think of all those who benefit from the Bill & Melinda Gates Foundation. Should we hold Bill and Melinda as spiritually inferior for making money? No. What matters is that we acquire our wealth with integrity and that we generously give back to life, give back to the earth, give back to our friends, family, and community.

"When in the marketplace you toilers of the sea and fields and vineyards meet the weavers and the potters and the gatherers of spices, invoke then the master spirit of the earth, to come into your midst and sanctify the scales and the reckoning that weighs value against value...And before you leave the marketplace, see that no one has gone his way with empty hands. For the master spirit of the earth shall not sleep peacefully upon the wind till the needs of the least of you are satisfied." — Kahlil Gibran, *On Buying & Selling*[124]

Aligning our livelihoods with spiritual life, in the end, is an expression of bodhicitta, the intention to awaken our hearts and minds for the benefit of all, for our Self. So again, whatever work we do, we can do it with this aspiration in our hearts and minds, whether it's expressed through our attitude at work, the work itself, or through our generosity to give back.

Exercises & Reflections

Is there anyone in your life who you are trying to "help" rather than "support"? Your child or even your spouse, perhaps? Are you forcing your own values and standards onto them, judging them based on your own ideals? What would happen to that relationship if, instead, you made a sincere effort to understand their aims and values, and then supported them in a way that is beneficial to them, even if that meant stepping out of their way?

When you see this tendency in yourself to help or fix everything, look inside yourself. Do you have a soft spot? Are you carrying past feelings of unworthiness, shame, embarrassment, etc.? Why is it that we want this person to be who *we* want them to be or to value what *we* value? Again, look for a wounded inner child, and then wrap that little boy or girl in unconditional love.

9. MIND

"The mind's nature is as vivid as a flawless
piece of crystal, intrinsically empty, naturally
radiant, and ceaselessly responsive."
– Shabkar

Opening to the mind itself is both a thrilling and harrowing adventure, vast in scope and endless in its creative endeavors. Every heroin and villain, every god and demon, every ghost and spirit, every friend and foe are created and play out their drama here, in the mind. Fear, shame, pride, love, and lust, again, all unfold here, in awareness. The mind is all we really know. It is all we can ever know. It creates our entire lives—our perception of the people we love, our goals, dreams and aspirations, our values and interests, our beliefs and understanding. It is the substance and context of all things.

Yet, when we look for it, when we look for the mind, for awareness itself, we realize there is nothing to find. But this no-thing, as we look closer, is not simply nothing. Though there is no mark to it, though there is no form, no shape, no color, there is a knowing quality, a radiance, vividness, and brightness, as well as a natural purity—a natural warmth, connectedness, and lovingness.

This fundamental nature of mind is described in many traditions, each with their own emphasis. Some describe the mind like the sky, entirely open. Clouds come and go, storms, hurricanes, lightning, and thunder all arise in it, but the sky (or the mind) remains unchanged. A mirror is another popular metaphor to describe the mind. A mirror reflects on its surface everything that comes before it, the ugly and beautiful, without discriminating. It doesn't become the things themselves. It doesn't take on their qualities or characteristics. It remains the same—pure, clear, unscathed, unchanged, accepting, and unbroken. Again, it allows each object to simply arise and be known in its own place, on this single plane of knowing. Further, the mirror is only known or seen through the objects that arise on it. Another common analogy is space. There is nothing that space does not encompass. Even the objects in space are, in some sense, made of space.

The Buddha lays a crumb trail for us to discover the empty, elusive, radiance of mind when he says, "Suppose bhikkhus[125] there was a house with a peaked roof with windows on the northern, southern, and eastern sides. When the sun rises and a beam of light enters through a window, where would it become established?"

"On the western wall, venerable sir."

"If there were no western wall, where would it become established?"

"On the earth, venerable sir."

"If there were no earth, where would it become established?"

"On the water, venerable sir."

"If there were no water, where would it become established?"

"It would not become established anywhere, venerable sir."

If you follow this crumb trail, replacing light for awareness, ask yourself, "Where can awareness be established?" Go ahead, look directly at your mind. Look for the foundation, for the source, of awareness. Can awareness be established anywhere? Is there a center to it? Is there some point from which awareness emanates? Or is it instead the always-enduring, all-pervasive radiance that lies awake, without beginning or end, even in complete darkness, where there is nothing to be illuminated?

In Christianity, we find parallels in Saint John of the Cross's book Dark Night of the Soul, which says (and I'm paraphrasing here), "A ray of sunlight that enters a room free from dust is less visible than a ray of light that enters a room filled with dust. This is because it is not the light itself that is seen but, rather, the light is the means by which those objects it strikes may be seen. In striking these objects, however, the light itself is also seen, through its own reflection of them. Were it not for this, neither the light nor the objects would be seen. Thus, if a ray of sunlight entered one window and passed out another on the other side, and if it met nothing on the way, the room would be no lighter than before; the light would be invisible. This is precisely what the Divine ray of contemplation [or mindfulness] does in the soul [or mind]... By leaving [the soul or mind] empty and in darkness, contemplation [or mindfulness] purges it and illumines it with the Divine spiritual light.

As you come to understand the mind through your own direct investigation, I hope you get a glimpse of its purity, love, and infinite creative power. Often, our first discovery of awareness can be exhilarating, quite the spiritual feeling. There is something sacred, reverent, and reassuring about knowing that our fundamental nature is entirely pure, boundless, unborn, and undying. Sometimes the discovery can be spontaneous. But more often it takes time and practice to notice. It's just that it's so subtle, fickle, flitting, and elusive. It has no marking and can't be measured by its coming and going, like the objects of awareness. And our attention too easily collapses into the mind's creations, its dream vapors.[126]

That is why, in this chapter, we will turn to the Buddha's third arena of training, training in cognition. Here, we will work on sharpening three mental faculties—effort, concentration, and mindfulness—so that we can learn to see more clearly the mind's true nature, its love, purity, and creative power. We want to see and understand directly that no matter what arises in the mind, however beautiful or terrifying, this is not who we ultimately are. The more we can see and understand this, the more we can settle into an open, easeful, and loving state of being, where we can take the artist's brush and paint freely the kind of life we want to live. As Ajahn Chah said:

> "About this mind. In truth, there is nothing really wrong with it. It is intrinsically pure. Within itself, it's already peaceful. That the mind is not peaceful...is because it follows moods. The real mind doesn't have anything to it. It is simply Nature. It becomes peaceful or agitated because moods deceive it... Sense impressions come and trick it into happiness, suffering, gladness, and sorrow, but the mind's true nature is none of those things. That gladness or sadness is not the mind, but only a mood coming to deceive us. The untrained mind gets lost and follows these things. It forgets itself. Then we think it is we who are upset or at ease or whatever.

> But really this mind of ours is already unmoving and peaceful... really peaceful!... If we know fully the true nature of sense impressions, we will be unmoved. Our practice is simply to see the Original Mind. So we must train the mind to know those sense impressions, and to not get lost in them... Just this is the aim of all this difficult practice we put ourselves through."[127]

Virya | Effort

What will you do with this precious gift of life? Whatever it is, you will need effort to do it. Effort is the source of all achievement. It fulfills our aspirations, breathes life into our values, and turns our intentions into lived expressions of our being.

Now, virya—the Pali word for "effort"—is actually a much bigger word than effort alone. It has many nuances and flavors to it, which include energy, strength, courage, vigor, vitality, resolve, and perseverance of body, heart, and mind. In its most basic meaning, though, we can think of virya as the capacity for activity, the power to get shit done, our willpower. As I said, it is the source of all our endeavors and achievements. So, virya is intimately connected with our motivations and intentions. Together with concentration and mindfulness, it breaks us free from the inertia of our behavioral habits and tendencies of mind and allows us to move toward a more intentional life.

In the context of the Eightfold Path, we apply virya to free ourselves and others from suffering, to rid ourselves of greed, hatred, and delusion, to establish peace of heart and clarity of mind. We apply effort to keep us on the path of fulfillment and awakening. This, the Buddha suggests, requires us to point our virya at what are called the Four Great Endeavors:

1. To prevent any unwholesome states from arising
2. To abandon any unwholesome states that have already arisen
3. To cultivate and develop wholesome states of mind
4. To strengthen wholesome states that have already arisen

This is a tremendous goal, of course, one that will last our whole lives. Virya isn't something that, once we have it, we have it for good. No, it takes continual practice and adjustment to find the right balance, like riding a bike or walking a tightrope. It's a refined art. We need to stay aware of our current state of mind and adjust the effort to what's needed in the moment. The Buddha compared it to tuning a lute—the strings can't be too tight or too loose. We need to continually find the sweet spot between effort and surrender. This may seem like a contradiction, but understanding this paradox is pivotal to our practice and a vital piece of knowledge to carry with us on our spiritual journey, or really any endeavor we pursue.

So, how can we work toward an aim or intention and, at the same time, avoid the trap, frustration, and energy-drain of over-efforting? How do we apply effort and at the same time surrender to reality? This brings up one of the biggest misunderstandings of Buddhism I hear from people—that Buddhism leads to total withdrawal and surrender from the world or from personal interests and endeavors, that it leads you to sink into the blissful meditative oblivion of oneness. This is far from the truth.

Thich Nhat Hanh was a major activist not just in Vietnam, where he was born and eventually exiled, but he also marched with Martin Luther King, Jr., and continued marching for peace the rest of his life. Surrender doesn't mean passive resignation. It means we surrender to the dhamma. It means we face the truth of the present moment's experience, rather than pretend things are otherwise. It means that we take a stand in reality, that we take a stand in truth. It is the same attitude or posture we explored in Chapter 4, when discussing equanimity, the same posture or attitude that James Baldwin expressed so well.

This kind of acceptance still allows us to make effort, to work toward our goals and aims, but it does so without the grasping or aversive mind, without causing unnecessary agitation to the system. It is an easeful effort that knows its aim but is not strained by expectation, strained by wanting things to go or be a certain way. We can be mindful of the bigger perspective, our goal, but also stay present, open, relaxed, and responsive in each moment.

Joseph Goldstein uses the analogy of climbing a mountain, which needs a similar balance of perspectives.[128] When you climb a mountain, you need to know your aim, to hike to the peak of Mount Raymond, say, a local favorite of mine. But you also need to be aware of each step. You need to be aware of the terrain beneath your feet so that you can adjust as you go. Similarly, with our spiritual journey, we can keep our larger goal in mind while also paying precise attention to where we are in the moment, allowing us to balance our effort as needed. When there is rocky terrain or we're close to the cliff, we need to tighten up our attention. But when we're in an open meadow filled with flowers, we can loosen up a bit.

So, how do we know if we're applying too much or too little effort? Well, to begin, try to pay attention to those moments when you feel overstrained, desperate, disappointed, frustrated, restless, or agitated. Are you expecting things to go a certain way? Are you waiting for something to happen? Do you want something about your experience to be different than it is right now? Do you feel like you are leaning into the next moment or leaning into the next task? We even see this on the meditation cushion—it's as if we are trying to anticipate the breath, trying to catch it. We might even be thinking about our next meditation, about how we will really be mindful for our next sit. We get too far out in front of ourselves.

These are all signs that our effort is too tight. Rather than being open and receptive to experience, laid back, seeing experience with wisdom, we are trying to catch and hold onto something, anticipating or expecting something to happen. There's an element of control, often from the little doer in our heads. At bottom, it is this feeling of wanting that can signal to us that we are over-efforting.

Effort becomes unhelpful when there is a forcing of the mind. Again, watch out for expectations or for any idea of gain you might be holding onto—the "in-order-to-mind" or the "if-then" mind. Does the mind feel tight and contracted or does it feel open and receptive to what is here? Are you trying to push the river along? If so, remember, it doesn't need your help. It's time to loosen the strings. It's time to sink down and back, to soften our heart and open the mind. We need to give up some control and settle into the dhamma, the truth of the ever-flowing moment. We need to work with and be with what's here, with equanimity, interest, and compassion. Remember, you're not producing anything in your experience, and you're not producing your awareness of it either. So, sit back and simply receive it. Even if we need to take action or respond to a situation, we can do it while we remain on top of our feet, settled into the moment. Don't get ahead of yourself and fall flat on your face.

Now, if on the other hand you find that the mind feels lazy, lethargic, apathetic, dull, bored, cloudy, or stagnant, this may be a sign that more effort is needed. When energy is low, when we are drifting or falling into a daze, falling into mindless reveries or daydreams, we leave ourselves vulnerable to delusion. Our effort is too loose. We need to tighten it. We need to straighten up our postures, check our attitude, and bring forward some strength, courage, investigation, and/or perseverance.

One way to do this is by taking a walk, going to the gym, or doing some Tai Chi or some other physical exercise that gets the energy in the system moving. Another thing to consider is eating lighter meals. It is quite the energy drain to metabolize food, especially in large quantities. Clean, moderate eating can take you a long way. You can also try being a little more active in your mental noting. And I don't mean becoming analytical of your experience. I mean to simply note it in a way that helps you bring a bare attention to the objects of awareness. So, the note should just be a soft mental note: tingling, pleasant; sleepiness, neutral; dullness, neutral; doubt, unpleasant.

See if, instead of five notes a minute, you can make ten notes about experience. Again, we just want to put a small frame around the experience to allow us to see it more clearly. We don't want to lean into the object. Just receive it. Finally, if you are still feeling sleepy, your body might be telling you it's time to take some rest. Listen to it. Just be careful that it's not sloth and torpor[129] trying to deceive you, trying to prevent you from facing a challenge, trying to prevent you from confronting some difficulty in your life, etc.

Remember, like all things in life, this practice will take some trial and error to tune-up. I actually just heard a funny story from Jack Kornfield that is relevant here. He said that when his energy was low, one of his teachers would have him sit on the edge of a deep water well to meditate. That ought to straighten up your posture and bring some energy to the system. Like I said, balancing our effort is an art. Have fun with it. And remember it will take time to learn the appropriate balance.

But to support you, let's explore some of the different forms and functions of virya so you can start to play around with the dials and see what works best for you at various times along your way.

One function of virya is to provide strength or support. Virya, in this form, serves to support wholesome factors[130] of mind—mindfulness, concentration, investigation, joy, tranquility, memory, and equanimity. The second-century monk Nagasena, in his famous dialogues with the Indo-Greek King Milinda, which we explored in Chapter 3, said that virya has the quality of shoring up our skillful practices and insights—when they are shored up by virya, none of our skillful dhammas are lost.[131]

The Buddha emphasized something similar in the Dhammapada, saying that when we put in the effort and practice, wisdom grows; and when we don't, wisdom wanes. So, like I said earlier, it is this quality of virya that keeps us on the path of fulfillment and awakening. It supports wisdom from waning. "Here," the Buddha says, "the noble disciple dwells as one who has produced strength; for the sake of abandoning unskillful dhammas and arousing skillful dhammas one is firm, of steady valor, unrelinquishing in purpose with regard to skillful dhammas."[132]

Another aspect of virya is courage, an unrelenting expression of heart. This quality of virya is profoundly energizing and is critical when, at times along our path, we run into difficult landscapes of mind that make us want to retreat to a place of comfort. While the hindrances sloth and torpor cause us to retreat from challenges, courage does the opposite. It is energized by challenges, inspired by them. When we cultivate virya in this form, we rise to the occasion and move onward to our aim. It doesn't mean we aren't scared or that we don't have doubts. It means we are willing to act in the face of those fears, in the face of those doubts. It welcomes fear and doubt and understands them as necessary elements of our growth.

"The only time a man can be brave is when he is afraid." — Ned Stark, *Game of Thrones*

Jesus demonstrated this quality of courage in an extraordinarily beautiful way. In Jesus's unwavering commitment to love, while his hands and feet were nailed to the cross, crowned in thorns, bruised and torn, he cried out, "Father, forgive them, for they know not what they do." Jesus had many opportunities, as well as every reason, to retreat from Jerusalem, to escape persecution. But courage kept him on his path, to become a living symbol of love not only for his people but for all humankind.

Now, you may be thinking, "Well sure, Jesus can do that. But he's the Christ, the Son of God and Man. I'm just a plain Jane." This quality of courage, though, isn't reserved for saints, heroes, and legends. Nor is it a fixed quality, something you have or you don't. It's a quality of mind that can be cultivated and strengthened with practice. And we see it everywhere in the hearts and minds of ordinary folk like you and me. We see it in so many mothers, who sacrifice their bodies, their time, and their careers for their children. We see it in extreme athletes, like the Wim Hofs of the world, who continually test the limits of their bodies. We see it in our schoolteachers, who keep showing up for their students, despite their low pay. We see it in our police officers, firefighters, and other first-responders, who continually face trauma without the proper resources, support, and pay. We see it in the women who spoke up against offenders in the #Me-Too movement. We see it right now in the people protesting in Iran for basic human rights.

We too can cultivate this quality of courage. As we learned in Chapter 4, we can skillfully build up this muscle by teasing the boundaries of our comfort levels, by briefly peaking over the edge. It takes courage to challenge ourselves, to extend our limits, to really see what is possible. As the Burmese meditation master Sayadaw U Tejaniya said:

> "Avoiding difficult situations or running away from them does not usually take much skill or effort. But doing so prevents you from testing your own limits and from growing. The ability to face difficulties can be crucial for your growth. However, if you are faced with a situation in which

162

the difficulties are simply overwhelming, you should step back for the time being and wait until you have built up enough [virya or courage] to deal with it skillfully."[133]

This is wise advice. We don't want to simply jump into a situation without giving it any thought. We want to discern with wisdom whether doing so is a skillful means to our end. Sometimes it isn't. Sometimes we simply aren't ready, and facing the challenge will just lead to more suffering. So, we need to step back and seek out some smaller wins before we come back to the bigger challenge.

There are some small practical ways you can start cultivating this element of virya, depending on your own personal conditioning. Maybe you can put yourself out there socially, pushing that comfort level. You can face your fear of rejection as you try to make some friends. You can put your art or writing out into the world, even though you fear people won't like or appreciate it. Or maybe you can apply for that job you've always wanted but haven't because you fear you'll get turned down. With your meditation practice, maybe you can sit for just a few minutes longer than you are comfortable with. You can commit to not move a muscle during one of your sits, no matter how uncomfortable it may be. You can also try running a 5- or 10k, or even a marathon. You can start going to the gym regularly. You can read a certain number of pages a day. There are many options here. When you push any of these boundaries, though, just make sure to pay attention to the energy that comes from teasing the boundary.

I really came to explore virya up in the mountains with my Snow Leopard. Every summer solstice, we would hike a bit further than we ever had before. Near the beginning, for one of our first summer solstice adventures, we hiked a trail in the Wasatch called Desolation Trail, an 18-mile hike with about 5,500 feet of elevation gain to Desolation Lake, where we camped for the night before making the 18-mile trek home. The next year, we went there and back in the time the sun was up, clocking in 36 miles in one day. And the next year, we did 48 miles in two days, bagging six peaks over ten thousand feet. Before each of these hikes, and especially during them, there was a big part of me that thought there was no way I could do it. Several times, I had the thought that this was it—I must simply lay down and die. But each time I thought my body would give out on me, this courageous dimension of virya came to the rescue and gave me the energy I needed. It showed me that my mind can propel my body much further than I ever could have imagined.

If you need some energy in your life, seek out some challenges. Play at the boundaries of your comfort levels. Know what you want and go get it, despite your doubts and fears. Let the bodhisattva's roar of courage motivate you: "Let only my skin and sinews and bones remain, let my blood dry up. I will not give up until I have accomplished what can be done by human effort and endeavor."[134]

The final dimension of virya we'll explore in this chapter is perseverance. Where courage gives us strength to face challenges, perseverance is all about the long game. It is the power of the long-enduring mind. This dimension of virya is not one to be underestimated. It is vital to our goal of liberation, which, as I said, is a life-long commitment and journey. Suzuki Roshi, in Zen Mind, Beginners Mind, says:

> "After you have practiced for a while, you will realize it is not possible to make rapid extraordinary progress. Even though you try very hard, the progress is always little by little. It is not like going out in a shower, in which you know when you get wet. In a fog, you do not know you're getting wet. But as you keep walking, you get wet little by little. If your mind has ideas of progress, you may say, 'oh, this pace is terrible,' but actually it is not. When you get wet in a fog, it is very difficult to dry yourself, so there is no need to worry about progress. Just be sincere and make full effort in each moment. This is enough."[135]

This is how practice works. It takes time. You can't just learn to rhyme like Eminem overnight. He's been at it consistently for decades. The other rappers who collaborate with him are astonished at the effort he puts in, saying he treats it like a 9–5 job. Despite what some Buddhist suttas say about people becoming fully Enlightened beings at the snap of a finger, it takes time to master the hindrances, to free ourselves of greed, hatred, and delusion, to free ourselves from suffering, especially in our complex, modern world. Our practice unfolds steadily over time when we apply this persevering dimension of virya.

There's a great story about the famous Tibetan master Milarepa, who, as legend has it, at a young age went on a revengeful killing spree at his mother's request. Later in his life, though, after he had encountered the Buddha's teachings, he realized he needed to get enlightened or else his karma would catch up to him.[136] So, he went and lived and practiced in many caves until he perfected his heart and mind, and then spent the rest of his life

164

teaching, and singing joyously.

Over the years, Milarepa grew very close to his chief disciple and shared many of his teachings with him. But the chief disciple thought Milarepa was saving the highest teaching, the real esoteric teaching, the secret transmission, for the end. So, not long before Milarepa died, the two of them trekked off to some remote place in the mountains. And when they got there, Milarepa had the chief disciple set everything up perfectly, really setting the stage for something special. The disciple was stoked, super eager to receive the secret transmission. So, finally, when everything was ready, Milarepa came very close to his disciple, turned around, bent over, lifted his robe, and showed his disciple the calluses on his ass—the secret transmission: virya in the form of perseverance.

What's the secret to success? Put in the work and don't give up. The long game is tough, no doubt. Whether it's raising kids, going to school, maintaining a relationship, putting in the years to get your dream job, working through grief or chronic depression, or just sticking with your spiritual practice, there will inevitably be times when we run low on hope and fuel. So, here are a few tools to keep in your bag for when you find yourself in those situations and need a little virya in the form of perseverance.

First, see if you can connect again to what first sparked your interest in your journey. Was it some personal experience, maybe of tremendous joy or interest, or maybe of suffering? Was there a deep thirst for meaning or purpose in your life? Were you desperate for freedom or understanding? Was it compassion for another? Whatever it was, see if you can reconnect with this motivation, interest, or inspiration. Let it rekindle some fire in you.

Second, you can try contemplating the inevitability of death and the preciousness of this human life. We too often take advantage of the unbelievable conditions we've been given—this miracle of life, this precious human birth, this awe-inspiring experience. Somewhat unconsciously, we think we'll never run out of time or that we'll be able to pursue our interests or deepest passions later. But thinking the conditions will always be favorable is simply a delusion. Eventually, we will get sick. We will grow old. And we will die.

Just a couple weeks ago, we had a friend over to our home. And that night she was working through a headache, which she expressed had been there for a couple weeks. A few days later, the headaches got bad enough to make her go to the hospital. Turns out, her entire life changed in an instance. She was diagnosed with a diffuse midline glioma, an aggressive and rare type of brain tumor.

Our life, this human body, this experience, this very moment, is precious. The Buddha said that we have arrived at a great treasure island, the treasure island of this precious human birth. Here, now, with this body, with this life, with this opportunity, with this day, with this hour, with this moment, we can come to understand and cultivate the causes of peace, happiness, and freedom. And this moment will never come again.

"Cherish your body," says the 14th Century Monk Tsongkhapa. "It is yours this one time only. The human form is one with great difficulty. It is easy to lose. All worldly things are brief, like lightning in the sky. This life, you must know, is a tiny splash of a raindrop, a thing of beauty that disappears even as it comes into being. Therefore, set your aspiration and make use of every day and night to achieve it."[137]

Mindfulness | Establishing Our Foundations

Spirituality is not a religion. Like chemistry, physics, medicine, or biology, spirituality is a field of study—the study of our own direct nature, the study of our subjective experience, of our mind-body processes, of our precious human life. We want to understand ourselves, the world, and our relation to it. We want to understand the causes and conditions of our joys and sorrows. We want to understand where to find value and purpose in our lives. We want to know what it means to be alive and what it means to die. We want to be loved, felt, and seen. And we want to love, feel, and see others in turn. We want to know what it means to be conscious, to be awake. We want to know what it means to live an examined life.

And just as the other sciences have tools to help them learn more about their subject matter, spirituality too has its own tools, the primary tool being mindfulness. Sam Harris compares mindfulness to the Large Hadron Collider—it is a tool for making profound discoveries about the nature of our own hearts and minds.[138] And like the other fields of science, which are committed to truth, spirituality too expresses a certain kind of passion for truth, a passion for discerning what is subjectively real in each moment.

Now, because we have already discussed the qualities of mindfulness in Chapter 3, we will not do so again here in much detail. Rather, we will explore how mindfulness—discerning what is subjectively real in each moment—can be formally cultivated using what the Buddha called the Four Foundations of Mindfulness. These foundations, he said, provide a direct path to awakening. They are: 1) the body, 2) feelings, 3) mind-states and emotions (or heart-mind), and 4) dhammas (categories or frameworks of experience). In the Buddha's words:

> "In regard to the body, one abides contemplating the body, ardent, clearly comprehending, and mindful, free from desires and discontent in regard to the world. In regard to feelings, one abides contemplating feelings, ardent, clearly comprehending, and mindful, free from desires and discontent in regard to the world. In regard to the heart-mind, one abides contemplating the heart-mind, ardent, clearly comprehending, and mindful, free from desires and discontent in regard to the world. In regard to dhammas, one abides contemplating dhammas, ardent, clearly comprehending, and mindful, free from desires and discontent in regard to the world."[139]

Before we get into the four foundations, however, let's quickly refresh what we learned about mindfulness. Mindfulness is the translation of the Pali word sati, which has several meanings and functions, all of which are critical to the development of wisdom. In Chapter 3, we learned that one dimension of mindfulness is remembering to be present. It is the opposite of absentmindedness or "spacing out." One teacher would often say to his students, "Sit and know you are sitting, and the whole of the dharma will be revealed to you."[140] I like to think of this dimension of mindfulness as a listening quality, an immediate or "bare" attention of what is here now.

Once, when asked what she says to god when she prays, Mother Teresa responded, "I don't say anything. I just listen."

"Well, then, what does god say to you?" the interviewer asked, puzzled.

"He doesn't say anything," she replied. "He just listens. And if you don't understand that, I can't explain it to you."[141]

This listening quality brings us close to experience without putting a story to it. It allows us to see experience without the clouds of papañca obscuring it. It allows the selfless, ever-changing, inter-connected nature of all things to shine forth. When we really listen, when we are truly mindful, we don't interfere with experience. We don't try to manipulate it or dominate it or control it. We simply open to what is already here, without judgment. That is, we cease to become distracted by thought. We don't collapse into some idea or image of who or what we or others are. When we are mindful, we remain entirely open and receptive to the always new and ever-changing flow of life, of energy, of experience.

In addition to this bare presence, to this listening quality, we also learned that mindfulness requires meta-awareness—an awareness of awareness itself. When experiencing an object of awareness, we also need to witness the knowing quality of mind, that the object and the known are inseparable, two sides of the same coin. We need to hold both the ultimate and the relative, the universal and the particular. We need to remember that we are not-two

Finally, we learned that mindfulness asks us to stay there in the middleness of all things, that we live from a place of equanimity. In other words, mindfulness requires that we don't look at experience through the lens of greed or aversion, that we don't grasp at the pleasant or push the unpleasant away. It asks that we hold every piece of experience, fully and intimately, with unconditional acceptance. It asks us to remain completely open and receptive to the dharma.

Okay, well, now that we have recapped what we learned about mindfulness, let's go ahead and apply it, first, to the body.

Mindfulness of Body

"In regard to the body, one abides contemplating the body, ardent, clearly comprehending, and mindful, free from desires and discontent in regard to the world." – The Buddha

"In regard to the body, one abides contemplating the body internally or externally, or one abides contemplating both internally and externally. One abides contemplating the nature of arising in the body...the nature of passing away in the body...or the nature of both arising and passing away in the body. Mindfulness that 'there is a body' is established in one to the extent necessary for bare knowledge and continuous mindfulness. And one abides independent, not clinging to anything in the world...." – The Buddha

If you put this book down for a moment and try to observe ten breaths, you will quickly discover that you don't have much freedom—freedom from distraction, freedom from mindless attention—and that it is primarily thought that robs you of your freedom. This is okay, of course. The mind thinks, and for good reason. The thinker in our heads is our little problem creator and problem solver. Ultimately, the practice is not to get rid of thought. But rather to notice thoughts clearly, not just their content but as a phenomenon, as a matter of direct experience, as a changing wave of energy in the mind, without losing the thread of awareness.

In the beginning, however, I think you will find that thoughts easily sweep you away. Suddenly, you will find that you are down some rabbit hole of a thought, with no idea of how you got there. You were supposed to be paying attention to the breath, say, to develop concentration, but there you were, thinking without realizing you were thinking. So, one of the first insights in our practice is to confront the sobering truth that there really is no one in the driver seat. As Stephen Batchelor puts it, "The comforting illusion of personal coherence and continuity is ripped away to expose only fragmentary islands of consciousness separated by yawning gulfs of unawareness."[142]

Grounding attention in the body helps us to close these gulfs of unawareness. It helps us to stay grounded in our bodies and environment, to not "space-out." It may not be the appropriate entrance for all people, like for people with autism who have underdeveloped proprioception. But amidst the endless stream of thoughts, which can toss us every which way, the simplicity of the body is always here for us to come back home.

To support mindfulness of the body, I find it incredibly useful to make it a habit throughout the day to make the soft mental note 'there is a body.' Immediately, this simple mantra tends to reconnect me with my body, to feel into its relationship with space and the immediate environment. Again, this is a great way to lasso me back down to earth from up there in the clouds.

As I mentioned earlier, old traumas from being sexually abused as a kid resurfaced for me and sent me into a storm of thoughts and emotions, which lasted months. I can't express enough how useful it was to be able to continually return to the skeletal frame 'there is a body.' No matter how wild life gets, we can always come back to the simplicity of the ever-changing field of sensations in the body—tingling, pressure, vibrations, heat, cold, whatever's there. We can always plant our feet back on solid ground. "Again, monks, when walking, one knows 'I am walking;' when standing, one knows 'I am standing;' when sitting, one knows 'I am sitting;' when lying down, one knows 'I am lying down;' or one knows accordingly however one's body is disposed."[143] Once we come back to the body, we can realize that it was the creative dimension of our minds that played out this entire drama. But here we are, just hanging out at home or whatever. We are safe.

Now, as you likely know from your own experience, the difficult emotions we face in our lives are experienced in the body—in the heart, stomach, throat, or other places in and even seemingly around the body. So, it can appear counterintuitive to ground ourselves in the body when we are caught up in some emotion. But often, what I have found, is that when we are caught in an emotion, like sadness or fear, though we feel the emotion in our body, even rather strongly, we are not actually seeing the emotion clearly, as an impersonal pattern of changing sensations—of tightness, pressure, heaviness, or whatever. Instead, we are primarily in our thoughts. We go into storytelling, judging, analyzing, or problem-solving mode. And as our thoughts proliferate, so do our emotions. We get caught in a feedback loop of thoughts and emotions. When we truly focus on the body, however, we take ourselves out of this cycle of thought. As the mindful recovery leader Kevin Griffin says, "There are no words in my body."[144]

Another reason it is important to bring our bodies into awareness, especially our postures, is because they are also a means of expression—they communicate to other people. They make a statement about our attitudes, about how we feel and relate with others and the world. What is your posture saying? Is it telling people you are lazy and disinterested? Is it aggressive and tense? Is it judgmental or skeptical? What vibes is your body sending out? Hard, cold, and closed-off vibes, or soft, warm, and open ones?

Our postures also shape our internal landscape. Sitting slumped forward with your head hanging low—belly-gazing—brings a different kind of energy to the system than standing tall with your arms out wide and your chin raised high to the sky. Is your back strong and tall? Are your shoulders rolled back and relaxed? Is your chest open? Is your stomach relaxed? Is your jaw relaxed? Is your forehead relaxed? Are your fists clenched or open and soft? I highly encourage you to start opening to your body postures so that you can restore the alignment between your body and mind. We only get this beautiful temple of ours once, and it is incredibly fragile, exceedingly precious.

Okay, before moving to mindfulness of feelings, let's explore one more important dimension of the body—our breath. The power of the breath to cut through the complexities of discursive thinking should not be underestimated. The Buddha's instruction here is fourfold. First, we start with the simple instruction, "Breathing in, one knows, I am breathing in. Breathing out, one knows, I am breathing out."[145]

Then, as the mind settles from this increased concentration, to further refine our attention, the Buddha asks us to note, "When breathing in long, one knows, I am breathing in long. When breathing in short, one knows, I am breathing in short."[146] Again, we're not trying to control the breath. We are simply opening to the experience of the breath directly, keeping it very simple. Refining our attention around the breath is a great way to settle the mind and sturdy our attention, which allows us to deepen our insight.

Next, the Buddha asks us to take a more active role, saying, "One trains thus: I shall breathe in experiencing the whole body... I shall breathe out experiencing the whole body...I shall breathe in calming the body... I shall breathe out calming the body."[147] As you know, it is always much harder to accomplish anything when we are not calm. River, my partner, before I met her and our kids, had established and instilled into the kids three rules, which are relevant here. The first rule is 'don't freak out.' The second is, 'take deep breaths.' And the third is, 'work through your problem.'

Like the Buddha emphasized with his shift in language—from knowing to training—staying calm is an important skill we must train in ourselves. It's like trying to surf or ride a long board. If we are tense and rigid, we are going to create all kinds of disasters for ourselves. But if we can stay calm, there's a natural flow and flexibility that allows us to move through the world with more grace. This is true with our practice as well. Not only can we respond more wisely to each situation when we are calm, but we can also set ourselves up to deepen insight. Think of those times when you were trying to learn a new subject in school, say, and you were too tense, too worried. It was much harder, wasn't it? When, on the other hand, we are relaxed, it's much easier to learn or accomplish a task.

So, first, we open to the whole body through each breath, and then we calm the body with each breath. Breathing in, I feel connected to the whole body. Breathing out, calming. Or simply, "Calm, calm, calming." This is a mantra I use all the time to keep me relaxed, receptive, and capable.

Now, like our bodies, many of us also take our breath for granted. Even though I had been practicing mindfulness for over a decade, I really didn't come to appreciate just how much that was true for me until I sat ayahuasca for the first time. All over the retreat center, there were signs posted that said, "Remember to enjoy your breath." My first thought upon seeing these signs was, "That's a bit elementary. Couldn't they have placed signs that carried a bit more depth or wisdom to them?" And then I sat my first ceremony...

Having that constant pillar there, the reminder that I am alive, that my body is breathing, really helped to keep the roof from collapsing in on me. The breath not only provides us with direct access to the truth of change, which helps keep us open, but it literally sustains our life. On average, we take 900 breaths an hour. That's 900 opportunities in this next hour to be grateful for this intake of life-sustaining oxygen, which is being pumped through our blood, giving our body the energy necessary to think, to move, to smile, to laugh, and to love. This very next breath is sustaining your life.

One last thing about the breath which I love to bring to awareness is that it is such a clear demonstration of our connection to the outside world. The outside world is continually flowing through us. We cannot be without it, we are inextricably linked, entirely at one, with the wide-open sky. Simply recognizing this can often bring much more space to awareness. It can push outward on every wall of our being.

Okay, well, let's move on to the second foundation of mindfulness—mindfulness of feelings.

Mindfulness of Feelings

"In regard to feelings, one abides contemplating feelings, ardent, clearly comprehending, and mindful, free from desires and discontent in regard to the world." – The Buddha

"Whatever feeling one feels, whether pleasant, unpleasant or neutral, one abides contemplating impermanence in those feelings, contemplating fading away, . . . contemplating relinquishment. Contemplating thus, one does not cling to anything in this world. When one does not cling, one is not agitated. When one is not agitated, one personally attains Nibbāna."[148] – The Buddha

In Buddhism, "feeling" (*vedanā* in Pali) has a very narrow definition—it is the pleasant, unpleasant, and neutral feeling tones that accompany every object of awareness, which should be thought of as a spectrum or dial rather than discretely. In English, we often use the words feelings and emotions interchangeably. But in the Buddhist frame, emotions are much more complex. They can contain many feelings associated with them. Anger, for example, can have pleasant feeling tones associated with that "honeyed tip" or "sweet justice" while also containing unpleasant feeling tones associated with indigitation or frustration.

Feeling tones are an incredibly important dimension of experience to bring into awareness because they are what condition our habits and preferences, moving us through the world. When a pleasant feeling tone arises with an object of mind, we usually try to grasp onto the object, we try not to let it go, we desire it and seek it out. And when an unpleasant feeling arises, we usually push it away, we resist it, we run and hide from it. And when a neutral feeling arises, we generally ignore it, we let it move through awareness with little attention around it, we become blind to some aspect of experience.

When it comes down to it, feeling tones are what bring experience to life. For this same reason, feeling tones are what toss us into the spiraling abyss of self-concern. They are what collapse attention into the contents of awareness. So, it's important to include feelings in our practice because, without becoming aware of these powerful forces, we will get dragged around by them. Just consider how many of your actions throughout the day are due to avoiding an unpleasant feeling or acquiring pleasant feelings. Notice too how your sense of self gets tied up in these feeling tones, how you become identified with them. We take these fleeting energy states to be our own—my pain, my anger, my sadness.

The Thai master Ajahn Chaa once sat retreat by himself in a little hut near a village where, one night, the villagers were celebrating with loud music. At first, Ajahn Chaa was annoyed, "Don't they know I'm here on retreat?" He quickly realized, however, that the problem wasn't the music. It was his own mind. "They're just having a good time down there," he thought to himself. "It's me who's making myself miserable up here. The sound is just sound. It's me who is going out to annoy it. If I leave the sound alone, it won't annoy me. It's just doing what sound does. It makes sound. This is its job. So, if I don't go out and bother the sound, it's not going to bother me."[149] This is interesting to note because, often, we feel like it is something we are attached to—a person, a material object, a food, or whatever—when in reality, it is the feeling tone the mind attaches to.

So, when we can get below the concept or preference—I do or don't like this object, emotion, or mind-state—and instead meet the raw experience of the feeling itself, we can start to get ahead of our reactions, we can begin to relate to things with wisdom, impersonally. It's not about "me" or "it" anymore. It's just nature, it's just biology, the old survival parts of the brain that are trying to protect me. There are no reasons or rationalizing here, just instinctual reactions meant to push us away from danger and move us toward food, sex, and other Darwinian needs, however outdated or unskillful in manner. All we need to do, then, is accept the feeling and relax into it. We can give up the fight and, instead, hold the feeling with unconditional love, without judgment or reactivity.

As we develop our ability to be with feelings in this way, noticing their impersonal and ever-changing nature, without judging or reacting to them, we start to get a taste of true equanimity. And as our equanimity grows, so does our capacity for freedom, our capacity for responding with discriminating wisdom rather than reacting automatically. We will have the choice to respond to people and situations with love, compassion, and joy rather than automatically react from a place of desire, aversion, or delusion. This, in turn, will lead to a deeper sense of calm, which allows us to be more concentrated, which will allow us to develop more insight and wisdom. As you can see, there's a reason the Buddha singled out feelings as one of the four foundations of mindfulness. The more we open to them, the more our life will spiral upwards.

So, what instructions does the Buddha provide for us? Well, as always, he keeps it simple and straightforward:

> "When feeling a pleasant feeling, one knows, 'I feel a pleasant feeling.' When feeling an unpleasant feeling, one knows, 'I feel an unpleasant feeling.' When feeling a neutral feeling, one knows, 'I feel a neutral feeling.'"

Again, to cultivate more mindfulness around this dimension of experience, as a feeling arises, whether pleasant or unpleasant, our goal, once again, is not to change it. We don't push it away if it's bad or hold onto it tightly if it's good. We simply drop down and back into our wide-open hearts. We open ourselves to the feeling. We investigate it directly, without reacting to it. And again, I don't mean conceptually. We don't analyze the feeling's relation to the object—the thought, sensation, or emotion. We simply become interested in the feeling tone as a matter of direct experience, as a raw phenomenon.

What do the feelings associated with anger, joy, or sadness feel like? What is this unpleasant feeling in my back like? What's its character or quality? Again, we just need to allow it into awareness, accept it, become interested in it. We don't judge it. We don't analyze it. We don't compare it. We don't ask why it's happening to us. We just note, "this unpleasant feeling feels like this. This pleasant feeling feels like this. This neutral feeling feels like this."

Now, because so many feelings are arising and disappearing all the time, it can be helpful in the beginning to open primarily to those bodily sensations that really pull at your attention. Make a soft mental note of the sensation—tingling... pleasant; tension... unpleasant. And when it no longer pulls at you, note its disappearance and go back to the frame 'there is a body.' Do this too with strong thoughts. Notice how thoughts trigger different feeling tones in your mind and body. Maybe you recall a person you love, and it triggers a wave of pleasant feelings in your emotional heart. Or maybe you recall someone, and it triggers a wave of pleasant feelings in your genitals and, at the same time, perhaps unpleasant feelings related to the emotional sensations of shame. In either case, see if you can simply open to the feeling tones, without reacting to them. You might even consider doing a quick body scan every morning when you wake up and again at night before you go to sleep. From head to toe, see if there are any pleasant, unpleasant, or neutral feeling tones in the body.

And if you ever find it too difficult to sit with particular feelings, see if the power of curiosity can save you. See if you can become more interested in the feeling. Ask yourself where in the body you feel it. Where do I feel anger, sadness, or fear? Is it a feeling in the face? Is it a contraction in the heart? Is there a stiffness in the spine? A tightness in the fists? A tingling in the genitals? A twisting of the stomach? Again, become curious of the feeling as it is directly experienced, not conceptually but as a raw experience. Try to notice it as a wave of energy.

Another skillful thing to do with feelings, whether they are on the physical or spiritual plane, is to contemplate and notice directly their impermanent and changing nature. Just consider that every feeling you have ever experienced, every feeling associated with embarrassment, rejection, shame, hatred, jealousy, grief, or doubt, every single unpleasant feeling you have ever experienced has come and gone all on its own. This feeling too will pass away all on its own. There's no need to resist it. Just hold it like a newborn baby, with love, care, and compassion.

Well, before we explore the third foundation of mindfulness, mindfulness of mind-states, let's explore one more aspect of feeling tones—the difference between worldly and unworldly feeling tones, as the Buddha called them. Worldly feelings are all the feelings associated with our senses—e.g., we eat some chocolate and there are sensations in the mouth accompanied by pleasant feeling tones. Unworldly feelings, however, refer to feelings associated with our ultimate nature—feelings associated with love and wisdom, those mind-states that don't seek anything, like renunciation, generosity, kindness, compassion, mudita, and equanimity. The more you can awaken to the subtle warmth of these feelings, the less likely you will be lured by your senses, by desire, aversion, and delusion.

As we saw in Chapter 5, most of us seek happiness through pleasant sense experiences. And we also explored the pitfalls to this approach. First, they are unreliable and unsatisfactory because they are so fleeting. Second, some of our desires are harmful on their face, like certain drugs, sex with minors, particular types of thrill-seeking, etc. Third, when we think of our sensual desires in terms of addiction, we see how much they control our lives and how much dis-ease this brings to our system. Just consider if we wanted to have sex all the time with everyone we saw, and we wanted to eat all the foods, and have all the things, etc. Our lives would be a living hell. The Buddha captured this well when he said, "What the world calls happiness, I call suffering; what the world calls suffering, I call happiness."[150]

With the unworldly pleasures, however, the Buddha is pointing us toward pleasures that don't have these hidden (or not so hidden) dangers, and which eventually become the basis for our awakening. So, you may find it extremely skillful to start opening awareness to these unworldly feelings. As you increase your direct awareness of them, the wanting mind will naturally settle, and you will slowly grow into a warm, relaxed, and contented state of being.

Okay, let's move on to explore the third foundation of mindfulness—mindfulness of mind-states and emotions, or mindfulness of heart-mind.

Mindfulness of Heart-Mind

"In regard to the mind, one abides contemplating the mind, ardent, clearly comprehending, and mindful, free from desires and discontent in regard to the world."[151] – The Buddha

"Here one knows a lustful mind to be 'lustful,' and a mind without lust to be 'without lust.' One knows an angry mind to be 'angry,' and a mind without anger to be 'without anger.' One knows a deluded mind to be 'deluded,' and a mind without delusion to be 'without delusion;' one knows a contracted mind to be 'contracted,' and a distracted mind to be 'distracted.'"[152] – The Buddha

The translation here for the fourth foundation of mindfulness is mindfulness of *citta*, the Pali word for heart-mind. In many Asian countries, they don't distinguish between the heart and mind. If you asked them to point to their mind, they would point to their heart. This may seem a bit strange for those of us who grew up in a Western culture and have been so strongly conditioned to live from our headspace, to operate from our ego center. But believe it or not, there is another way to be. We can orient, live, and relate from the wholeness of our heart-mind, which encompasses the ego or thinker but is not confined to it.

Loch Kelly,[153] a meditation teacher who I describe as an architect of mind and a real warrior of love, truly one of the kindest and wisest people I have met, tells a relevant story about one of the first scientific researchers to travel to Nepal to study the brainwaves of monks. After the researcher arrived with his trunk full of equipment, he started to show the monks what he had planned on doing. So, they sat there politely as they watched him pull out his equipment. Then, the researcher took out the EEG cap, which he placed over the top of his head, and the monks began to laugh. Surprised, he asked, "What's so funny?"

"Why would you look there, in your head? This is where we experience meditation," they said, as they put their hands on their chests, "in our heart-mind."

I think this story helps to capture both the vastness and the intimacy of the third foundation of mindfulness. With mindfulness of citta, or heart-mind, we not only train ourselves to become aware of all the mind-states, moods, and emotions that arise and how they color and condition our hearts and minds, but we train ourselves to become mindful of our attitude or posture toward them. Rather than viewing the inner and outer worlds in terms of liking and disliking, we open to the full range of experience, to all mind-states, moods, and emotions with mindfulness. In short, we open to the three unwholesome roots—desire, aversion, and delusion. So, really, it is a practice of shaping the right attitude toward experience, as the Burmese Sayadaw[154] U Tejaniya puts it.

Sayadaw U Tejaniya encourages us to ask throughout our sitting and throughout our day, "What is the attitude in the mind right now?" I will also at times frame this as "What is my posture to experience right now?" or "What is the posture in the mind?" Am I leaning into or away from some element of experience or am right here with it, observing and learning from the experience as it is? Am I wanting things to be different than they are or am I settled back, open, and interested in what is unfolding? Am I trying to control experience, trying to anticipate it, expecting that something will happen, or am flowing along with it, responding with wisdom?

A mind free of compulsive liking and disliking is what allows us to see things clearly as they are, in a relaxed and alert way. "Whatever you are experiencing in this moment," U Tejaniya reminds us, "is the right experience... No experience out there is better than the present experience. An experience is an experience. An object is an object. It is neither wholesome nor unwholesome!"[155] It is our attitude toward experience that matters. Are we looking at experience through the lens of desire, aversion, or delusion? Again, what's the attitude in the mind right now? Often, when I simply ask this question, I tend to notice a softening in my body, heart, and mind.[156]

It's important to see that dissatisfaction arises from the delusion that things are not the way we think they should be. We see this all the time with the yogi or meditator mind. We sit and our whole experience is bright, clear, and open, and so we think we had a good sit. Then, the next day, we sit and our whole experience is cloudy, painful, and dark, and so we think we had a bad sit, or that we are a bad meditator. This is the attitude we are trying to avoid. It closes the mind and hinders our practice. As the fifth-century Zen master Jianzhi Sengcan said:

> "The Great Way is not difficult for those who have no preferences. When liking and disliking are both absent, everything becomes clear and undisguised. Make the smallest distinction, however, and heaven and earth are set infinitely apart. If you wish to see the truth, then hold no judgements for or against anything. To set up what you like against what you dislike is the disease of the mind. When the deep meaning of things is not understood, the mind's essential

peace is disturbed to no avail."[157]

Now, we all will have unskillful attitudes from time to time. That is a part of being human. So, again, rather than double down on our aversion, rather than condemn an unskillful attitude, we can instead accept it, relax into it, and learn from it. How does this attitude help or hurt our aim? Remember, the mind itself, knowing itself, is already wholesome, it's already pure, it's already at peace.

Okay, well, before moving on to the final foundation of mindfulness, mindfulness of dhammas, let's briefly explore an important dimension of our practice and our lives—that is, our moods. Moods are tricky because not only are they difficult to open to but they are difficult to stay open to. They are nebulous. They work under the surface, and can last for days and sometimes even weeks or months. If we're not mindful of them, they can wreak havoc on our lives—on our jobs, on our relationships, and on our own hearts and minds. So, it's important to stay mindful of whatever moods we have operating. One skillful way to do this is to keep a journal of your moods, to track them. You can also tell those close to you that you are in a particular mood, and then ask them for whatever support or boundaries you need.

Another reason moods are tricky is because they get so entangled in thought. We build entire superstructures of self around them, skyscrapers and even entire cityscapes. If we're not careful, if we don't stay aware of the impersonal and ever-changing nature of all the bodily and emotional sensations, their corresponding feelings, and associated thoughts (all of which we simply denote as "depression," "anger," etc.), the mood reinforces our sense of self. And if it endures, it can even end up defining our entire lives. It can become our root identity: "I am just an angry or depressed person." Again, our moods can consume us if we're not ardent in our mindfulness.

This was an extremely hard lesson for me that took many years to understand. The emotions of sadness, which stemmed from thoughts of loneliness, from not being seen and understood by my family, friends, and community, and which also stemmed from physical and sexual abuse as a child, slowly morphed into a more permanent mood, which I eventually identified so heavily with. This mood then caused more suicidal thoughts, which produced more emotions of sadness and loneliness, which often lead to panic attacks, and on and on it went. It was mindfulness that finally saved me. Like I said in Chapter 5, it didn't make these thoughts and emotions go away. But it allowed them to arise without forcing my "self" onto them. It allowed them to be here, without struggle, which really helped to deflate the seemingly permanent mood.

If you commonly experience a certain mood, like depression or anger, let the people in your life know. Express what boundaries or support you need. You don't have to go at this alone. And you don't need to feel ashamed for having these moods. The humility and courage to express how you are feeling and what you need will give others the courage to do the same. And when we are all able to communicate more openly and honestly with each other in this way, all of us will be better situated to support one another.

Alright, well, let's turn to the fourth foundation of mindfulness, mindfulness of dhammas.

Mindfulness of Dhammas

> "In regard to dhammas, one abides contemplating dhammas, ardent, clearly comprehending, and mindful, free from desires and discontent in regard to the world." – The Buddha

> "In regard to dhammas, one abides contemplating dhammas in terms of the five hindrances. And how does one in regard to dhammas abide contemplating dhammas in terms of the five hindrances? If sensual desire [aversion, sloth and torpor, restlessness and worry, or doubt] is present, one knows, 'there is sensual desire [etc.] in me'; if sensual desire [aversion, sloth and torpor, restlessness and worry, or doubt] is not present, one knows 'there is no sensual desire [etc.] in me'; and one knows how unarisen sensual desire [etc.] can arise, how arisen sensual desire [etc.] can be removed, and how a future arising of the removed sensual desire [etc.] can be avoided." – The Buddha

The Pali word *dhamma* can create a lot of confusion because it has such a wide range of meanings, depending on the context. As we have already learned, dhamma (or *dharma* in Sanskrit) can be used to mean the truth of the moment's experience, or simply "law," "reality," or "truth." It can also be used to mean "the teachings of the Buddha," or specific elements of the mind and body—each of the mental and physical elements is called a "dhamma."[158]

In the fourth foundation of mindfulness, however, we can think of dhammas as categories of experience, or the different frameworks that organize the principles of the Buddha's teachings—how different elements of experience interact and function. In other words, rather than a dry verbal exploration, the Buddha is showing us how we can skillfully investigate these dhammas for ourselves and apply his teachings to our moment-to-moment experience. Now, though the Buddha's frameworks include 1) the five hindrances, 2) the five aggregates of clinging, 3) the six sense spheres, 4) the seven factors of awakening, 5) the four noble truths, and 6) the eightfold path, here, we will focus only on the hindrances. And more specifically, we will primarily focus only on the last three hindrances—restlessness, sloth and torpor, and doubt—since we have already explored in some detail desire and aversion.

As you likely know, no matter how dedicated you are to practice, there are times and seasons in our lives when everything feels off. We're not concentrated. We can't connect well to others or to our experience. Our emotions may be either dry and unfeeling or in extreme turmoil. And it's nearly impossible to watch even a few breaths without becoming distracted. This, of course, is completely natural. It's a universal experience for each of us at times to be flooded with obstacles that cloud our hearts and minds and prevent us from staying open, connected, and receptive to the ever-changing flow of experience. That's why I thought we'd take this space to look a bit closer at the hindrances. We'll practice identifying them, opening to them, and working skillfully with them. We'll learn how to embrace them as a part of our path rather than treat them as personal failings or something "bad" we have to avoid.

Let's begin by briefly going over each of them—1) desire, 2) aversion, 3) sloth and torpor, 4) restlessness, and 5) doubt. Desire, as you know is that sense of reaching out for pleasure, wanting it, grasping it, longing for it, whereas aversion is any kind of pushing away from experience. (I just want to point out that the aversion I am speaking to here, this pushing away, must come from a place of ill-will. Remember, we can put up healthy borders if we do so out of love.) Aversion includes things like hatred, anger, boredom, resistance, or irritation toward the unpleasant. The third, which we haven't addressed head-on, is a low energy state, which is traditionally boxed into sloth and torpor, but which we can also think of as lethargy, sleepiness, drowsiness, dullness, heaviness, laziness, cowardice, or a lack of driving power. The fourth is an overly energized state, a frenetic and excited one, which is often expressed as restlessness, worry, anxiety, and panic. And finally, the fifth is doubt, which expresses itself in a multitude of ways: self-doubt, uncertainty, fear, confusion, or indecision. It's that feeling of going back and forth or, at its extreme, that feeling of being paralyzed, unable to make a decision or do anything at all.

Again, there are no hard lines here. Experience is fluid. These are just useful concepts to identify and work skillfully with the obstacles that block our path of fulfillment and awakening. And I chose to stick with these five because, again, they encompass most of the general disturbances we face, especially if we look at the energetic quality of each of them—that is, reaching out, pushing away, collapsing in, bursting out, and paralyses.

To see these energetic states more clearly and how they impact the mind, the Buddha used two metaphors. In the first, the mind is thought of as a clean and tranquil pond that reflects our image clearly. When desire is preset, however, it is as if the pond has been colored by a dye—the "rose-tinted lenses" metaphor. Our desire, our wants and fantasies, color our perception of things. They give the objects of experience qualities they don't really have. A body is a body. Lust is not a quality of the body itself. When, on the other hand, the heat of aversion, ill-will, hatred, or anger is present, it's as if the water is boiling. So, again, we can't see our reflection clearly until the water cools down. Sloth and torpor are like having algae growing heavily across the pond, making it slimy and murky. There is a stagnation of mind that prevents us from seeing the mind's true nature. Restlessness, anxiety, and worry are like the wind agitating the surface of the pond. The body and mind are tossed around by a tense and overactive nervous system. And doubt is like a pond filled with a thick, sticky mud. We can't see anything well and so we don't know what to make of it, let alone how to move through it.

I mentioned the second metaphor already in Chapter 4 when talking about finding joy in the subsiding of the hindrances. But I will repeat it again here because it gets at the idea that these defilements are only visitors. Once we start to see the defilements and how they impact our minds, as the first metaphor shows, we can begin to open awareness to the quality of the mind itself. When you can stay mindful of greed, how does it feel when it finally subsides? Does it feel as if you've just been released from a debt? What about aversion, anger, hatred, or ill-will? Does it feel like you've just recovered from an illness? What about apathy and lethargy? Does it feel like you've just been released from a dark prison cell? What about restlessness, anxiety, and worry? Do you feel like you have just been given your freedom, released from servitude? What about doubt? Do you feel like you have just made it out of the desert alive? Whenever a hindrance subsides, can you experience the wide-open space of awareness and its natural purity?

Rather than look at these as clever metaphors, let them point you to your own direct experience of what the mind is like when the hindrances are present and when they subside. See if you can pay particular attention to moments of transition, when you go from being lost in one of the hindrances to being mindful of them? What is that transition like? I bet the more you pay close attention to the subsiding of the hindrances, the less you will be captured so easily by them. You will learn that we can simply let this desire or worry pass all on its own. Nothing is permanent. This hindrance too will pass. There's no need to struggle with it.

Okay, let's take a closer look at sloth and torpor. To begin, sloth and torpor are actually two different mind-states, but we will consider them together since, really, they are a package deal. Sloth is a sluggishness of mind, which disperses energy. It is a lack of will power, a sinking into the earth. And torpor, which always comes along for the ride, is a weakening of mental faculties. Torpor strips us of our mental prowess, agility, pliability, focus, and memory. We feel it when we nod off to sleep as we are trying to pay attention to a lecture or meeting or whatever. It's a mind made of butter that is too hard to spread.

Sloth and torpor are a common experience when we first begin to meditate, especially if we live on fast-forward, always doing this-that-or-the-other-thing, conditioned for busyness. Most of us run on external stimulus—the city buzz, interactions with others, social media dings, the pressure of productivity, coffee or energy drinks, etc. So, when we first begin to meditate, we often confront a lot of boredom and dullness. But as we enter deeper into ourselves through meditation, we discover an incredible source of natural energy that allows our mind to become increasingly awake and alert on its own, in a very easeful way. We meet the mind's naturally quality—it simply knows.

At this point, however, sloth and torpor may begin to show up in a different way. We start to see a subtler dimension of sloth and torpor, which we explored when discussing virya—that is, the tendency to retreat from challenges and difficulties. When we are not mindful of this aspect of sloth and torpor, we are likely to strengthen our tendencies toward laziness, lethargy, apathy, and passivity. And once it grabs hold, this hindrance is hard to release. It's comfortable and, therefore, seductive. So, it's important we catch it as soon as it starts to creep in.

The first step, again, is to simply note, "When sloth and torpor are present, one knows this is a mind filled with sloth and torpor." And when it fades, we open awareness to what the mind is like without it. Finally, after we become more familiar with its presence and absence, we can start to explore and familiarize ourselves with its causes and conditions. The Buddha helps to support our investigation by suggesting that its primary cause is unwise attention, a careless attention towards mental states like discontent and boredom. Sam Harris captures this well when he says:

> "What we discover when we begin practicing meditation is that there is no such thing as a boring object of attention. Boredom is simply a lack of attention. We only become convinced that we are bored because we have not found something compelling enough to capture our attention. Our attention is normally so blunt an instrument that we need something thrilling or terrifying to capture us. What pleases us most in those moments when we are fully captured by experience is the state of complete attention to the present. If you can muster that on your own through meditation, then any arbitrary object—the feeling of the wind past your hand as you walk—can be an exquisitely pleasurable thing to notice... Concentration is intrinsically pleasurable."[159]

Another thing to watch out for is sloth and torpor masquerading as self-compassion. We might feel tired or lazy, and then sloth and torpor come in with a seductive voice that tells us, "You've been working so hard, my friend, you deserve a break. Go rest child." Now, of course, like I said earlier, sometimes we do need to rest. But very often, if you are honest with yourself, I think you'll find that this is sloth and torpor causing you to retreat from life. We feel defeated by work or family or some other aim. It's not that there isn't enough energy in the system, but rather we just want to retreat to our comforts, to our couch and to our shows, movies, or phone, rather than show up in our role as parent or spouse or friend. If so, try to kick-start the system—get up and move around, go to the gym, take a walk. Draw, paint, do something creative and spontaneous. It's especially important to move our bodies for those of us who spend our entire day at a desk, which slows our energy and metabolism.

Unacknowledged emotions, strong or even traumatic emotions, are another cause for sloth and torpor to arise. If this is the case, a great deal of sensitivity is required because, often in these situations, sloth and torpor are acting as a defense. They are trying to protect us, regulating how much and how quickly repressed feelings should be sent to the surface of awareness. This doesn't mean we should overanalyze everything or search for some deep hidden meaning or emotion, but it should signal us to hold our experience tenderly while we look inside to see what's happening. You might even consider doing this with a therapist.

Before we move on to explore restlessness, let me briefly just mention and recap some common remedies for sloth and torpor. First, is mindfulness—the watcher on the wall. Can we be with the hindrance mindfully until it disappears? The (big) mind itself is not tired. See if you can notice that this sleepiness has an experiential or energetic mark—it is a visitor. The true nature of mind, however, is always wide awake and clear. It is what knows this sleepiness. Second, we can bring some energy to the system by increasing our noting, bringing the energy of investigation. Third, we can get up and do some activity—go on a walk, fold the laundry, call a friend, explore our emotions in a journal or diary, etc. Fourth, we can reflect on death and the preciousness of this moment. And finally, if you are still tired, go rest, my friend. Just as we need to watch out for self-deception, we also need to beware of being too hard on ourselves by denying the body rest when it needs it.

All right, well, moving on to restlessness. The Pali word for restlessness is *uddacca*, which can also mean agitation, excitement, or distraction. It is that feeling of not being settled on any object of experience but hovering shakily around it. And closely related is *kukkucca*, the Pali word to describe the mind-state of worry, regret, and anxiety. We often experience this after we have done something harmful or when we didn't do something we should have done. At other times, we worry about some imagined future. We anticipate problems—what I like to call the what-if mind. We also get anxious when we find ourselves comparing ourselves or judging ourselves about who we are or what kind of progress we've made.

Again, the first instruction for working skillfully with restlessness is to simply note it when it arises. "If restlessness and worry are present . . . one knows 'restlessness-and-worry are present. . .'; if restlessness and worry are not present . . . , one knows 'restlessness-and-worry . . . are not present.'"[160] See if you can watch it subside, then, as with the other hindrances, investigate their causes and conditions.

One of the most important causes of restlessness is the balance between concentration and energy. The restless mind, I have found, is often due to a lack of concentration, which stabalizes and calms the mind. When the mind is concentrated on something, this is synonymous with saying the mind is still. It is abiding in quietude. It is focused or settled on a particular object.

If we are still imbalanced, however, there are a few more things we can investigate. Generally, the most common cause for the restless mind is when our attention gets drawn into the contents of our thoughts, which love to go racing, as you know. This is especially true for us analytical and verbal types, like the Buddha's chief disciple Sariputta, and like those of us with OCD, autism, and ADHD. Really, all of us carry this inclination for thinking, but there are definitely some of us whose dials are turned up.

I saw a hilarious demonstration of this contrast when two friends of mine, a husband and wife, asked me to sit with them while they tried magic mushrooms for the first time. The wife, once under the influence, couldn't stop talking about and analyzing every little aspect of her experience. It was as if I was listening to a sports announcer, who gave me a play-by-play into her mind. The husband, on the other hand, couldn't formulate a single word. Responding to my question whether he wanted a drink of water seemed to be a damned-near impossible task. There was no analyzing, no talking for him, just ineffable experience.

For those of you like me, who have your analytical dials turned up, it may take us more time to break through the clouds of papañca, like it did for the Buddha's most trusted disciple Sariputta, since we are conditioned so deeply to orient from thought, from concepts and percepts. And that's okay. This can be a great strength in many ways—in business, in communicating, in teaching, in planning and organizing, in strategizing, etc. And once we finally do break through the clouds of papañca, we may have a lot to offer the world.

But, it's important to understand that there is a whole realm of insight and wisdom that cannot be gained from discursive thinking. There is insight and wisdom that can never come through the thought process, only through direct experience. Let me stress this again. No matter how much we read and think and talk about raising a child, running a company, traveling to space, tasting chocolate, it will never give us the actual experience of any of them. No matter how much we read and think and talk about the selfless, ever-changing, interconnected nature of all things, this alone will never give us the direct experience and understanding of it.

Wisdom must be lived. Too many of us read book after book, trying to intellectualize our way through everything, including spiritual life. If you are one of these people, I invite you to explore a couple things in yourself. First, become curious whether there is an element of control underlying your need to constantly conceptualize—read and think and talk—your way through everything. In a world of chaos and change, it is a natural impulse for us humans to seek security, order, and control through storytelling, through gaining a conceptual understanding of things. Without this, we often live in a state of agitation, worry, and uncertainty. But as soon as we give a story or explanation to something, or sometimes even a name, much of our worry dissipates. We now have a box to contain it in. In some sense, it is no longer a (conceptual) mystery. Now, again, it is not a bad thing to seek a better conceptual understanding of the world. We just need to make sure our sense of self isn't hiding out here. If we let go of concepts, if we let go of the analytical mind, is the self worried it will disappear? Is it worried it will no longer be needed? Really, this is getting at our deep-seated fear of death.

Second, if you are constantly getting pulled into restless thought, obsessive planning, or needless worrying, I encourage you to explore whether you believe thinking leads to wisdom, to peace of heart and mind? Some people, like me, carry a soft spot from childhood, a wound that tells us we aren't smart enough, and so we feel we need to overcompensate. We can never let our intellectual guard down. We can see this in ourselves when we examine what we value in others. Are we always noticing the "smart" person (or kid) in the room, maybe even to the detriment of the kind, or creative, or courageous, or humble person (or kid)? Why is this quality so important to us? Check to see if there is a soft spot in you that needs a little love, care, and attention. And again, remember that wisdom requires us to let go. Until we are willing to lose our 'self,' to embody emptiness, intellectualizing will only lead to further division, isolation, and loneliness. Once we die so that we may live fully, however, we can bring the thinker back into the fold to work harmoniously with the rest of our being.

To tie this all back to concentration as a remedy for the restless mind, see if you can focus not on the contents of thought, but on thought as it is directly experienced. What is a thought as a phenomenon? Again, not its contents but as an energy state? All of us think all the time. We are often obsessed with the contents of our thoughts. But how many of us actually stop to examine what a thought is in itself? Can you notice how these things that have so much power and control over us are little more than nothing? For those of us who have extraordinary imaginations, yes, thoughts can be quite gripping. But for most of us, most of the time, thoughts are little more than passing puffs of smoke in the mind.

Another major red flag to watch out for with the restless mind is loquacious and frivolous chit-chat. Loquacious and frivolous chit-chat, whether you are a participant or receiver, is a sure way to send your mind into a storm of scattered, racing thoughts. Make sure to pay attention to this not only in others but in yourself. How much oxygen are you taking up? What is your word count in this conversation? Watch your WPMs (words per minute). Let's make sure we give people the room to respond to one point before moving on to another...and another...and another, whether we're with our friends or in a meeting at work. The world is so fast paced right now, we're getting far too ahead of ourselves. Let's slow it down. Is what I am saying honest? Is it beneficial? Is it affectionate? Is it skillful? How can we truly explore the intentions and motivations of our words when our mouths are moving too fast?

Another skillful thing you can do for yourself in this arena is to get off social media. Get off the internet. Go outside and touch grass. Turn all that shit off. Is it really making you better off? Be honest with yourself. Is it adding value, or is it mostly frivolous, harmful, time-consuming, and distracting? Now, of course, there are exceptions. It may be a great place for teachers, artists, and similar creators to share and promote their work. Just make sure to stay mindful and honest about your activity online. Who is in control—the algorithms or you? Is the digital world filling your head with noise or is it keeping you on your path, pointing you toward your deepest aims and intentions?

Another way I get caught in the restless mind is by obsessing over hurtful things I've done. Now, don't get me wrong, it's important to feel remorse for what we have done. We want to learn from those painful experiences so that we can do better in the future. Sam Harris gives a pointed example of this with a thought experiment.[161] Assume, he says, we have created a pill that can take away our feelings of shame and guilt. Now, imagine a mother takes a bath with her baby on her chest. During the bath, the mother accidentally falls asleep. And when she wakes up, she discovers that her baby had drowned. The mother is obviously suffering immensely. So, the question is, when do we give her the pill? An hour after? A week? A month? A year? A decade?

Remorse, as I tell my kids when they are feeling bad about something they have done, is just a message from Love, a reminder to prevent us from causing harm again. Rather than carry it negatively, we can be thankful for that reminder. But once we have learned from it, we don't need to punish ourselves unnecessarily. Rather, we can reconnect with our commitment to non-harm and let that be our object of concentration. When we are calm and concentrated, focused on our commitment to non-harm, we will be less likely to cause harm in the present, therefore creating more ease for ourselves in the future. We can live with the peace of non-remorse.

Okay, before we move on to doubt, let me mention one more trick to deal with the restless mind. Often, when our mind is frenetically running about, we think it's impossible to stay mindful. But remember, there is no certain way the mind needs to be in order for us to practice mindfulness. Every mind-state is perfectly suited for practice. Sometimes we just need a small shift in frame. One note given to me by Goldstein, which has been of tremendous help, is, "A lot of thinking."[162] This way, it's no problem that the mind is spinning out. We can keep the thread of mindfulness by simply noting this is the way the mind is right now. And that's okay.

Moving on to doubt now, the first thing I want to make clear is that there is a healthy kind of doubt, which asks us not to take things on authority. Dogma is a poison of the mind. Don't just do or believe things because god, a prophet, a parent, a book, a teacher, a sign, a fortune-teller, an astrologist, or anyone or anything else tells you to. This just leads us to become unthinking, uncritical, brainless, walking zombies, who don't take responsibility for ourselves. It is this kind of blind faith that leads to the Holocaust, the Christian Dark Ages, Jihadist suicide bombers, and so much more. To doubt authority, to doubt dogma, to doubt tradition, is something I highly encourage, and so too does the Buddha. The world needs more critical thinkers. We are all becoming far too passive, simply accepting whatever information or news is thrown at us in our echo-chamber.

The kind of doubt that is harmful, however, is the doubt that freezes us. We come to a fork in the road and just sit down. We waver back and forth and so we never move anywhere. This can be a strong hindrance for those of us who feel like everything we do must be perfect. But as we learned in Chapter 1, the only way to progress is through our mistakes. So, when we come to a crossroads and don't know which way to go, as we all must at times in our lives, act! Not carelessly, not without thought. But once you have done your due diligence, take a risk, follow your gut. If we aren't willing to move forward in the face of our uncertainty, again, we will never move anywhere or do anything at all. We will never give ourselves the opportunity to know whether we took the wrong turn, and so we will never be able to course-correct.

Now, doubt in the Buddha's philosophy typically applies narrowly to dharma practice and the support systems around it, but I'm going to speak to it more broadly, in a way that encapsulates both the practice and our lives. After all, like me, I'm sure many of you face doubt in your relationships, in your education, in your career, in your art, and in other areas of your life. How do I know if this is the person I want to commit to, establish a life with, have kids with? Am I worthy of this person? Do I really know what I'm doing in my career? Do I stay at my job, which gives me a kind of security, or do I take a risk and chase after my dreams? Again, I hope to present doubt in a way that is applicable to any arena of your life.

One way in which doubt shows up for many of us, especially for those of us who have been burned by religion or some spiritual teacher, is in the presentation of any framework or belief system. And of course, this is for good reason—fool me once, shame on you; fool me twice, shame on me. So, when we come across the Buddha's teachings, or any new practice or framework, we may question its legitimacy. This kind of doubt can be extremely skillful if we use it to fuel our own investigation of the Buddha's claims, or any other. There's a passion and a vitality behind healthy skepticism that keeps our faculties sharp.

Where this kind of doubt becomes a problem, however, is when it triggers an automatic rejection of things presented to us. This is a sure way to stunt our growth and limit our understanding. So, it's important that we remain open, that we hold frames lightly. We just need to make sure we have the support and protection of reason so that we don't become a pawn in someone else's game, a prophet's puppet, or so that we don't download and install a bad operating system.

Another way doubt appears in the context of the Buddha's teachings, which also applies to life more generally, is when we never commit ourselves long enough to anything—that is, we constantly doubt our path, practice, method, work, partner, etc. Spiritual growth, like any skill, takes time. Again, it's not like understanding something conceptually. It takes experience. It takes practice. If you try to start a fire by rubbing two sticks together, quit after a few seconds because it isn't working, try another approach, like hitting two rocks together, and then quit again, you're never going to get a fire. So, if you decide to try a practice, then really try. Give it enough time and devotion. Too many of us in our culture want the easy way out, the quick fix. This isn't how spiritual practice works, or anything else for that matter. Now, of course, there will be many practices out there that are not the right fit for you, so it is okay to explore and try on different things. But to make real progress, in any avenue of life, whether it be a skill, a career, a relationship, a spiritual practice, you must sincerely devote yourself to it. We can't just half-ass it for brief stints of time.

The next kind of doubt is self-doubt, which has two flavors I'd like to explore. The first is imposture syndrome, the experience of feeling like a fraud. We fear that people will discover who we truly are—not experienced enough, capable enough, or qualified enough. I have had so many people in my life who have done well in their careers express this to me: "I'm just waiting for the day when someone finally busts me, when they realize that I've just been 'winging it' the whole time." Listen, I tell them, we're all just a bunch of kids playing in this cosmic sandbox without a clue about much of anything. All these CEOs, executives, and managers are in the same position. They're just kids trying their best to figure this out. You have gotten to where you are because you have demonstrated yourself through your work ethic, or creativity, or organizational, problem-solving, or people skills, or whatever it is. Own that. And remember, you're not alone in your doubt. A little doubt helps to keep us humble and grounded. Just don't let that doubt grow to a point where it debilitates you.

Another way I see self-doubt express itself is through self-sabotage. How many times must we undermine ourselves, our strengths and talents, our values, dreams, and aspirations? Why do so many of us procrastinate doing what is most important to us, and instead focus on the tedious, comfortable, unimportant things? Why do we self-medicate with drugs or alcohol? Why do we lash out at those we love most? Why do we constantly find ourselves putting others' needs before our own, even though we're drowning? Why do we comfort eat or, in extreme cases, engage in self-harm?

There are many reasons for these behaviors but, most often, it is from past traumas and the beliefs we have built around them. So, the primary key here is mindfulness, specifically of our repetitive thoughts. These patterns, however, can be extremely hard to notice and break on our own. So, it may be beneficial, especially if you have thoughts or behaviors of self-harm, to see a licensed therapist, particularly one who pairs mindfulness with something like CBT (cognitive behavioral therapy), which helps to methodically rewrite some of the scripts and behaviors we have running.

For those who find themselves sabotaging their relationships, there is often some hurt that needs to be held with the loving, tender care of mindfulness. To develop deep and meaningful relationships requires us to be vulnerable. And if being vulnerable in the past led us to pain, distrust, abandonment, or neglect, it's no wonder we have this little protector in us who is doing their best to prevent that kind of hurt from happening again. So, again, exploring these emotions and fears with a licensed therapist can useful. It can help us to understand our relationship patterns that developed in childhood and to identify our triggers for self-sabotaging behaviors. But you can also take steps yourself by journaling and communicating your habits, fears, and emotions to your partner. I also highly recommend looking into Loch Kelly's work. He artfully and skillfully weaves together non-dual mindfulness practices with the Internal Family Systems model, opening a ton of space for self-compassion to arise. And lastly, you can make it a practice to extend some love to yourself every day when you wake up and again every night before you go to sleep.

All right, well, let's move on to our final training of the mind—training in concentration.

Concentration

The Buddha said a mind without concentration is like a fish out of water, flopping around with no control. We need concentration to stick to our tasks, goals, and aims. We need it to stay grounded in our motivations, frameworks, and understanding. We need it to bring stability to our journey, to bring clarity, continuity, and harmony to our experience, to bring unity to our life.

Sadly, I fear concentration is waning in our culture. We are constantly being ripped and pulled apart by distractions. We slice, dice, and juggle our attention with emails, text messages, DMs, Slack, Zoom, and other platforms. We stay up with our notifications from Metta, Instagram, Medium, WhatsApp, TikTok, news sources, and all the other platforms that strategically fight for our attention. All the while we have music, a podcast, or an audiobook in our ears, or maybe even a show or movie playing in the background, maybe even while we eat our food.

By the end of the day, we are utterly and entirely fractured, thousands of pieces of ourselves are scattered across the open field of awareness. And many of us even have to remain plugged into work through our phones late into the evening. It makes it very difficult to be present, to worship our partners and children, to shower them with our full, undivided attention. It leaves us in disharmony.

Something has to give here. It won't be easy to fix this as a culture, but we need to work out a different way. We need to bring back our focus. We are so lost in the weeds that we have little clarity in our moment-to-moment experience around our deepest values and aims, and their underlying motivations. I fear this has led and will continue to lead to much of our suffering, to many feelings of isolation and lack. It's preventing us from staying connected with what matters most to us. It is leading to our own destruction.

So, as we step into our final workout for our training of the mind, completing the Eightfold Path, I invite you—in your role as employer, employee, parent, child, partner, friend—to hold this dimension of the path with a reverence, humility, and willingness to see how it is affecting your own life. Then, hopefully any insights you gain will allow you to find ways to bring some unity and clarity back into your life and the world around you.

Okay, what is concentration and how does it fit into the Noble Eightfold Path? Well, the first thing to make clear is that concentration is not an end in itself. It is a means to insight and wisdom, a means to love and understanding. So, its primary role is to provide a penetrating clarity and stability, a kind of sharp lens, to our mindfulness practice, to our lives, and to our experience.

Concentration brings things into view. Like a lens that collects and focuses the light, concentration gathers and puts together the fractured pieces of our being. It gathers all the faculties of mind and points them at the task at hand, bringing a unity and harmony to our being and to our aims. When it is well cultivated, like a laser that can cut through steel, concentration can cut through the hindrances, allowing us to penetrate more deeply into experience so we can gather more insight and wisdom.

Concentration's primary role is to aid us along the Eightfold Path by keeping us seamlessly and firmly rooted in our mindfulness practice. It keeps us calm, sharp, and collected, pointed at wisdom. It prevents us from becoming fractured and isolated. It keeps us safe from the hindrances and defilements. It keeps us whole.

Okay, great. So, how do we cultivate concentration? Well, the Buddha lays out two practices: 1) one-pointed or fixed-object concentration and 2) continuous, momentary, or fluid concentration. Let's explore these two in turn.

One-pointed or fixed-object concentration is a meditative or contemplative concentration. It fixes the mind on a single object to calm and steady the mind, to slow down the discursive and proliferating thought process. When this one-pointed concentration is strong, we start to feel a peace in our lives that comes from an ability to focus firmly on what is in front of us, without getting agitated, unsettled, and tossed about by desire or worry, without becoming distracted and dragged around by the restless mind.

The Abhidhamma, or Buddhist psychology, points out that this faculty, this kind of one-pointed concentration, arises to a degree in every moment of experience. If we had no one-pointedness at all, we would never be able to connect with anything in our experience. Our minds would continue to fly around and never stop for even a moment to make contact with the objects of awareness—sights, sounds, smells, tastes, thoughts, feelings, etc. So, we need this one-pointedness to unify, collect, and center all the faculties of mind—our sense faculties, our memory faculties, our perceptual faculties, our thinking and reasoning faculties, our creative faculties, etc.—on the objects of awareness.

To take a narrow example, let's consider the visual system. When the eyes move from one object to another, there is no unity, no collection of attention, and so there is no clear picture of anything until you land on an object. These quick movements, which are called saccades, allow the eyes to concentrate on specific parts of the visual field to gather data, move onto different points to collect more data, and ultimately sketch and paint a cohesive picture of the world in our minds. This process, however, is selective. The visual system doesn't have the bandwidth to focus on every data point in the visual field. It needs to focus on what information is important.

This highlights the necessity of our underlying frameworks, especially our aims, which orient our focus or point of concentration. If we are in the "Tinder or Grinder frame," for example, we will focus on physical beauty, facial symmetry, or whatever pleasant qualities draw our attention. If we are looking for a new car, our focus will land on the makes, models, shapes, and colors of different cars on the road. If we are competing in the victim olympics, we will concentrate on reasons to be pitied and viewed as a victim. If we are looking for truth, beauty, and goodness, we will focus on things that are true, beautiful, and good.

Again, we need this one-pointed concentration to unify, collect, and center all the faculties of mind to build our perception of the world, to know its objects, to keep our experience stable and centered. It is what allows for a central point of focus—the spotlight of attention. Now, though some degree of one-pointedness is always present, as you probably know from your own experience, this faculty is often weak and unstable. The mind loves to jump, swim, fly, and frolic around every which way. It loves to go chasing squirrels. We can all relate to the flighty, untrained mind. Just consider how often you get lost in thought while trying to read, having to reread everything? So, again, we need to strengthen and develop this faculty of one-pointedness to keep our mind centered and our mindfulness practice fruitful. As the Buddha said, "The mind, hard to control, flighty, alighting where it wishes, one does well to tame. The well-trained mind brings happiness."

The Pali word for meditation is *bhāvanā*, which literally means "causing to be developed." I highlight this because it is important to understand that concentration isn't something we have or we don't. Just as our bodies get stronger through physical training, concentration grows through mental training. We can develop this faculty, we can strengthen and intensify it, we can make it a practice to focus the mind on a single object. Now, I know it is hard to introduce any new practice or routine into our life. So, let's keep it simple and 'habit stack' this onto our already existing mindfulness practice. For the first minute or two of practice, I suggest you work on sharpening your focus by continually bringing attention back to a single object, like the breath, before you open the mind to the whole range of experience, as we do with our open mindfulness practice.

Now, the object of concentration doesn't need to be the breath. It can be anything. It's less about the object and more about the focus. So, again, you can pick anything that calls to you—an image, an idea, a virtue, a word, a mind-state, or whatever. But we can also be a bit more strategic about the object we use. If, for example, anger is a close companion, you can concentrate on loving-kindness, the unconditional wish that you and others be happy, that you and others be free from anger and hatred, that you be at peace. If your personality tends to be particularly lustful, you can contemplate the impermanent,, unsatsfactory nature of sexual pleasure, or on a more holistic view of the human body and all its inner workings—its blood, guts, puss, and organs. If restlessness is a constant visitor, you can focus on a calm body of water. If you are the devoted type, you can focus on the three jewels: the Sangha, Buddha, and Dharma. If you lack fuel or motivation, you can contemplate death and the preciousness of life. If you want to improve your visual imagination, you can bring to life in your mind a seed blooming, growing, decaying, dying, and being reborn from one of its seeds. If you are often tense and contracted, you can focus on space, the space in the room or in the galaxy, or the space between thoughts, sounds, feelings, and emotions. And of course, a very popular place for beginners is the breath. The breath is always there and speaks volumes about your current state of being. It keeps you connected to the body, connected to the fluid, impermanent, and ever-changing nature of all things, with the arising and fading of each breath. And it can also promote the slowing down and stilling of thoughts, especially if you emphasize the out-breath.

And last but certainly not least, you can focus on your sila, or morality. Not in a way where you just beat yourself up over all your past transgressions, but in a way that acknowledges the good intention, the light, in you, your commitment to non-harm. The Buddha often taught that sila is the foundation for concentration. When we haven't witnessed and acknowledged the goodwill in us that wishes well for ourselves and others, and then established a moral framework from this foundation that keeps us pointed at living in harmony with life, it can be very difficult to grow concentrated. Just consider honesty alone. When we are dishonest, we have to juggle our lies. We have to remember what we said to whom and work really hard to paint a consistent picture. Usually, we just end up fabricating more and more lies to save face. Dishonesty tears us apart and makes our lives very complicated, as do other intentions rooted in ill-will.

Sila also helps prevent guilt and shame from arising, which can cause tremendous ripples in our experience, since it keeps us rooted in non-harm. That way, even if we do cause harm, sila can transform the guilt or shame we carry into remorse, a loving reminder that our actions impact both ourselves and the ones we love. Again, not to punish us but to keep us pointed at our aim, non-harm; to remind us of the love we carry. Reestablishing our commitment to non-harm, we can let go of guilt. We don't need to allow shame to become a part of who we are. We can still have remorse for those actions that hurt ourselves and others. But instead of getting lost in or identifying with the guilt or shame, we can connect again and again to our commitment of non-harm. We can really feel into our intention to live in harmony with life. This is who we are: Love. Not a small ego-based part that tells us we're not worthy or that we're disgusting, perverted, cruel, or whatever it may be.

Once you connect with this deep intention, whether for the first time or the thousandth, notice how you can be with memories of unwholesome or unskillful actions with more ease and stability. See how you can more easily learn from them and let them go. And on the opposite side, if you forget to once again establish yourself in sila, see how hard it can be to concentrate as you fall into worry or a shame-based identity. Sila fertilizes the soil for concentration to grow and strengthen. But again, only you can know this for yourself. So, check it out. See if there is a happiness, peace, and ease when you commit and recommit to non-harm. And see if this leads to a natural concentration and clarity in the mind.

Anyway, as you develop this one-pointed concentration, see what works for you through trial and error, whether it's the breath, sila, loving-kindness, an image, etc. You might even find it useful to concentrate on a new object every day. Just remember, the object isn't crucial here for what we are developing. What is crucial is that you practice consistently. So, give it a go and have fun! I'm excited for you to touch new levels of peace and clarity as this faculty strengthens.

Let's move on to explore the next kind of concentration—continuous or fluid concentration. Here, rather than concentrate on a single object, the idea is to stay continuously concentrated on the ever-changing quality or processes of experience. So, this too develops a steady and penetrating attention, but one that directly supports our vipassana practice. Without this steadiness of concentration, it is easy to collapse into or identify our 'selves' with feelings, perceptions, and thoughts as they arise, it's easy to fall prey to delusion. We try to hold onto the river. We take ephemeral, transitory states (or ostensible states or things) to be who we are, and then get carried away by trains of association and reactivity.

Without continuity of mindfulness, we would never be able to generate the power to go deeper, to penetrate the ultimate nature of reality, the ultimate nature of self, the ultimate nature of suffering. So, we need the support of concentration to keep the thread of mindfulness. We need it to see the microscopic arising and passing away of all phenomena until there is no granularity left, but instead the Everlasting Fire. Here, the illusions of solidity and separateness dissolve beneath our feet, as we free-fall into the unborn and unformed awareness that holds this miraculous floating world. Through a continuous concentration, we come to embody love and wisdom.

Now that we've explored the two types of concentration to aid us in our pursuit of love and wisdom, let me just finish by sharing a few tips and some words of encouragement. First tip, have confidence in yourself. No matter what you think, no matter what the world has told you about your capacity to focus, you can become more concentrated with practice. So, believe in yourself, and allow for imperfection.

Next, because so many of us—essentially all of us—have a slippery and scattered mind, a simple and skillful you can do is merely note whether concentration is present or not, both in your sitting and in your daily life. "If concentration is present, one knows concentration is present in me. If concentration is not present, one knows concentration is not present in me."[163] And something important to note here is that the Buddha doesn't say anything about judging yourself for not being concentrated. The practice is simply to discern the present state of mind. Here, in this non-judgmental and non-reactive space, we can simply get to know what the mind is like when it is concentrated and what it like when it is not, pressure free. Do this and I think you'll see that awareness has a way of taking care of itself.

Another skillful approach here, as I said above, is to start your meditation with a fixed-concentration practice before moving into vipassana. This will help slow down the sporadic and proliferating thought process. It will allow the mud to settle, bringing a peace and relaxed clarity to the mind. That's why many teachers have new students focus on nothing but the breath for long periods of time, whether for weeks or even months.

Another tool I love comes from my Snow Leopard, who would continually ask me as we traversed forests and ridges, talking about philosophy, "What are our roots?" I love this tool, which has now become a kind of mantra for me, because it keeps me sharp and pointed. It allows me to follow the threads of conversation and the threads of my own thoughts and understanding. It sustains my focus, which brings a stableness and a continuity to my words and relationships. And this in turn leads to a calm, connected, and receptive kind of clarity in life.

Finally, developing concentration isn't easy. The mind is difficult to steady, so it will require resolve, determination, and perseverance—that is, it will require virya—to keep bringing attention back to the object of mind. You will need to continually apply a balanced effort, a kind of gentle return to the object of concentration, where you are settled back and relaxed as you pass through the many distractions and hindrances in the mind, without adding agitation or resistance to the system.

And of course, there will be times when you feel like you just can't do it, you can't focus, times when you feel dull, cloudy, lazy, restless, or uninspired, and you think it is impossible to practice, so you don't even want to try. But just because these mind-states are present doesn't mean we can't have a continuity of concentration. Again, we might just need to adjust our framing. Rather than give up when our minds aren't concentrated, we can simply allow awareness to open to the sleepiness, cloudiness, or lack of concentration without trying to improve or change the situation. In this way, we can keep the thread, we can keep a continuous awareness around our sleepiness. With this frame, we don't limit ourselves by thinking that concentration practice requires us to be in a certain state of mind.

And with restlessness, don't forget the note offered by Goldstein, "A lot of thinking." When the mind is racing from thought to thought and it feels impossible to keep up and stay concentrated on anything, that's okay.

Again, we can maintain the continuity of concentration with the simple note, "A lot of thinking," without worrying about having to change our experience. Instead, we can be at ease with this bombardment of thoughts. "A lot of thinking." Remember, our practice is all-inclusive. It welcomes all mind states without trying to fix them.

Meditation

10. DEATH

"To die will be an awfully big adventure."
– Peter Pan

For the year 2023, I made the commitment to meet Death formally every day, not in a morbid sense but as a part of my spiritual practice. Death, if we witness it, if we get close to it, if we listen to it, allows us to live more fully. It can bring clarity to our aims and intentions, clarity to our experience, clarity to the majesty and mystery of our being. I decided to meet Death to get closer to life.

How does one meet Death? They sit with and acknowledge Her. They respect and hold reverence for Her. They listen to Her. They heed Her counsel about how to live, how to love, and how to be.

As it turns out, the universe seemed to agree with my commitment. On the second day, January 2, 2023, Death quite literally knocked on my front door. My partner and kids were going skiing for a couple days with grandma and grandpa, so my partner River and I had the kids get in the car as we finished up a few things in the house. Suddenly, we looked out the window and saw a young deer next to the car where the kids were.

I went out to say goodbye to the kids and asked them if they had noticed the deer, which was on the other side of the car from where I was standing. They hadn't. So, I opened the sliding side door on the opposite side of me with the keys, and there it was.

Something seemed off about it. It appeared a little tired and weathered. I spoke softly and gently to it, and it moved toward the house. I said goodbye to the kids, and then went inside. For the next little bit, the deer stayed by the side of the house, where I could see it from the window. I took a couple pictures, and then went to work at my desk upstairs.

A few hours later, I heard a knock at the front door, so I went downstairs and opened it, where I once again found the young deer. I didn't want to disturb it since it seemed a little uneasy, so I let it be and went back to my work. Over the next few hours, I occasionally checked in on it and, soon enough, it became clear to me that it had decided this would be its final resting place. I brought it water and did what I could to make it feel safe and comfortable.

Several hours later, when I came to check on the precious thing, it had laid down on its side and extended its neck. I could see it breathing, and it turned its head a bit to look at me. But other than that, there was not much movement. I went ahead and sat down next to it and rubbed my hand gently across its body. It looked me softly in the eyes.

For the next thirty minutes, I gave myself fully to the deer, eyes locked. I stayed present, non-distracted, with a heart and mind full of love and compassion. A tremendous sense of peace and reverence filled the space around us.

Finally, a Ranger from the Sheriff's Office came and respectfully ended the deer's pain and suffering before taking the body. I went inside and took time to reflect on the day and on death in general. I acknowledged that this would one day be me. The life force and vitality that brings light to my eyes would one day dissipate and leave behind a cold, heavy corpse, which would decay and return to the earth.

A Brief History of My Relationship With Death

Death had been on my mind a lot the year prior. Actually, it had been on my mind for most my life. Through my early teens to mid-twenties, as you know, I struggled with suicidal ideation, with a growing intensity over the years. And as a young adult, in a rather short period, I also had several people close to me die.

At 19, I spent the final six months of my father-in-law-to-be's life in the VA hospital. Five years earlier, he had received a double lung transplant because he had contracted Idiopathic Pulmonary Fibrosis after being exposed to hazardous materials as a Marine in Desert Storm. And double lung transplants at the time typically lasted about five years, which was the case for him. So, for the last few months of his life, he was connected to life support, with no prospects of surviving. We stayed with him for as long as he needed to find the strength to say goodbye. And when the time finally came, we—his wife, kids, and parents—watched him, consumed by fear, take his final breaths.

About six months later, my sister-in-law left her baby for the first time with a babysitter and came home to find her baby in the crib, purple and not breathing. We all rushed to the hospital, where I saw my 6-month-old niece lie lifeless on the emergency room table. There were drugs, needles, machines, and the signs of every attempt to bring that child back to life. Her mom. Her poor mom. The grief. The pain. The confusion. The anger. The weight of that room, I will never forget.

Not long after, my childhood friend and neighbor, who had Type 1 Diabetes like me, died suddenly in the night. The way his dad spoke with silence and tears at his funeral filled me with a reverence I had never known until that point. His son. His only son. Taken from him without notice. No parent should have to bury their child.

And in that same period, two of my grandparents and my childhood dog of 16 years died—my grandpa from a stroke in his early seventies and my grandma from brain cancer shortly after. I remember my dad went out and buried our dog by himself in the backyard. It was only a couple weeks after he had lost his dad. I think he needed the space to himself to mourn.

Anyway, throughout this time, I grew deeper into depression until, finally, I hit rock bottom in my first year of law school at the age of 22. Nearly every day, I would find myself on top of the law school building, seven stories up, waiting for the impulse that would send me plummeting to my death. I wasn't unfamiliar with death. It consumed me. I knew it would come for me, whether I took matters into my own hands or let Nature take its course.

"Valar Morghulis." (All men must die.) – Game of Thrones

As you know, during that time, I met a therapist who introduced me to vipassana, or insight meditation, which dramatically transformed my life. For the next few years, after marrying Buddhist philosophy to my practice and really putting in the work, my relationship with death changed dramatically. I understood and related to death from an entirely new perspective, the perspective of Love. My suicidal thoughts faded slowly, along with their intensity. And behind that dark cloud of thoughts opened a clarity and spaciousness, as well as an immense gratitude and thirst for life! My mind continued to reach profound levels of peace and joy. My heart opened. My eyes wide and interested. Everything within and around me became brighter and more vivid. I felt lighter and more alive, like a young child again, filled with awe and wonder. Death took a backseat to Life.

In my late twenties and early thirties, though, a lot changed for me. And with change, there is always an element of loss. I stepped into an entirely new life. I went from being single, living alone, with no responsibilities toward anyone but myself, to becoming a committed partner and full-time parent, caretaker, and homeschool teacher to four remarkable children (and three dogs).

Before becoming a parent, I had made peace with death. But now I had before me the prospect of my children's death, along with the fear and anxiety that stem from the thought of my own death, leaving them without my love and support. This, coupled with two other painful losses, had me once again examining my relationship with loss, grief, and death.

Recent Experiences of Grief

In the first few years of my vipassana practice, there was a honeymoon period, where the developing concentration and mindfulness led to an incredible sense of rapture and joy in the heart and mind. As I said, it's like I got to experience the world as a child again, with the same kind of love and wonder, but with the wisdom of an adult.

The thing is, though, if meditation has taught me anything, it is that nothing lasts. And life is full. There isn't just the pleasant. There is the unpleasant too. And I was about to get a good dose of it. When I met these recent losses with the polished attention I had gained over the years from my mindfulness practice, I experienced the unpleasant—the loss, the hurt, the anger, and the grief—with a vividness I hadn't known before.

The first loss had happened slowly over the years. I had been growing apart from my best friend—my Snow Leopard Guardian Angel, someone I considered to be my human for many years, until finally it came to an end. We hiked over a thousand miles together along the Wasatch Range, as we discussed philosophy, challenging each other's ideas and beliefs, pushing each other's growth. We grew up together on the mountains, walking along the high ridges, atop the world, traversing through sun, rain, and snow, smelling the pines and wet dirt, listening to the wind murmur through the aspens, learning how to push through our pain, testing the limits of our body and mind.

With all my heart, I am thankful for sharing such a rich and expansive journey with that human. I am filled with the utmost gratitude to have so much of my being wrought from his hammer. And to be holistic and truthful, he hurt me. He really hurt me. He went down a path, which I tried to follow out of the motivation to love and understand him. But in the end, that motivation became more of a wedge than a dab of glue. It became clear that we were headed in two very different and incompatible directions. It was time to say goodbye.

The grief and all its attending emotions from this split lasted for almost three years. It was extremely challenging. It had me examining myself, my history, my beliefs. It made me question my value and my worth, my intellect and my heart. Only recently do I feel I have been able to put it to rest. Though I know he will always be a part of me, I finally recognized it was time to let go. It was time to move on and rebuild myself from the ashes. It was time to transform the grief back into love.

The second loss I experienced was a challenging and complex loss. Amidst the separation from my Snow Leopard and its attending grief, my partner and I had a miscarriage, which hurt me so badly I suppressed it and hid from it for a long time. It really wasn't until a year or more after, when I sat a silent retreat at Spirit Rock,[164] that I was able to face the full force of this grief.

For my whole life, I wanted to be a mama, a caretaker. Before meeting River, though, as I moved into my late twenties, more and more, I thought this would never happen. I was just too particular, too solitary, too stuborn, too skeptical, too independent, and too queer (in every sense of the word) to find someone I could share a life with, let alone raise kids with. I loved and still love to be alone. With my free time, I like to study, read, write, and meditate. I like the silence, the stillness. I like my own space, clean and organized, everything where it belongs. I like growth and development, and can come off as overly upright and disciplined, which others in my space can feel. It puts a kind of pressure on them, an unfair pressure to be sure. And when I do socialize, I have little patience for shallow conversation. I like to get deep. I like to be real and honest, which can make me seem too abrasive. I like to ask the hard questions and to be asked the hard questions in turn. I like the conversation to be an exploration of each other's beliefs, an exploration of the mysteries of life, consciousness, and experience. Add the fact that I'm an unusual breed of queer, bi- or pan-sexual, typically attracted to people who walk the line of both genders, and that I myself express that same kind of non-conforming gender, then you can see why I thought a relationship might have felt like a long shot for me.

Anyway, in my mid- to late-twenties, I had finally made peace with the prospect of being alone. Really, thanks to my vipassana practice, I had made peace (or at least I thought I had made peace) with whatever life had in store for me, even if that meant I would be a hermit with no kids or family. But then, at 28, I went to Peru with my brother to meet the Shipibo and partake of their sacred plant medicine, Ayahuasca, as well as some other plant medicines like San Pedro and Sapo Toad venom (5-MeO-DMT, otherwise known as the "God molecule"). As it turns out, the peace I had made came into question that trip. During the Aya ceremonies, I couldn't escape from my desire to be a mama. And on the final day, when we took San Pedro and spent the day by a river in the Sacred Valley, my heart cracked open. I sat with my brother and cried on his shoulder, expressing my heart's deepest wish to have a kid, and confronted the possibility that it may never happen.

Not more than a few months later, the love of my life and mother of my children showed up at my doorstep. Immediately, I was struck by her eyes. They demanded my full presence and attention. I felt naked, utterly exposed. Nobody, I felt, had seen me as deeply as she did in those first moments. Nobody's presence had I felt so profoundly. She was really there. A spark of hope lit up in me. I felt as if I wasn't alone in this world, after all.

In any case, when River and I were first dating, we thought there was a possibility she had become pregnant. The excitement, the fear, the love—filled me. I hadn't known a feeling like this. Turns out, though, we weren't pregnant. Then, a few months later, I flew out to the East Coast, where my partner, her ex-husband, and kids had lived. It was the start of a new chapter for all of us. I drove her and the kids across the country to start a new life with me in Utah. And along that drive, we re-explored the idea of having a child together.

But after giving it much thought and discussing it in depth, in the end, as we passed the border into Colorado, we decided that we didn't want that big of a gap between kids. And I also had four new kids to smother with my love. Plus, I had years of catch-up to do with them. So, I decided my focus should be there, on those precious little humans. I wanted them to feel and know deeply the unconditional love and acceptance I had for them, and for them to feel deeply in their bones my commitment to them.

It was strange. Before that point, I didn't realize how strongly I wanted to create a child, to be a part of the whole process—to find love, make love, witness the whole miracle of pregnancy and birth, hear the child's first cries, and feel the child wrap its hand around my finger for the first time. My whole life, I actually imagined I would adopt. My parents adopted two of my younger siblings. And my family was also a shelter home while I was growing up, so I knew how many kids were in desperate need of loving adoptive parents. So, this really surprised me. Anyway, I ended up crying through the whole state of Colorado.

Over the next year, we weren't doing anything to prevent pregnancy because I had my fertility tested and found out it was very unlikely that we could conceive. As it turns out, though, River did get pregnant, but ended up miscarrying. I had known many people and couples who had miscarriages, but I never really understood the full complexity and pain behind them. It is hard to put into concepts. And to make things harder for the women and men who experience a miscarriage, there is no real cultural ritual or support. There's no formal grieving process. The expectation is essentially to suck it up and get on with life.

Anyway, like I said earlier, I don't think I've ever suppressed emotions like I did here. I was already experiencing so much grief in my life, which I had attributed to losing my Snow Leopard, since that's where so many of my thoughts were. I had stories to sort through with my friend, conversations and a history to examine, a conflict and disagreement to consider. With the miscarriage, though, with our Gabriel, there were no real concepts or stories. There was essentially just hurt to feel. To throw salt in the wound, River ended up getting a hysterectomy because of a cancer scare. So, the prospect of bringing new life into this world with her officially ended.

Almost two years after our miscarriage, I was still trying to work through and feel all that pain, along with the debris and shrapnel it sent into my relationship with River. Alongside the loss, I also had to work through some feelings of guilt for not being present or working through the grief with River at the time it happened, leaving her feeling abandoned and alone, left to grieve in isolation.

Thanks to my commitment to meet death, though, which led me to write a lot of this down and share it with her, we were able to express and release our emotions together, and to sink into one another's hearts and arms. It was incredibly healing. River was also able to see and understand why she wasn't able to connect fully with my grief, since much of it stemmed from the fact that I would never be a part of the whole process of birth—like I said, to find love, make love, witness the miracle of pregnancy and birth—which she got to experience with our precious little ones. This allowed us to tease apart and share the many layers of this grief.

I can't express how grateful I am to have a human that can communicate so effectively and honestly, and with such maturity. Yes, it's hard to face the struggles in any relationship. But to not face them, like many couples do, only makes you feel more isolated in the relationship. It leads to anger, resentment, and frustration. Again, I am so grateful that River was so willing and capable to work through such an emotionally complex three years. I have no doubt that because we made it through this difficult beginning, still able to experience so much joy, peace, and love in all the darkness, we will only grow closer in the years to come. I love that human so fully and completely.

Anyway, in addition to these two losses, there were a few more incidents that pushed me to make the commitment to meet death formally for the year. During my silent retreat in September, 2022, as with most traditional vipassana retreats, the teachers pointed us to the impermanent nature of all things. They pointed us to our nature to get sick, age, and die. They highlighted the fact that we will one day lose everyone and everything we cherish.

This got me thinking about everyone I love, with a profound clarity of mind. On my drive home from the retreat, from California to Utah, I really came face-to-face with my dad's inevitable death, which struck me deep in the heart. I will never be able to express how much love I have for that human. There is honestly nobody like him. His love is the purest love this world knows. He is the most humble, hard-working, selfless, and generous servant of love. He has always been a tremendous example as a parent. Whenever I enter stillness or silence, I find his love there.

Then, about a month after the silent retreat, I returned to Peru to sit with Ayahuasca again. While there, two days before the first ceremony, I received a video call from back home. It was my brother and mom. Immediately, I felt the pain and reverence in their expressions and voices. It was my grandma. She had been hospitalized. Her heart was nearing its end. Tears filled my eyes as I thought back to the many years of influence she had on my life. My mom was babysitting our kids while we were in Peru, and I thought of the many times my grandma had babysat me and my siblings when my parents had left town.

Gratitude filled me as I witnessed this generational support, this interconnection, this inter-being. My heart grew vast, holding both the joy and the sorrow. And then the tears started to stream when I realized that I may not be able to hold her head to mine and say goodbye for the final time.

Two days later, when I walked into the first ceremony, I reflected on the fact that my grandma would have to surrender completely. We all must surrender completely. One day, each of us must let go of everything. Why not, I thought to myself, let go now. All the wisdom traditions have, after all, been pointing me to this—to selflessness, to Love. Do I have the courage to let go entirely?

'We'll do it together,' said a soft voice in my heart and mind. And then my grandma, on her death bed, came into view. I was there with her, my forehead pressed against hers. And suddenly, I too was on my death bed, old and wrinkled, lying next to her, with her hand in mine. Our arms began to expand, forming a circle, extending further and further outward until we embraced all of existence. Then, the imagery quickly began to take shape of the Icaros, the sacred healing songs sung by the Shamans during ceremony that become geometrical patterns in the mind, which are believed to represent the harmonious energy field that pervades all of life. The many dissolved into one. Life and death became one, two sides of the same coin. We do not get one without the other.

Letting Go

You and I are of the nature to get sick, age, and die. Have you really taken the time to face this truth? Don't avoid your own mortality until it's too late. Imagine yourself on your deathbed and examine your life from this perspective. What changes does this reflection suggest you should make to your life? Is there anything you are putting off, thinking there will be time in the future? Are there any plans and dreams you aren't making space for? What about conversations you might be avoiding? Are there relationships you have left unresolved? Are you holding onto any hatred or anger rather than reaching for forgiveness? How much time and energy are you wasting on things that, in the end, don't really matter? Did you hold your partner or your kids tenderly in your hands today and tell them how much you love and appreciate them?

While often feared and avoided, the contemplation of death can be a potent tool for unlocking deeper insights into the true nature of our being. Not only can it point us to our empty, selfless nature, thereby acting as a catalyst for spiritual transformation and growth, but it can bring a brilliant clarity to our values, priorities, aims, and intentions, here, now. With death in view, every moment can become an opportunity to align ourselves, our heart and mind, with our deepest values and aims. When we confront the reality of our mortality head-on, the petty grievances and trivial pursuits that once consumed our attention pale in comparison to the overarching questions of meaning and purpose. We no longer take anyone or anything for granted. In the face of death's undeniable presence, we are compelled to reassess our priorities, to discern what truly matters in the grand scheme of things, and then to keep our focus there.

In embracing the wisdom of death, we come to understand that impermanence is not something to be feared but, rather, something to be embraced as an integral part of the natural order of things. Just as the seasons turn, bringing new life, so too does death signal the inevitability of transformation and renewal. In embracing the impermanence of all things, we find a profound sense of peace—a knowing that, in the grand tapestry of existence, our individual threads are but a small part of a much greater whole. This allows us to hold the things and people we love with an open hand, which allows us to let go more easily and to love more freely, to love unconditionally. The person across from you is the most valuable thing in the world because they will one day die. This moment, now, is precious because it will end.

The contemplation of death is a celebration of the miracle of life. By embracing the wisdom of death, we are reminded of the preciousness of each moment, the beauty of each breath, the weight of each tear. Death empowers us to live fuller, more authentic lives. It reminds us to embrace the journey with open hearts and open minds, knowing that, in the end, it is not the destination that matters, but the journey itself.

Get close to death, so that you may live fully now. May you embody lasting peace.

John P. Driggs
August 1, 2024

THE UNBOUND HEART

MORE FROM JOHN

The Love & Understanding Podcast

loveandunderstanding.com

johndriggs.org

ENDNOTES

1 Xenophanes DK, B 16 and 15.

2 Xenophanes DK 18, 35, and 34.

3 Thales A 15.

4 Anaximander A 11.

5 id.

6 For its relation to the wheels or circles see Aristotle De Caelo 289b10-290b10.

7 Xenophanes DK B23 – 26.

8 Heraclitus B 88, 60, 58, 102, 78, and 123.

9 Parmenides B1: 29; See also B2.

10 For more information about falsifiability, see Popper's Problem of Demarcation; see also Popper, Conjectures and Refutations, Routledge & Kegan Paul (1963).

11 DK 68B9; Galen, De Med. Etnp. (DK B125), a fragment edited by H. Schöne, 'Eine Streitschrift Galens gegen die empirischen Arzte', Sitzungsberichte der königlichen preussischen Akadetnie der Wissenschaften zu Berlin, Jahrgang 1901, Bd II, p. 1259. (Some scholars think that the dialogue, which Galen attributes explicitly to Democritus, is Galen's own invention.); see also Popper (1963).

12 See Karl Popper, The World of Parmenides, Routledge (1998), Essay 1, XI.

13 Karl Popper, All Life is Problem Solving, Routledge (1999), first published in German 1994 by Piper Verlag, Munich.

14 see Herodotus, The Histories

15 Protagoras DK80B1

16 see Plato's works Apology, Crito, and Phaedo.

17 see Thucydides' History of the Peloponnesian War.

18 For Plato's discussion of Pindar's naturalism, see esp. Gorgias, 484b; 488b; Laws, 690b; 714e/715a; cp. also 890a/b.

19 See Sir Ernest Barker, Greek Political Theory, Methuen (1925), Antiphon, On Truth; see also Karl Popper, The Open Society and Its Enemies (1945).

20 Plato, Republic, 469b–471c, especially 470b–d.

21 see Plato, Republic; note that I have paraphrased the discussion.

22 see Republic, 434a–c.

23 The important passages from the Laws: Laws, 739c, ff. Plato refers here to the Republic, and apparently especially to Republic, 462a ff., 424a, and 449e. (A list of passages on collectivism and holism can be found in note 35 to chapter 5. On his communism, see note 29 (2) to chapter 5 and other places there mentioned.) The passage here quoted begins, characteristically, with a quotation of the Pythagorean maxim 'Friends have in common all things they possess'. Cp. note 36 and text; also the 'common meals' mentioned in note 34. (2) Laws, 942a, f.; see next note. Both

these passages are referred to as anti-individualistic by Gomperz (op. cit., vol. II, 406). See also Laws, 807d/e.

24 Republic, 389c/d; cp. also Laws, 730b, ff.

25 Republic, 466b/c. Cp. also the Laws, 715b/c, and many other passages against the anti-holistic misuse of class prerogatives.

26 Republic, 496c–d; cp. the Seventh Letter, 325d.

27 Republic, 489b/c

28 see Meno; Plato's theory of epistemology starts to take a turn in Phaedo and Phaedrus and, in the Republic, it transitions entirely from an optimistic and fallible epistemology to a pessimistic and infallible theory of knowledge or epistēmē.

29 Meno 81b–d

30 Cp. Phaedo, 72e ff.; 75e

31 Letter to Henry Fawcett, September 18, 1861

32 see The Milindapanha; O'Brien, Barbara. "King Milinda's Questions and the Chariot Simile." Learn Religions, Apr. 5, 2023, learnreligions.com/king-milindas-questions-450052.

33 see One Strange Rock (2019), National Geographic, Netflix.

34 See Joseph Goldstein, Bare Attention, Insight Hour with Joseph Goldstein, Podcast audio, Episode 112 (Dec. 31, 2021); see also Joseph Goldstein, What Mindfulness Is (& Isn't), Insight Hour with Joseph Goldstein, Podcast audio, Episode 113 (Dec. 31, 2021).

35 Anālayo, Satipatthana: The Direct Path to Realization, Windhorse Publications (2003); See Anālayo's books Satipatthana: The Direct Path to Realization and Satipatthana Meditation for more information on the process of papañca, as well as the practice of vipassana in general.

36 See Joseph Goldstein, Bare Attention, Insight Hour with Joseph Goldstein, Podcast audio, Episode 112 (Dec. 31, 2021); see also Joseph Goldstein, What Mindfulness Is (& Isn't), Insight Hour with Joseph Goldstein, Podcast audio, Episode 113 (Dec. 31, 2021).

37 Goldstein, What is Mindfulness? (2021).

38 Goldstein, Bare Attention (2021).

39 Tara Brach & Jack Kornfield, Becoming a Mindfulness Meditation Teacher, The Radical Compassion Institute (https://courses.tarabrach.com/courses/becoming-a-mindfulness-meditation-teacher)

40 William James, The Principles of Psychology, Vol. 1, Dover Publications (1890).

41 Jose Ortega y Gasset, On Love: Aspects of a Single Theme, Trans. by Toby Talbot (a series of essays originally written for the Madrid newspaper El Sol and posthumously published in English)

42 Thomas Merton, Love and Living, Commonweal Publishing Co., Inc. (1965)

43 Anālayo (2003); Goldstein, What is Mindfulness? (2021).

44 Jack Kornfield, A Path with Heart, Bantam Books (1993).

45 Jack Kornfield, The Wise Heart, Bantan Books (2008).

46 Jalal al-Din Rumi, The Essential Rumi, trans. by Coleman Barks (2004).

47 St. John of the Cross, To Reach Satisfaction in All.

48 Meister Eckhart, Beati Pauperes Spiritu, Sermon on Matthew 5:3; see also The Complete Mystical Works of Meister Eckhart, trans. and ed., Maurice O'C. Walshe (Crossroad: 2009), 422.

49 Meister Eckhart, Qui Audit Me, Sermon on Sirach 24:30. See The Complete Mystical Works of Meister Eckhart, trans. and ed., Maurice O'C. Walshe (Crossroad: 2009), 298.

50 Joseph Goldstein shared this story in a Dharma Talk at the IMS Retreat Center in Barre, MA.

51 Hafiz, The Gift, trans. by Daniel Ladinsky, Penguin Books (1999), The Sun Never Says.

52 Thich Nhat Hanh, Being Peace, Parallax Press (2005).

53 See Joseph Goldstein, Insight Hour with Joseph Goldstein, Podcast audio.

54 See the Waking Up App by Sam Harris. Though I use many different practices from many different teachers, I use Sam's app for my daily practice. It is my staple.

55 If you find it difficult to extend loving-kindness to yourself, you may want to start with a benefactor, maybe even a pet. Or you might play around with extending loving-kindness to the child you once were.

56 Karl Popper, All Life is Problem Solving, Routledge (1999), trans. by Patrick Camiller.

57 Kornfield (1993).

58 See Joseph Goldstein, Insight Hour with Joseph Goldstein, Podcast audio.

59 Effective Altruism [add clip about Sam Bankman-Fried], https://www.effectivealtruism.org

60 Dilgo Khyentse Rinpoche, The Heart Treasure of the Enlightened Ones, Shambhala Publications (1992).

61 Sam Harris, Ethics and Emptiness, the Waking Up App, a conversation with Diane Musho Hamilton.

62 Hanson, R. and Mendius, R. (2009) Buddha's Brain: The Practical Neuroscience of Happiness, Love, and Wisdom. Oakland, CA: New Harbinger; see also "Simon-Thomas et al. An fMRI study of caring vs. self-focus during induced compassion and pride. Compassionate motives are linked to parts of the brain that give rise to feelings of connectedness and meaningfulness.

63 Thich Nhat Hanh, Making Space, Parallax Press (2011).

64 Gil Fronsdal, Equanimity, Insight Meditation Center, essay adapted from a talk given by Gil on May 29th, 2004; https://www.insightmeditationcenter.org/books-articles/equanimity/#:~:text=The%20Buddha%20described%20a%20mind,a%20different%20aspect%20of%20equanimity

65 https://tricycle.org/magazine/cultivate-equanimity/

66 Kakacupama Sutta: The Simile of the Saw, trans. by Thanissaro Bhikkhu (1997).

67 Kornfield (2008).

68 Sharon Salzberg, Lovingkindness, Shambhala (2002).

69 Notes from Underground (1864)

70 Pema Chodron, The Places That Scare You, Shambhala (2002); Chogyam

Trungpa, Training the Mind, Shambhala (1993).

71 Chodron (2002).

72 Trungpa (1993).

73 Chodron (2002).

74 Kornfield (2008).

75 Joseph Goldstein, Insight Hour with Joseph Goldstein (Be Here Now Network), episodes 75, 76, and 81.

76 Dhammacakkappavattana Sutta, 56.11

77 Sallatha Sutta; Samyutta Nikaya 36.6.

78 https://www.ncbi.nlm.nih.gov/pmc/articles/PMC9518606/

79 Sallatha Sutta; Samyutta Nikaya 36.6.

80 Sallatha Sutta; Samyutta Nikaya 36.6.

81 Joseph Goldstein, The Experience of Insight, Shambhala (1987).

82 John Calvin, The Institutes of the Christian Religion: Books First and Second (Altenmünster, Germany: Jazzybee Verlag, 2015)

83 Kornfield (2008).

84 Kahlil Gibran, On Joy and Sorrow

85 Merton (1965).

86 https://ifs-institute.com

87 See Joseph Goldstein, Insight Hour with Joseph Goldstein, Podcast audio.

88 See Joseph Goldstein, Insight Hour with Joseph Goldstein, Podcast audio.

89 See Joseph Goldstein, Insight Hour with Joseph Goldstein, Podcast audio.

90 See Joseph Goldstein, Insight Hour with Joseph Goldstein, Podcast audio.

91 Dr. Oliver Sacks, Sudden Sight, After a Lifetime of Blindness, The New Yorker (May 2, 1993).

92 Sacks (1993).

93 The Baltic German biologist coined the term umwelt to describe this individual view for each organism, claiming that organisms have different umwelten even though they share the same environment.

94 Bhikkus here simply means someone who practices the Buddha's teachings.

95 See Tittha Sutta: Sectarians, trans. By John D. Ireland; see also The Udana: Inspired Utterances of the Buddha, trans. By John D. Ireland, Kandy: Buddhist Publication Society (1997).

96 Mark Twain, The Wit and Wisdom of Mark Twain, Chartwell Books (2016).

97 See Friedrich Nietzsche, The Gay Science (1882); see also Nietzsche, Thus Spoke Zarathustra (1883 & 1885).

98 See Chapter 2.

99 Anālayo, 5.

100 Jack Kornfield and Paul Breiter, eds., A Still Forest Pool: The Insight Meditation of Ajahn Chaa (Wheaton, IL: Quest Books, 1984, 2004), 162.

101 Sam Harris, The Necessity of Thought, Waking Up App

102 Bhikkhu Bodhi, The Eightfold Path, Buddhist Publication Society (1984), second edition (revised 1994).

103 James M. Barrie, Peter Pan, Simon & Schuster (1904).

104 Examples: They defame someone like Sam Harris, for example, by taking his words entirely out of context (again, because they saw some small clip on social media). The poor man has an evil doppelgänger out there that is even more famous than he. Or, as another example, these justice warriors see a Palestinian child pulled from the rubble, for example, and immediately start shouting into the digital void about how awful Israel is, without putting in the slightest effort to understand the ideological, ethical, and historical context. They say they support human rights, yet they stand behind Hamas, who refuse to give women rights, who regularly kill gays, infidels, and heretics, and who are not interested in a liberal democracy at all but rather a global theocracy, and who have been launching rockets endlessly at Israel for decades. This is not honesty. It's laziness and cowardice, a peddling and perpetuation of misinformation. We need to step out of the digital space and have conversations in person. I think people would be less hostile if we looked each other in the eyes when we communicate. Nor do I think people would take such strong positions, knowing that they don't have the actual knowledge to back themselves up in a live arena.

105 Anthony D. Smith, Behind the Scenes of Sarcasm, Psychology Today (Dec. 14, 2020).

106 Bhikkhu Bodhi, The Noble Eightfold Path, The Way to the End of Suffering (1999), https://www.accesstoinsight.org/lib/authors/bodhi/waytoend.html

107 Mark Twain, Notebook, 1894, The Wit and Wisdom of Mark Twain, Chartwell Books (2016).

108 Ryuho Okawa, The Essence of Buddha, Irh Press (2016).

109 I could not find the source of this quote, though I have noted that it is from Thich Nhat Hanh. Searching for the source, I was, however, able to find this: https://dharmanet.org/coursesM/24/Hindrances5b.htm

110 Anguttara Nikaya 10:176

111 Etty died in Auschwitz in 1943 at the age of 29. This quote is from "An Interrupted Life", Picador (1996). It contains a compilation of her diaries and letters.

112 Khalil Gibran, On Teaching, The Prophet, Penguin Random House (1923).

113 Deborah Adele, Yamas & Niyamas, On-Word Bound Books (2009).

114 Deborah Adele, Yamas & Niyamas, On-Word Bound Books (2009).

115 We'll learn more about restless, sloth and torpor, and the three remaining Buddhist hindrances in Chapter

116 Sam Harris, Freewill, Free Press (2012).

117 Alan Watts, Preservation and Curation of the Original Recordings, alanwatts. org

118 Deborah Adele, Yamas & Niyamas, On-Word Bound Books (2009).

119 Jack Kornfield & Joseph Goldstein, The Seeking the Heart of Wisdom, Shambhala (2001). This is likely a loose interpretation of a passage from the Itivuttika 26.

120 Kahlil Gibran, On Giving, The Prophet (1923).

121 Gibran (1923).

122 Gibran (1923).

123 Gibran (1923).

124 Gibran (1923).

125 Bhikkhus means someone who is on the Path.

126 There's a story about a hermit monk who was a talented artist. And for many years, he meticulously painted a tiger onto the wall of his cave. When he finally finished the painting, the monk looked at his painting and, because it was so realistic, he jumped back in fear. How many times do we do this each day? (Excerpt from: Joseph Goldstein, Mindfulness, Sounds True (2016)).

127 Ajahn Chah, A Taste of Freedom, The Sangha Forest Monastery (1980).

128 See Joseph Goldstein, Insight Hour with Joseph Goldstein, Podcast audio.

129 We'll discuss sloth and torpor, as well as the other hindrances, later in this chapter.

130 Mind states that lead us away from harm, discontent, and unnecessary suffering

131 Ānāpānasati Sutta, trans. by Rupert Gethin, The Buddhist Path to Awakening, Oxford, England: Oneworld Publications (2001), 78; see also Joseph Goldstein, Mindfulness, Sounds True (2016).

132 Ānāpānasati Sutta, trans. by Rupert Gethin, The Buddhist Path to Awakening, Oxford, England: Oneworld Publications (2001), 117; see also Joseph Goldstein, Mindfulness, Sounds True (2016).

133 Sayadaw U Tejaniya, Don't Look Down on the Defilements (2006), 57.

134 Appativana Sutta, trans. By Thanissaro Bhikkhu (2006).

135 Shunryu Suzuki, Zen Mind, Beginner's Mind, Shambhala (2011).

136 Again, I don't subscribe to this kind of dogmatic belief in karma.

137 This quote is commonly attributed to Je Tsongkhapa (1357–1419).

138 Sam Harris, Waking Up (App), Lessons: Fundamentals

139 Bhikkhu Anālayo, Satipatthāna: The Direct Path to Realization (Cambridge, UK: Windhorse Publications, 2003), 3–4.

140 Anagarika Shri Munindra (1915 – October 14, 2003). Joseph Goldstein often recalls this in his dharma talks.

141 Stephen Carter, Civility (New York: Harper Perennial, 1999); I first heard this story in a Dharma talk given by Joseph Goldstein.

142 Stephen Batchelor, Foundations of Mindfulness, Tricycle: The Buddhist Review (https://tricycle.org/magazine/foundations-of-mindfulness/)

143 Anālayo, 4–5.

144 Kevin Griffin, There Are No Words in My Body: How the four foundations of mindfulness can help us practice with—and diffuse—difficult emotions, Tricycle: The Buddhist Review (Feb. 2022); https://tricycle.org/article/four-foundations-of-mindfulness/

145 Satipatthāna Sutta: The Foundations of Mindfulness

146 Satipatthāna Sutta: The Foundations of Mindfulness

147 Satipatthāna Sutta: The Foundations of Mindfulness

148 Ñānamoli and Bodhi, The Middle Length Discourses, 347.

149 Amaro Bhikkhu, Small Boat, Great Mountain (Redwood Valley, CA: Abhaya-giri Buddhist Monastery, 2003), 67.

150 Dvayatanupassana Sutta: The Noble One's Happiness 3.12

151 Bhikkhu Anālayo, Satipatthāna: The Direct Path to Realization (Cambridge, UK: Windhorse Publications, 2003), 3–4.

152 Anālayo, 8.

153 See Loch Kelly, the app Glimpses; see also Loch Kelly, Shift Into Freedom, Sounds True (2015); see also Loch Kelly, The Way of Effortless Mindfulness, Sounds True (2019).

154 Sayadaw means venerable teacher.

155 Sayadaw U Tejaniya, Relax & Be Aware: Mindfulness Meditations for Clarity, Confidence, and Wisdom, Shambhala Publications, Inc. (2019).

156 Though this stems from Sayadaw U Tejaniya, it was Joseph Goldstein who introduced me to and encouraged this practice.

157 The Third Patriarch of Zen, Hsin Hsin Ming by Seng-T'san, trans. from Chinese by Richard B. Clark, featured in Jack Kornfield, Teachings of the Buddha, Shambhala (2007).

158 See Anālayo, Satipatthana: The Direct Path to Realization, Windhorse Publications (2003); see also Joseph Goldstein, Mindfulness, Soundstrue.

159 Sam Harris, Waking Up

160 Anālayo, 9.

161 I could not trace this reference. I believe Sam used it in a conversation on his podcast, Making Sense. But it has stuck with me for many years.

162 Goldstein gave this note to me in an online Q&A in 2022.

163 Satipatthāna Sutta, trans. by Bhikkhu Anālayo

164 Spirit Rock is a highly regarded vipassana retreat center in Northern California, created by Jack Kornfield, Sylvia Boorstein, Anna Douglas, and other early pioneers of the dharma in the West; see https://www.spiritrock.org.

www.ingramcontent.com/pod-product-compliance
Lightning Source LLC
Chambersburg PA
CBHW071713140626
46557CB00011B/72